THE WRITER'S COMPLETE
FANTASY REFERENCE

THE WRITER'S COMPLETE FANTASY REFERENCE

AN INDISPENSIBLE COMPENDIUM OF MYTH AND MAGIC
FROM THE EDITORS OF WRITER'S DIGEST BOOKS

INTRODUCTION BY **TERRY BROOKS**

W

WRITER'S DIGEST BOOKS
CINCINNATI, OHIO

02   01   00   99   98   5   4   3   2   1

Library of Congress Cataloging-in-Publication Data

The writer's complete fantasy reference / from the editors of Writer's Digest Books.—1st ed.
        p.   cm.
Includes index.
ISBN 0-89879-866-3 (hardcover : alk. paper)
1. Fantastic fiction—Authorship. I. Writer's Digest Books (Firm)
PN3377.5.F34W75   1998
808.3'8766—dc21   98-27642
                                                                          CIP

Edited by David H. Borcherding
Production Edited by Michelle Kramer
Cover Designed by Candace Haught
Cover Illustration by Robin Wood

ABOUT THE AUTHORS

Terry Brooks

Terry Brooks has more than fifteen million books in print world-wide. He published his first novel, *The Sword of Shannara*, in 1977 and it became the first work of fiction ever to appear on the New York Times Trade Paperback Best-seller List, where it remained for over five months. *The Elfstones of Shannara* followed in 1982 and *The Wishsong of Shannara* in 1985. *Magic Kingdom for Sale— Sold!* began a best-selling new series for him in 1986. The Heritage of Shannara series, a four book set, debuted with the publication of *The Scions of Shannara* in 1990.

His new novel, *A Knight of the Word*, is the second book in a contemporary fantasy series that began in 1997 with *Running with the Demon*.

Daniel A. Clark

Daniel A. Clark is a former English teacher who now works in information systems. He has published in *Studies in Popular Culture*, *The Journal of General Education* and the *Masterplots* young adult literature supplement. He dabbles around in short fiction, but mostly tells stories to his son Thomas, who likes stories about trains and "mouses."

Sherrilyn Kenyon

Sherrilyn Kenyon is the best-selling author of four science fiction and fantasy novels which have won numerous awards. Her current SF release, *Born of Fire*, is the launch title for the new electronic publisher, Dreams-Unlimited.com.

A former editor and agent, Sherrilyn has written two reference books for Writer's Digest, *Everyday Life in the Middle Ages* and *Character-Naming Sourcebook*. She is currently under contract with HarperCollins for three historical novels.

Allan Maurer

Allan Maurer has been published in *OMNI*, *Starlog*, *Twilight Zone*, *Fantastic Stories*, *Playboy*, *Modern Maturity* and many other magazines. He was Senior Writer on *OMNI*'s *Continuum* book (Little Brown, 1982) and the author of *Lasers, Lightwave of the Future* (Arco, 1982). His work for OMNI's "Antimatter" column was included in *OMNI's Book of the Bizarre* (OMNI Books, 1974).

Maurer attended the 1974 Clarion Science Fiction and Fantasy Writer's Workshop, taught by such luminaries as Harlan Ellison, Kate Wilhelm and Damon Knight. He has founded several regional magazines, including *Charlotte's Best Magazine* and *Beaufort (NC) Magazine*.

P. Andrew Miller

P. Andrew Miller has published a number of fantasy stories in a variety of publications. His stories have appeared in *Sword & Sorceress #13*, *Dragon Magazine*, *Valykyrie*, *Odyssey* and many others. He has been an attending author at the International Conference on the Fantastic in the Arts for the last five years. Miller is also a member of the Science Fiction Writers of America. He lives and teaches in Cincinnati, Ohio.

Michael J. Varhola

Michael J. Varhola is a freelance editor, writer and publisher who lives and works in the Washington, D.C., area. As a journalist, he writes news and feature articles on many subjects, especially those involving world cultures, military history and the Middle East. As a senior editor, he has helped found or run several publications, including *Living History* magazine, *Renaissance* magazine, *SKIR-MISHER!* on-line gaming magazine and *The Achiever*. Varhola also served in the U.S. Army during Desert Storm with the 3rd Armored Division, and during the Cold War with the 1st Infantry Division (Forward), in Stuttgart, Germany, where he was part of a successful effort to safeguard Europe from invasion by the former USSR. He earned a B.S. in Journalism at the University of Maryland, College Park, with a minor in history. Varhola also studied European Culture at the American University of Paris, in Paris, France.

Renee Wright

Renee Wright is Managing Editor of *Charlotte's Best Magazine* in Charlotte, NC. She was a founding editor of *Beaufort (SC) Magazine*. Wright published a long-running column in several Charlotte publications, covered the Carribbean for a travel book series and art-edited a collector-coveted NASCAR season retrospective. She works frequently as a writer, editor and researcher with Allan Maurer and researched his 1982 book on lasers. Wright is near completion of a Master's Degree in Psychology and travels the U.S. in an RV with her daredevil mother.

TABLE OF CONTENTS

INTRODUCTION
Terry Brooks

I remember vividly, twenty years later, what Lester del Rey repeatedly used to tell me about writing fantasy. Lester was a longtime writer, critic and editor in the fantasy/science fiction field, and I was fortunate enough to be able to work with him during the first fifteen years of my professional career. Most of what I learned about being a commercial fiction writer, for better or worse, I learned from Lester. Lester used to say that it was harder to write good fantasy than any other form of fiction. Why? Because a writer of fantasy is free to invent anything, unfettered by the laws and dictates of this world and limited only by the depth of imagination and willingness to dream. The temptation to free-fall through a story chock full of incredible images and wondrous beings can be irresistible— but, when not resisted, almost invariably disastrous.

What he was telling me was that in creating a world populated by monsters and other strange life forms, reliant on uses of magic, and shimmering with images of childhood tales, legends and myths, a writer runs the risk of losing touch with reality entirely. Given the parameters of the world and characters that the writer has created, something of that world and those characters must speak to what we, as readers, know to be true about the human condition. If nothing corresponds to what we know about our own lives, then everything becomes unbelievable. Even the most ridiculous farce must resonate in some identifiable way with truths we have discovered about ourselves. Even the darkest sword and sorcery epic must speak to us of our own harsh experience.

Achieving this end as a fantasy writer demands mastery of a certain skill, one not uncommon with that required of a ship's captain charting a course at sea. When putting together a fantasy tale, a writer must navigate a treacherous passage that bears neither too hard to starboard nor too far to port in order to avoid arriving at an unforseen destination or, worse, ending up on the rocks. Fantasy writing must be grounded in both truth and life experience if it is to work. It can be as inventive and creative as the writer can make it, a whirlwind of images and plot twists, but it cannot be built on a foundation of air. The world must be identifiable with our own, must offer us a frame of reference we can recognize. The characters must behave in ways that we believe reasonable and expected. The magic must work in a consistent and balanced manner. The book must leave us with a feeling of comprehension and satisfaction at having spent time turning its pages to discover its end.

How does a writer accomplish this? This latest offering from the people at Writer's Digest Books is a good place to start. Fantasy stories work because the writer has interwoven bits and pieces of reality with imagination to form a personal vision. Here are some examples of what I mean:

- An elfin culture in an imaginary world incorporates a religion similar to that of the Maori.
- The hero journeys to a castle of wraiths that has battlements, parapets and a gatehouse with a deadly murder hole which will figure strongly in the resolution of a crucial battle.
- Lizard soldiers man a monstrous siege machine that functions like a trebuchet.
- Secrets that can end a war between black and white witches can only be revealed by the proper use of ophiomancy.
- The hero of the tale is a simple Adamist, who falls under a Wiccan spell and must gain freedom through mastery of an enchanted Khopesh.

I've used strange words to suggest other times and places, other worlds and lives, but all their definitions are fixed in the cultures and myths of our world. All can be found within the pages of this book. Understanding the possibilities is a requirement to making choices, and writers of fantasy can discover a good many of those possibilities if they read on. Various chapters look closely at forms of magic, types of weapons and armor, fantasy races and creatures, and ancient societies on which speculative fictional worlds and characters can be based. Each writer must choose the ones that work and make them the building blocks of a story's foundation.

Description lends weight and substance to ideas, and nowhere is that more important than in a world that doesn't exist—at least outside the pages of the writer's story. So giving the reader an understanding of how a world looks, tastes, smells, sounds and feels is crucial. In fantasy, more than in any other form of fiction, the reader must feel transported to the world being created, while at the same time readily comprehending what it is he or she is experiencing. When an otherworldly character is introduced, the reader must be made to see the differences, but must recognize the similarities as well. Details ground the story's larger images and keep the reader engaged.

I happen to favor rather strongly the practice of outlining a book before trying to write it, and I would recommend it to beginning writers, in particular, for two reasons. First, it requires thinking the story through, which eliminates a lot of wasted time chasing bad ideas. Second, it provides a blueprint to which the writer can refer while working on a story over the course of months or even years. Use of an outline is not a popular practice because it is hard work. It isn't easy thinking a story through from start to finish. But writing a hundred pages that have to be discarded because they don't lead anywhere is a whole lot more unpleasant. Moreover, outlining gives a writer a chance to add to the details of the book, to pen notes in the margins, to decide how all those bits and pieces of reality I mentioned earlier will fit with those grand landscapes of imagination.

This seems a good place to stress the importance of "dream time" in the creative process. All good fantasy requires a certain amount of gestation, a period before pen is set to paper, or fingers to keyboard, in which a writer simply gives free rein to imagination and waits to see where it will go. After a path reveals itself, a writer should start to map that path, carefully noting which side roads are offered, what travelers await, where dangers might lurk, and how lessons could be learned. If the writer is patient enough, eventually a story will present itself. If it is the right story, it will demand to be written. It simply won't stand to be cooped up. But this is a process that is difficult to rush and one in which the writer must trust. It sounds a bit mystical, but it really isn't. It's puzzle building without a box cover. It's outlining in your mind.

There is one final lesson Lester taught me that I want to pass on before I end this. Some years back I was fussing to him about finding an idea for a story that hadn't been used before. I wanted something new and original. He gave me one of his patented smiles—the ones that always made him look like a cross between your kindly uncle and Jack Nicholson in *The Shining*—and told me in no uncertain terms that new ideas did not come along that often and that when they did, they came in disguise. It was better to take old, established ideas and just turn them over and over in your mind until you found a new way to look at them. Then write about what you saw.

It was good advice then. It's good advice now. Go forth, and write something magical.

Terry Brooks

CHAPTER ONE

TRADITIONAL FANTASY CULTURES

Michael J. Varhola

A t the heart of most traditional fantasy milieux is a culture derived from that of the European Middle Ages, in large part the medieval societies of what are now Great Britain, France and Germany. This culture is a synthesis of both the Roman culture that dominated western Europe for some five centuries and of the Germanic culture that eventually overran and absorbed it.

Three major institutions formed the basis of medieval society and dictated how most people lived. These were feudalism, manorialism and Christianity.

FEUDALISM

Feudalism was a pyramidal system of contractual relationships in which lords granted lands to their retainers in exchange for oaths of loyalty and military service. Feudalism was most prevalent in France, Germany, England, Sicily, northern Spain and the Crusader states, and its specifics varied from region to region. The vast majority of people in medieval Europe did not participate in the feudal system, which was largely reserved for fighting men.

Under feudalism, local political, military and economic power was held by the lords. Each of them was subject to the lord above him, to whom they had sworn loyalty in return for **fiefs** (land, its occupants and resources), and who could, at least in theory, demand service from them. Castles garrisoned by an elite caste of professional knights and men-at-arms, as well as local levies and sometimes foreign mercenaries, were the bases from which lords exercised their control.

Feudalism declined for a multitude of reasons. A major cause was the inheritance of fiefs, which compromised the system of lands being granted in return for oaths of loyalty. Strong national leaders, changes in warfare that reduced the importance of armored knights, and the phenomena of scutage and liege homage also contributed to the decline of feudalism. **Scutage** was the practice of replacing personal military service with monetary payments. **Liege homage** was the practice of a vassal who had sworn oaths to more than one lord giving his primary allegiance to only one of them, thus eroding the basis of the feudal system. By the beginning of the fifteenth century, feudalism was for the most part dead.

Because the mounted knights that were at the core of the feudal system needed substantial economic support in order to arm, armor and equip themselves, and needed to spend much of their time training for combat, substantial amounts of land and peasant labor were needed for their upkeep. Thus, feudalism was complemented by manorialism.

MANORIALISM

Manorialism was an economic, social and administrative system that defined the hereditary relationships between the peasantry and the nobility. While only the military and political elite of any given area was affected by feudalism, nine out of ten people in most areas were subject to the conditions of manorialism.

As a rule of thumb, writers should assume that more than half the people in most medieval European areas were bonded peasants— serfs—who had few, if any, rights or freedoms and were completely subject to the landed aristocracy. In some countries, particularly Mediterranean regions like Greece and Italy, outright slavery was widely practiced.

Manorialism had its origins in the last years of the Roman Empire, when laws were enacted binding farmers to the land. When Rome fell in the fifth century, Europe was thrust into a state of chaos, descending into the Dark Ages, and farmers were vulnerable to violent, invading peoples. Thus, they were largely willing to cede liberties in exchange for security, maybe even in the early years hoping that the times of trouble would pass and things would return to "normal." Crises were normal enough that manorialism solidified and was strengthened in the ninth and tenth centuries when new waves of invasions by Magyars, Muslims and Vikings struck Europe. Manorialism reached its peak in the eleventh and twelfth centuries;

in the following centuries, it began a prolonged decline that did not end in some areas until the twentieth century.

In general, manorialism was a hereditary system under which a lord owned or controlled the land, and then allotted portions of it to the individual peasants who resided under him. In exchange, the peasants paid the lord in crops, money and labor. The specifics of manorialism varied from state to state (e.g., the proportion of their crop or yield; how much money, if any; how many days of labor per year; the size of land parcels).

Peasants throughout medieval Europe had severely abbreviated rights, especially by modern standards. Without the permission of their lord, peasants were not even allowed to travel or choose their own occupations. In eastern Europe, conditions like this persisted until the early years of this century. Lords had jurisdiction over many sorts of crimes committed on their lands and tried them in manorial courts. Such courts were a substantial source of revenue for the lords, who often stood to gain financially through fines and court fees regardless of the outcome of cases (or who might be tempted to sway the outcome of a case in a way favorable to themselves).

Conditions began to improve for the peasantry around the 1100s, in large part because of an agricultural revolution that was attributable to several factors. One was implementation of a three-field farming system in which one field was used for summer crops, another for winter crops and another left fallow, increasing output and avoiding soil depletion. Another factor was improved irrigation systems. Technology, too, played a part in improved productivity, and implements like the wheeled plow, horse collar, clearing axe and flail were of immeasurable value to medieval farmers.

Reclamation of land from the wilderness through the clearing of wooded areas and the draining of swamps contributed to greater availability of arable land, allowing for overall greater production. The Catholic church played a big role in such land reclamation as much of it was accomplished by monastic orders, who established their own manors, which were managed by abbeys and run much like their secular counterparts.

CHRISTIANITY

Christianity was the predominant religion of medieval Europe and was a social and political force as important as feudalism and manorialism, and frequently more powerful than either.

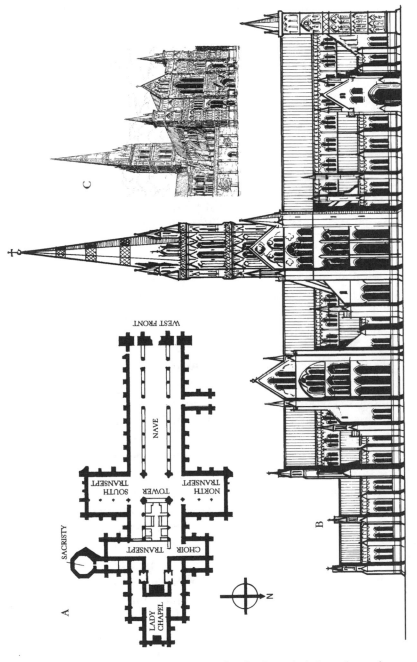

CATHEDRAL: A–Floorplan, B–View of north side, C–Angled view of west front

Indeed, the role of the Church in day-to-day life, the importance of religion to most people and their level of faith in general can scarcely be imagined by most people today. It was this level of faith that enabled the Church to muster entire communities to raise great cathedrals, the greatest works of architecture of the Middle Ages. Such centers of worship could take decades to complete, and thousands of laborers and craftsmen such as carpenters, glaziers and masons would participate in their construction.

The Church assumed many of the administrative functions that the government of the Roman Empire had once fulfilled, such as the construction of public works and the colonization of wilderness areas. It also served as a repository of knowledge and literacy, which had been nearly expunged in the chaos of the Dark Ages. (Most people, even kings and nobles, were illiterate until the last centuries of the Middle Ages). Histories and other information were recorded in tomes by monks, who copied and illustrated them (a process called illumination) in monastery scriptoriums. This work allowed many works from antiquity to survive and produced many valuable works of art.

Medieval Europe was considered as the heart of Christendom because of the important role played by the Catholic church in society. Nonetheless, in practice, the Christianity of the Middle Ages bore little resemblance to its modern counterpart and was intermingled at every level with elements from the violent, superstitious, essentially pagan world it was a part of. For example, many medieval Christian churches were built upon the sites of Roman, Germanic, even prehistoric pagan temples or worship sites. And, in Scandinavian churches, the iconography of statues of saints can be identified with that of the various Norse gods. Even today, at Catholic Easter masses in some rural villages in Belgium, handfuls of grain are ritually cast into a vat of green flames. Fantasy writers can put such phenomena to good use in their stories.

Veneration of the saints, frequently crossing the line into outright worship, was characteristic of medieval Christianity. Individuals, sects, cities, guilds and even entire kingdoms chose patron saints and sought their blessings and special benefits through votive masses, adoration of relics and special feast days (which frequently displaced Sundays as days of worship). Interestingly, the characteristics of patron saints often corresponded closely with those of the pre-Christian deities that peoples in the same regions had worshipped.

That is not to say that people did not have a strong belief in God, only that they saw Him as an unapproachably powerful, frightening being that could not be reliably called upon to intercede in their daily lives. (After all, it is much easier to believe in a benign and sympathetic god if one lives in a benign and reliable world.) In fact, so feared was God in the Middle Ages that many people refused to take communion because of His ominous presence in the host. This phenomena became so widespread that in 1215, the Fourth Lateran Council was forced to make annual communion obligatory.

THE SOCIAL ORDER

Titles of nobility are used to organize the upper echelons of an aristocratic society, and those used throughout Europe during the Middle Ages originated largely during the early Holy Roman Empire. Many were derived from Roman titles of rank, among them count and duke, while others were distinctly Germanic in nature, such as earl. Titles, especially the highest ones, were frequently linked to specific lands, powers and responsibilities.

Historically, hereditary titles usually passed from father to son or, in the absence of a suitable male heir, from older brother to younger brother. However, in the real world this varied by region and even by title, and the whole system and its study is rather arcane. Writers can certainly create a simple, clear-cut system, or may decide a complex, even impenetrable system is of more use to them.

In the following section, the feminine construction of the various titles appears in parenthesis after the masculine form. Such feminine forms can variously refer to the wife of a titled individual who wields incidental, if any, power, or to a titled individual who rules in her own right. Historically, such women sometimes took power when their husbands died or when their reigning father or brother died without a suitable male heir (e.g., Queen Elizabeth II of England). In a fantasy milieux, women might more frequently be entitled to hold such positions, and hereditary titles could even pass from mother to daughter.

The head of a state was usually a king (queen) or emperor (empress), and even he was theoretically subject to the will of God, an idea expressed in the concept of "the divine right of kings." However, this was largely a device to check both papal interference into the business of monarchs and to implement unpopular policies by dismissing accountability toward the populace. Lesser nobles might be the rulers of smaller states. Such nobles, in order of precedence, include princes, dukes, marquesses, counts, viscounts, barons, baronets and knights. Princes, dukes or other nobles might be the rulers of relatively small states.

It is possible for cultures to have aristocratic ranks beyond these. For example, German states also had the ranks of Furst (Furstin), Pfalzgraf (Pfalzgrafin), Landgraf (Landgrafin) and Freier (Freierin).

Writers should not forget that as colorful as aristocratic societies are, they are distinctly undemocratic. Even when measures that are perceived as democratic are instituted, such as the imposition of the Magna Carta, they are usually only intended by a lower echelon of the nobility to reduce the power of those above them, not to extend it to all segments of society. For example, when the Magna Carta was signed in 1215, serfs were worse off they had been before the Norman Conquest.

On the other hand, nobles frequently shouldered great responsibilities. In a dangerous and often violent world, it was the nobility that was responsible for administering the subdivisions of states, raising armies and leading troops into battle. Naturally, in many areas the various ranks of nobility frequently came to lose their original meaning or level of responsibility. For example, in the prerevolutionary France of the eighteenth century, a marquis was not responsible for guarding a marc, or border area, as was originally the case.

In some states, including most of the monarchies that still exist today, titles of nobility are often granted as a symbolic but nonmonetary way to recognize and reward service to the state. In other states, titles of nobility might be illegal or anathema. For example, the Constitution prohibits the United States from granting titles of nobility, and in republican Rome, there was a fear of anyone who was in a position to proclaim themselves, or be proclaimed, king.

NOTE: Royal titles are not capitalized unless used in conjunction with a name, unless they are in German, which capitalizes all nouns. Some of these are rough equivalents of the listed English titles.

prince (princess): Whereas the child of a monarch is referred to as a prince or princess, in some states the children of a prince or the spouse of a monarch might also hold such a title. Princes, if not the head of an independent state, usually have few powers and no land, but might also hold some other title. For example, the oldest son of the monarch of England is also the Prince of Wales. A state ruled by a prince is called a principality.

(French **prince, princesse**; German **Prinz, Prinzessin, Furst, Furstin**; Italian **principe, principessa**; Spanish **principe, principesa**)

duke (duchess): Derived from the Latin *dux*, or "leader," the duke is usually the most powerful of the landed nobility beneath the monarch and is the highest title in the English peerage (i.e., the nobles entitled to sit in the House of Lords). A state or area within a state ruled by a duke is variously called a dukery, duchy or dukedom.

In some societies, nonruling dukedoms have been bestowed upon princes in direct line of succession to the throne or upon generals who have won great victories in battle (such as the English generals Marlborough and Wellington). The first nonruling English duke was created by Edward III in 1337 when he made his oldest son, Edward the Black Prince, Duke of Cornwall.

Some states with many dukes distinguish the most powerful (or, for example, the siblings of the monarch) as "grand dukes." Grand dukes might wield great power within a state, as in Imperial Russia, or be the leaders of small states, such as the Grand Duchy of Luxembourg.

(French **duc, duchesse**; German **Herzog, Herzogin**; Italian **duca, duchesa**; Spanish **duque, duquesa**)

marquess (marchioness): Dating from the eleventh century, this title originally applied to lords who were responsible for guarding border areas, known as marches. In Germany, where the title Markgraf was bestowed upon counts who stood border guard for their monarch, such nobles could be further distinguished as *Landgraf* or *Markgraf*, depending on the sort of territory they controlled.

(French **marquis, marquise**; German **Markgraf, Markgrafin**; Italian **marchese, marchesa**; Spanish **marques, marquesa**)

count (countess): From the Latin word *comes*, "companion," a count is a powerful noble with authority over a province or similar area. The English equivalent is the earl, the oldest title in the English peerage. Derived from the Danish *jarl*, or "chieftain," the earl was originally the lord of a shire.

(French **comte, comtesse**; German **Graf, Graefin**; Italian **conte, contessa**; Spanish **conde, condesa**)

viscount (viscountess): Meaning the lieutenant or deputy of a count, the title of vice-count was probably created in the Holy Roman Empire prior to the reign of Frederick I Barbarossa. In some states, high-ranking soldiers have sometimes been rewarded with the title of viscount.

(French **vicomte, vicomtesse**; German **Vicomte, Vicom-tesse**; Italian **visconte, viscontessa**; Spanish **visconde, viscondesa**)

baron (baroness): Barons are the lowest level of noble who are granted land directly from a sovereign, and their name is derived from this meaning. The title came to England during the Norman Conquest, where barons became the lowest level of noble entitled to sit in the House of Lords. Historically, the baronage relished the power they lorded over those below them, but chafed at royal control. It was the barons of England that took advantage of the weakness of King John Lackland by foisting the Magna Carta upon him. An area ruled by a baron is called a barony.

(French **baron, baronne**; German **Baron, Baronin, Freiherr, Freiherrin**; Italian **barone, baronessa**; Spanish **baron, baronesa**)

baronet (baronetess): Baronets were originally English barons who lost the right of individual summons to Parliament in the fourteenth century. A hereditary order of baronets was created in England in 1611 by King James I and sold to gentlemen willing to set up plantations in Ireland. In 1624, baronets were also created for gentlemen prepared to settle in Nova Scotia. The title for the wife of such a noble would simply be "lady." Historically, only one woman was ever made a baronetess.

knight (dame): The term knight can be used many ways, and can refer to an individual honored with the nonhereditary title of knight; to individuals enrolled in an order of knighthood (see "Knighthood," page 16); or, used loosely rather than titularly, to refer to any armed and armored mounted warrior (e.g., any baron riding into battle might be referred to as "one of the king's knights").

It is with good reason that the rank of knight is associated with the mounted warriors of the Middle Ages, a class who enjoyed high social status. The French and German terms for a knight, do, in fact, mean "horseman," while the English word knight is derived from the Saxon word *cnyt*, or "attendant."

   (French **chevalier**; German **Ritter**; Italian **cavaliere**; Spanish **cabellero**)

Not all societies will have all of the listed titles of nobility, and they may not be as important in all societies. For example, in imperial Russia, the Tsar, or emperor, was at the apex of society. Below him were a vast number of princes and princesses, but because there was no law of primogeniture, as in many western states, the aristocracy was bloated, and many of these nobles were relatively unimportant and not in line for the throne. (A reading of some of Tolstoy's works will shed a lot of light on this subject.)

ECCLESIASTIC TITLES

Writers should not overlook the role of ecclesiastic officials in medieval society. The pope at various points in time had his own armies, extensive lands and a direct mandate from God that translated into great political influence over other monarchs. In short, he was a king as much as any other. Cardinals were not called "princes of the Church" without good reason. And powerful abbots might have controlled several manors, even a dozen or more, from their abbeys; in England, France, Germany and Italy, such Church officials were often the equivalent of barons or better, and could wield great economic power within a state and political power at court.

   In some states, political power was sometimes held jointly with ecclesiastic power. For example, the rulers of the mountain city-state of Salzburg in Austria were called "prince-bishops." Military power might also have been wielded by churchmen, and there are numerous examples of bishops and priests of other ranks leading troops into battle. One of the earliest examples of this is depicted on the Bayeux Tapestry, the chronicle of the Norman conquest of England.

   The basic hierarchy of the Church was based upon three sorts of churchmen, priests and bishops, and the pope.

abbot (abbess): An abbot, from the Hebrew *abba*, or father, was the head of an autonomous community of monks. Such communities were usually founded by the members of a monastic order, such as the Benedictines. In the Church hierarchy, an abbot was on about the same level as a bishop and tended to have at least as much political power as a baron. The community he controlled was called an abbey, which consisted of one or more monasteries.

An abbot was expected to govern his monks with both compassion and firmness, and, as Christ's deputy, his flock was expected to show him reverence and obedience. Abbots were usually elected for life by the senior members of the community from among a pool of qualified candidates, an appointment that usually required confirmation from the papacy or the head of the order.

Basilian monks usually called a leader of one of their communities a **hegumen**, while Russian and other eastern orders used the term **archimandrite**.

Like her male counterpart, an abbess was the head of one or more convents or cloisters of nuns. Historically, they did not tend to wield the same political power as abbots, who controlled powerful estates.

archbishop: Such churchmen were responsible for large areas, called provinces in England, with several bishops under them. For example, England has two archbishops—the Archbishop of Canterbury (the head of the Church of England) and the Archbishop of York. Such figures often had great influence, even beyond death. For example, when Archbishop of Canterbury Thomas Becket was slain by four knights of King Henry II, the site of his assassination almost immediately became a major pilgrimage center, and he was canonized a saint.

bishop: From the Greek word for "overseer," bishops were regional church leaders and had a cathedral as their seat. Cathedrals were among the most impressive and labor-intensive structures built in Europe during the Middle Ages, and it was indicative of the political, spiritual and economic power of a bishop who could muster the resources to have one built.

The ecclesiastic area governed by a bishop was known as a diocese; a political area ruled by a bishop was known as a bishopric.

cardinal: Originally, the term cardinal was applied to bishops whose dioceses had been overrun by barbarians in the sixth century and who were subsequently assigned vacant dioceses by the pope. Later, senior priests of certain parishes in Rome came to be known as cardinals. By the eleventh century, these churchmen had developed into the sacred College of Cardinals, and served as assistants and counselors to the pope. In 1059, cardinals became the church officers empowered to elect a new pope, and

later in the eleventh century, bishops outside of Rome began to
be appointed cardinals.

deacon (deaconess): Such ordained churchmen, immediately subor-
dinate to priests, were responsible for serving as their assistants,
in charge of the purification ceremonies connected with preparation for baptism and charged with the care of the poor and
unfortunate.

Deaconesses, probably ordained just like their male counterparts, were principally responsible for assisting at the baptism of
women and in helping them to prepare for that sacrament, and
also administered to the women of Christian communities. In
western Europe, such female officers were active until about the
eleventh century; in eastern Europe, they continued to function
for somewhat longer, and among certain sects in the Middle East,
served throughout the Middle Ages.

pope: Head of the Catholic church. During the Middle Ages, the
pope was also the head of western Christendom. (In the east, the
patriarch of Constantinople was generally acknowledged as the
supreme authority.) The pope was believed to be in a direct line
from Saint Peter, who was believed to have received his authority
directly from Christ. The seat of his authority was Rome as opposed to Vatican City, a relatively modern state.

In addition to the direct political authority the pope wielded
over Rome and its environs, essentially as a king, he also had
much influence over other states. For example, the pope
crowned the heads of the Holy Roman Empire, and could call
upon the monarchs of Europe to launch crusades—and not just
upon Muslims in the Holy Land, but also heretical communities
within Europe itself, as in the case of the Albigensians of southern
France, who were largely annihilated by a force of Norman
crusaders.

The pope could also excommunicate individuals or even entire
countries, making them ineligible to receive the sacraments until
reconciled with the Church. To most modern minds, this holds
little meaning. To the medieval man or woman, such a prospect
was horrible and held the threat of eternal damnation. Of course,
the power to censure secular rulers through excommunication
could backfire with dire consequences. For example, after being
excommunicated for divorcing his wife without papal consent,
King Henry VIII of England, once called "Defender of the Faith"

because of his devotion to the Church, founded the Church of England rather than beg the pope for mercy.

KNIGHTHOOD

Knights were frequently organized into orders of knighthood, many of which were fraternal or military associations of armed, armored and mounted expert soldiers fervently dedicated to God or some other noble cause. Just as such organizations can evoke colorful and powerful images of their role in history, so too can they be used to evoke powerful images in works of fantasy.

Some orders of knighthood owed allegiance to a specific sovereign, others received support from a variety of sources (e.g., the Hospitalers received men, money and material from several Christian states), while others were wholly independent and even established states for themselves (e.g., the Teutonic Knights, who carved the state of Prussia out of pagan eastern Europe).

The head of an order might have one of several titles, including Grand Master, Knight Grand Commander and Knight Grand Cross. The second highest member of an order was usually styled Knight Commander. Various other members might have held titles that denoted some office within the order, for example, Sergeant-at-Arms. Most of the other members of an order would likely simply hold the title of Knight.

Most orders of knighthood were very religious and ritualistic, like militarized sects, and many even had a cultlike quality, with complex initiations, sacred mysteries and increasing degrees of arcane knowledge.

Among the oldest and most distinguished of the historic orders of knighthood are the Sacred Military Constantinian Order of Saint George, founded in A.D. 312; the Sovereign Religious Order of the Knights of Saint Catherine of Sinai, founded in 737; the Equestrian Order of the Knights of the Holy Sepulchre of Jerusalem, founded in 1113; the Order of the Garter, founded in 1348; and the Order of the Golden Fleece, founded in 1429.

The following orders were especially representative, colorful or influential. All were formed in the Holy Land during the Crusades, but each evolved in different ways and is remembered for different accomplishments.

Hospitalers were members of the Knights Hospitaler of Saint John of Jerusalem, an order formed by crusaders in the eleventh century for clergy attached to a hospital that tended to sick and needy pilgrims to the Holy Land.

In the twelfth century, the order was reorganized and began to participate in military operations on behalf of the Latin Kingdom of Jerusalem. In 1187, Jerusalem fell to the Muslims and the order moved to Acre, a fortified coastal city, from which it continued to care for the sick, patrol the roads and crusade against the infidel. In 1291, Acre fell and the Hospitalers moved to Cyprus. A few decades later, in 1310, it moved to the Greek island of Rhodes, which it ruled as an independent state until it was conquered by the Ottoman Turks in 1522.

Holy Roman Emperor Charles V gave the island of Malta to the order in 1530. They successfully defended it against repeated and numerically superior assaults by Turkish forces, and remained there until 1798, when Napoleon Bonaparte ejected them from the island. After that, the Hospitalers entered a period of decline. Nonetheless, they still exist today, as the Sovereign Military Order of Malta.

Knights Templar were members of the Poor Fellow-Soldiers of Christ and the Temple of Solomon, who were also formed during the Crusades. Many nobles joined the order, and it quickly became a powerful, rich, proficient military organization. A grand master and a general council presided over the order, which was divided into knights, sergeants, chaplains and craftsmen.

Distinguishing characteristics of the knights included white cloaks emblazoned with red crosses, round churches and commanderies that they often used as banks. Indeed, after 1291, when the European crusaders were driven from the Holy Land, the main worldly pursuit of the Templars became banking and moneylending. Such was their financial influence upon the nations of Europe that they drew the envy and enmity of both secular rulers and clergy.

Beginning in 1307, monarchs in France, England and Spain raided and shut down the Templar headquarters. They arrested the knights and charged them with heresy, immorality and witchcraft, and sought to support these charges with confessions extracted by torture. The pope initially championed the Templars, but eventually renounced them for cynically political reasons. In 1314, the leadership of the Templars was burned at the stake in Paris. The charges against the Templars now appear to have been largely fabricated, and the order driven to extinction because of their success rather than their crimes.

The **Teutonic Knights** were founded in 1190 as the Brothers of the Hospital of Saint Mary of the Teutons in Jerusalem for the purpose of serving in a hospital during the siege of Acre during the Third Crusade. Despite its origins as a crusader order in the Holy Land, the knights forged a name for themselves thousands of miles away in Germany.

Within a decade, the Teutonic Knights had become a military order of nobles who took vows of chastity, obedience and poverty. In the thirteenth century, they relocated to Europe and began the work it became known for: unrelenting warfare against the pagan peoples of eastern Europe. Moving eastward, the knights conquered and colonized the state of Prussia, playing an important role in the expansion of German culture and influence.

In 1237, the Teutonic order merged with the Livonian Knights, an order that had carved out a domain for themselves along the Baltic coast. This combined order continued its eastward expansion, but in 1240 was defeated by a force led by Russian national hero Alexander Nevsky (who, incidentally, was a sworn vassal of the Mughal Empire, which at that time held Russia in the "Mughal yoke").

For the next two centuries, the order continued to war against Lithuania, Poland and Russia, but suffered as many defeats as victories. The order ceased to exist as a military force in 1525, when its grand master converted to Lutheranism and declared the militarized, monastic state of Prussia a secular duchy.

POLITICAL ENTITIES

Throughout the Middle Ages, a great variety of political entities were founded, existed and disappeared. In addition to innumerable tiny kingdoms, principalities and lesser states, several significant states and organizations emerged. Descriptions of the following entities are not intended to give a complete view of medieval Europe, but rather to give writers ideas for the kinds of organizations that might have a place in their worlds.

The **Holy Roman Empire** governed most of Germany, Burgundy and Italy for almost one thousand years, from A.D. 962 to 1806. Many of the great institutions of the Middle Ages were either founded within this great state, or greatly influenced by it. Two great precepts provided the moral foundation of the empire: the idea of a hierarchical political organization with a single ruler at its head, and the idea that all Christians were united.

In 800, Charles the Great—Charlemagne—became emperor of what he called the Roman Empire when he was crowned by the pope in Rome. This state, an ostensible restoration and continuation of the empire that fell more than three centuries earlier, lasted until 925, when it fragmented into a series of successor states.

In 962, Otto I of Germany and Pope John the XII collaborated to resurrect Charlemagne's Roman Empire (the adjective "Holy" was added in the twelfth century to emphasize its ostensible importance to Christendom). All of the successive Holy Roman Emperors were similarly kings of Germany, elected to the post by the region's princes.

Although the Holy Roman Empire was not really an empire, holy or Roman, its kings often had great influence throughout Europe, in no small part because of the respect for the concept of the empire and its leader. Because of this, German kings expended much financial and political capital to see themselves elected to the post and crowned in Rome.

The Holy Roman Empire declined with the end of the Middle Ages and was broken up by Napoleon Bonaparte in 1806 when he conquered Germany.

Crusader States, many no larger than fortified cities and their environs, were founded throughout the Holy Land, the Levant (modern-day Lebanon), Syria and Asia Minor (modern-day Turkey) by western European Crusaders in the eleventh, twelfth and thirteenth centuries. Among the most significant of these were the Latin Kingdom of Jerusalem and the Latin Kingdom of Constantinople.

The Latin Kingdom of Jerusalem was founded in 1099 by the commanders of the First Crusade and included Palestine (modern-day Israel), Beirut and Antioch. The Crusaders elected Godfrey of Bouillon the first king of Jerusalem, although he used only the title "Defender of the Holy Sepulchre." Jerusalem itself was lost to the Muslims in 1187, and the Latins were unable to recapture it, despite financial aid from Europe and the professional military assistance of various orders of knighthood. The kingdom was gradually whittled away and finally collapsed in 1291, when the fortified port city of Acre fell to the Muslim Mamelukes of Egypt.

The Latin Kingdom of Constantinople was founded in 1204 when a force of French and Italian Crusaders overran and sacked the capital of the Byzantine Empire, and chose Count Baldwin IX of Flanders to be Emperor Baldwin I of Constantinople. Dependant on French and Italian financial aid and requiring Venetian naval support, the state functioned as little more than a military camp during the six decades of its existence. It was also reviled in some circles because it had been established at the expense of the greatest Christian, albeit Orthodox, state in the east. In 1261, soldiers of the Byzantine emperor in exile recaptured the city and ejected the remaining Latins.

The **Hanseatic League** was a commercial alliance of Baltic and North Sea German cities that was gradually formed between 1250 and 1350. Leading members of the league included Danzig, Hamburg, Bremen and Riga, and the Teutonic Knights and the state of Prussia also cooperated with it. The league maintained offices (kontors) in non-German cities that included Bergen, Bruges, London and Novgorod where its merchants lived and traded.

Essentially a coalition of regional groups, which met regularly in a diet from 1356 to 1669, some two hundred different cities were members of the organization throughout its history, and about three dozen were part of the organization at any given time. Accomplishments of the league included suppressing piracy, defending members against aggression, lobbying for passage of beneficial commercial laws, preparing charts and other navigational aids, and obtaining valuable concessions for its members.

Enemies of the Hanseatic League included Denmark, which the league defeated in naval combat in 1370, and in the later Middle Ages, the Netherlands and England, which competed against the league commercially and curtailed its rights in their territories.

The league began to decline after 1500, and although never officially disbanded, effectively ceased to exist after 1669.

PERIPHERAL CULTURES
Beyond the borders of western Europe and its institutions of feudalism, manorialism and Christianity, lived many other peoples. To the fantasy writer, these peoples and their lands represent a source of colorful characters, stirring legends and exotic settings for adventures.

There were the pagan peoples, among them the Saxons, the Picts and the Vikings. There were also the Muslims, among them the Saracens and the Moors. Throughout the Middle Ages, all of them were the antagonists of the English, French, Spanish and Germans of Christendom.

Of course, the way such foreign peoples were perceived in contemporary literature and society does not necessarily reflect their true natures, and writers may wish to take this into account. For example, many medieval Europeans believed Islamic culture was a Satanic inverse of Christendom, with an antipope at its head and similarly evil counterparts to all other elements of their own society. Not only was this not true, but many informed rulers and scholars in western states found much to admire in Muslim culture, arts and science.

Several of the more interesting and influential of these peripheral peoples are described below.

The **Magyars** were a people who originated along the Volga River in northeastern Europe and adopted many of the habits of Turkish tribes they encountered, including their equestrian ways. In the late ninth century, they conquered the Carpathian Basin and then began to launch destructive raids westward into Germany. The mounted Magyar raiders moved further and further west until King Otto I, founder of the Holy Roman Empire, met and defeated them at the Battle of Lechfield in 955. Soon after, the Magyars converted to Christianity and established the Kingdom of Hungary.

The **Moors**, Muslim Berbers from North Africa, invaded Spain in the eighth century and occupied it for several hundred years. In the late fifteenth century, the Christian monarchs Ferdinand and Isabella systematically drove the Moors from Spain, but they were able to hang on in a few fortified cities until the seventeenth century. Moorish troops also invaded France several times early in the Middle Ages, but were always driven back. (A Moorish cavalry army was defeated in 732 by the French infantry under Charles Martel, who ordered his troops to aim the blows of their heavy axes and swords at men and horses alike.)

The **Mongols** swept into Europe in the thirteenth century, threatening Christendom and Islam alike, and even causing the two to briefly unite. Under Ghengis Khan, Mongol cavalrymen conquered much of the Old World, and by the time their great leader died in 1227, their empire stretched from the Black Sea to the Pacific Ocean and from Siberia to Tibet. As with Charlemagne's empire, however, that of the Great Khan could not long survive his death and was divided amongst his sons. By the fourteenth century, most of the Mongol successor khanates, or kingdoms, had collapsed, and by the beginning of the fifteenth century, their act upon the world stage had ended.

The **Normans** were the descendants of Viking raiders who settled along the coast of northern France in the tenth century. In 1066, the Normans, under their leader Duke William, conquered England and established a kingdom on either side of the Channel. A tough, martial people, the Normans were called upon by various popes to engage in several crusades, sold their services as mercenaries throughout Europe and the Mediterranean, and conquered Sicily.

The **Picts** were a mysterious people of unknown origin who lived in Scotland from ancient times and battled the Romans along their northern frontier and eventually harassed the English. Covered in blue paint and specializing in ambuscade, Picts are a constant enemy of the noble Prince Valiant. They reached the peak of their power in the mid-eighth century under King Angus, and a century later formed a unified kingdom with the Scots.

The **Saracens**—as Muslims in general, especially Arabs and Turks, were referred to throughout western Europe and the Byzantine Empire—represented one of the most persistent and real threats to Christendom. Turkish soldiers of the Ottoman Empire (founded in the 1300s) conquered the Byzantine Empire, the seat of Orthodox Christianity; overran most of southeastern Europe; and menaced Sicily, Italy, France and Austria, being stopped at the gates of Vienna every few centuries. Saracens were also the major opponents of the Crusaders and the villains of popular literature and lore, as in the *Song of Roland*, the quintessential heroic poem of the Middle Ages (even though in reality, Basques killed the figure Roland is based on).

The **Saxons** were a fierce Germanic people who conquered many of their neighbors and by the fifth century A.D., occupied Britain and what is now France and northwestern Germany. During the sixth, seventh and eighth centuries, the Saxons warred against various French kingdoms. Charlemagne led almost annual campaigns against the Saxons for thirty-two years in an attempt to end their dark pagan practices, which included human sacrifice. Although the Saxon chieftain Widukind opposed the Franks stubbornly, Charlemagne eventually defeated them through warfare, mass deportations and executions.

The **Vikings**, natives of the Scandinavian countries of Denmark, Norway and Sweden, and colonizers of Iceland, were certainly the best known, most colorful and most feared of the European pagan peoples. From the ninth to the twelfth centuries, the Vikings raided and traded along the coasts and rivers of England and Ireland, and penetrated into Russia, and even made incursions into the Mediterranean, Middle East and North America. Landing along unprotected shores in their dragon-prowed ships, the raiders would sack and burn local villages, take slaves and sometimes even capture horses and raid inland.

TERMS
The following terms cover many aspects of life in the Middle Ages, including the legal system that regulated people's lives under manorialism, and major events and phenomena.

ad censum: Term for the status of serfs who pay their rent in money rather than labor. Such a tenant was referred to as a *censuarius* (pl. *censuarii*).

ad opus: Term for the status of serfs who owe payment to a lord in the form of labor.

amercement: A fine.

assart: An area of wasteland or swamp that is reclaimed for agriculture.

assize of bread and ale: A royal law setting prices and standards.

bailiff: The chief official on a lord's manor.

balk: A raised strip of land left unplowed so as to separate the tracts assigned to serfs.

beadle: A manorial official, usually an assistant to a reeve.

bondman: A serf.

boon-work: The obligation of peasant tenants to provide special labor for a lord, primarily for his harvest.

bylaws: Rules made by open-field peasants to govern farming and grazing.

cellarer: The official of a monastery responsible for provisions.

champion country: Open country, which in the Middle Ages in northern Europe and England was settled by compact villages that were surrounded by their own fields. From the French *champagne*, or "open field."

charter: An official document, such as grant of privilege or a deed.

chevage: A payment made annually by a serf living outside the manor.

communitas villae: A term used to refer to the community of the village.

corrody: An old-age pension that provided room, board and incidentals, often purchased from a cloister for an annual premium by peasants.

cotter: The tenant of a cottage, who usually owned little or no land.

Crusade: A holy war called by the pope that was participated in by the military powers of Christendom. Nine Crusades were launched against the Muslims in the Middle East from 1095 to 1272 in an attempt to drive them from the Holy Land. Most were partially or wholly unsuccessful, largely because of a lack of cooperation between Europeans from opposing states. From the twelfth through the fifteenth century, numerous Crusades were launched against pagans and heretics in Europe.

curia: A courtyard.

custumal: A document listing the rights and obligations of serfs.

Dark Ages: A term for the period from the fall of Rome in the late fifth century A.D. through the ninth or tenth centuries, by various accounts. Although widely considered a period of decline, it was nonetheless a period characterized by some political, social and technological developments.

demesne: The portion of a manor cultivated directly on behalf of a lord, through the obligatory labor of his tenants.

dies amoris: An opportunity given to litigants to reconcile their differences. Also known as **love-day**.

distraint: An arrest or summons to court.

essoin: A delay permitted to a defendant in a court case, or an excuse for not appearing in court.

estate: The sum total of a lord's holdings, often consisting of several manors.

extent: A document listing the lands, rents and services of a manor.

eyre: A royal circuit court.

farm: A lease.

fief: Land granted to a vassal in return for services, usually military in nature.

frankpledge: A legal device under which every member of a tithing was responsible for the conduct of other members. An English system that predated the Conquest.

furlong: A subdivision of an arable field.

gersum: An initial fee for taking possession of a tenancy.

glebe: Land designated for the support of the parish church.

gore: An odd-shaped piece of arable land created by irregular terrain or the convergence of plowed strips.

hallmote: A manorial court of justice.

hamlet: A small, agricultural settlement that lacked some of the characteristics of a village, such as permanency. Such communities were typical of the Dark Ages and in frontier areas, or during times of political unrest.

hamsoken: An assault upon a victim in his or her own home, considered more serious than an attack upon neutral ground.

headland: A small section of land left at the end of plowed strips used for turning the plow around.

heriot: A death duty paid to the lord, usually in the form of the deceased's best animal.

hide: A variable unit of land, in theory one hundred twenty acres, used for purposes of tax assessment.

house hire: The rent paid by a serf for his house. Also **heushire**.

hue and cry: A system under which all within earshot were required to try to apprehend a suspected criminal.

hundred: An administrative division of an English county theoretically consisting of one hundred hides.

hut, sunken: Characteristic of the early Middle Ages, the sunken hut was the smaller of the two basic peasant structures (the other being the longhouse). Used as dwellings, workshops and storage rooms, such huts were dug up to a yard into the earth and roofed with A-frame structures of wattle and daub or thatch, and were usually about ten feet wide by twenty feet long.

infangenthef: The right of a lord to prosecute a thief caught on one of his manors and to confiscate his possessions upon execution.

leirwite: A fine levied against an unmarried woman for sexual misconduct.

longhouse: One of the two basic sort of structures built by peasants throughout the Middle Ages (the other being the sunken hut). Village longhouses tended to be some twenty to fifty feet long and perhaps fifteen feet wide, with wooden frames, wattle-and-daub walls and thatched roofs. They were not very sturdy, and hoodlums often broke into houses simply by battering through a wall. Also **byrehouse**.

Exterior of a sunken hut
Art by Sharon Daugherty. © Writer's Digest Books.

Magna Carta: The document signed under duress by King John Lackland of England in 1215, guaranteeing various political and social liberties to freemen and the nobility. Considerably more than half the population were not freemen, however, and thus did not benefit at all from the "Great Charter."

manor: An area consisting of a lord's demesne and the land allotted to his serfs.

merchet: A fee paid to a lord by a serf when his daughter married.

messor: A minor manorial official, the assistant to a reeve. Also **hayward**.

messuage: A house and its yard.

Middle Ages: The period in Europe between antiquity and the Renaissance, generally reckoned as the millennium from the fall of Rome in A.D. 476 to the fall of Constantinople in 1453.

mortuary: A death duty paid to the parish church upon the death of a serf, typically his second-best beast. Compare with **heriot**.

multure: A portion of flour kept by a miller as payment for grinding grain.

Norman Conquest: The 1066 invasion of Saxon England by Duke William of Normandy, possibly the most formative event in the nation's history. The Normans defeated the Saxons at Hastings and established a Norman dynasty.

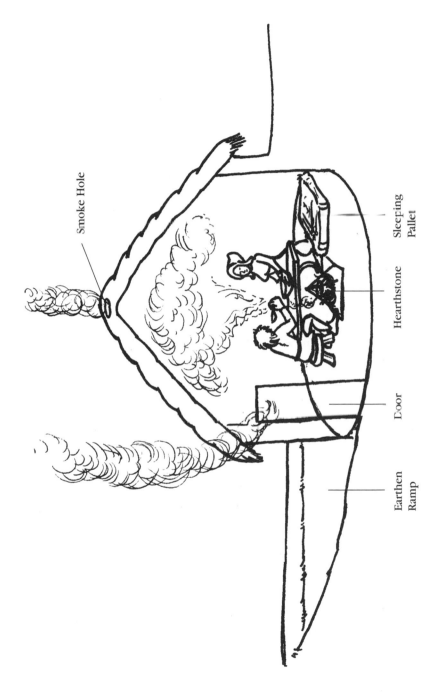

Interior of a sunken hut

Art by Sharon Daugherty. © Writer's Digest Books.

Exterior of a longhouse
Art by Sharon Daugherty. © Writer's Digest Books.

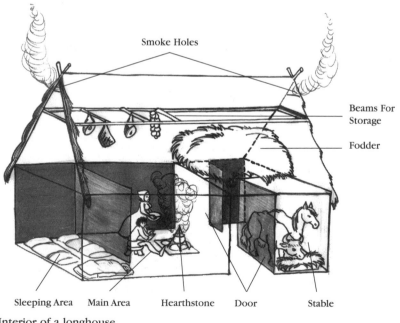

Interior of a longhouse
Art by Sharon Daugherty. © Writer's Digest Books.

open-field system: An agricultural system of northwestern Europe and England characterized by nucleated agricultural communities; i.e., compact villages where farmfolk dwelled, surrounded by their fields.

pannage: A fee paid by peasants to a lord to allow their pigs to forage in a wooded area.

pinfold: A lord's stockade for stray animals.

pledging: A legal device by which one peasant guaranteed the conduct of another (e.g., the payment of a debt, appearance in court, good conduct).

plague: Various epidemics ravaged Europe throughout the Middle Ages, especially in areas of relatively dense population. Major visitations of the plague began in A.D. 767 and reached a horrifying peak in the Black Death (bubonic plague) epidemics of the fourteenth century, which slew from one-quarter to one-half of the continent's population. Fleas, borne by rats, carried the diseases.

quarter: A unit of volume equal to eight bushels.

reeve: The main manorial official under a bailiff, always a serf.

ring: A unit of volume equal to four bushels.

seisin: Legal ownership of a property.

selion: A narrow strip of plowable land, up to several hundred yards in length.

serf: A manorial peasant with obligations that included merchet, tallage and week-work.

steward: The supervisor of a lord's manors and the chief official of his estate. Also **seneschal**.

tallage: A tax levied annually by a lord upon a serf.

tally stick: A notched stick used by a reeve to account for a manor's deliveries, expenditures, production and receipts.

tithe: A payment to a church equalling one-tenth of agricultural produce, sometimes including a monetary levy for other things such as livestock.

tithing: A unit of ten or twelve village men mutually responsible for one another's conduct.

toft: The yard of a house in a village, usually facing the street, surrounded by a fence or ditch and containing pens and buildings for animals and their fodder.

tota villata: A term for the body of all the people in a village.

village: A permanent, organized farming community of the Middle Ages that also included some craftspeople, which began to appear from about the tenth century onwards. From the Roman *villa*, the agricultural estates that were the center of many settlements in the early Middle Ages (cira A.D. 500 to 900). In England and northwestern Europe, the village buildings tended to cluster around the manor house and the church and were surrounded by fields. In Mediterranean countries, the village tended to be built within the walls of fortified hilltops, with fields, vineyards and animal pens on the plain below.

villein: Term used in England for a serf.

virgate: A unit of land, ranging in size from eighteen to thirty-two acres, ostensibly sufficient to support a peasant family.

wardens of the autumn: Officials appointed by peasants to help oversee harvest work. A similar official appointed by a lord was the reap-reeve.

wardship: The right of guardianship exercised over a minor by a lord.

wattle and daub: A lattice work of wooden sticks coated with clay and used for the walls of peasant huts throughout medieval Europe.

week-work: The main labor obligation of a manorial serf.

woodland country: Forested areas that in the Middle Ages were settled by isolated farmsteads, hamlets and non-nucleated or spread out villages. Woodland areas were often settled as a first step in clearing them for more intensive agriculture.

woodward: A manorial official in charge of a lord's wooded areas.

CHAPTER TWO

WORLD CULTURES
Michael J. Varhola

Fantasy cultures can be as varied, colorful and exciting as the real world and more so, if writers make the effort to craft these most critical backdrops. Nonetheless, many fantasy novels today seem to be set in an unending series of northern European countrysides; the villages, castles and taverns inhabited by Germanic, English or Scandinavian peoples; the forests, streams and caves haunted by trolls, orcs and goblins. Think twice before doing the same with your novel because you are covering ground many other writers have already visited and will continue to tread.

Beyond Europe, however, there are thousands of potential world cultures to use for inspiration or as a base for your fantasy cultures. Several cultures are profiled on the following pages. One intent of these profiles is to hint at the great variety of foreign cultures available to writers from every inhabited part of the world and from every period of human development. Another intent is to inspire and guide writers to seek out more information about these exciting cultures and incorporate them into their own worlds.

Writers should consider what point or points in a culture's development they are going to portray. Each has its particular allure and interesting characteristics. Cultures cannot remain static for long and are constantly changing, expanding and contracting. Is the culture in the ascendent, with dynamic leaders striving to carve a place in a world of dangerous competitors? Is it a strong, powerful state, secure against all but the most dangerous enemies? Is it an ancient, now-decadent culture with indifferent leadership and on the brink of imminent decline? Or has that decline already begun, with collapse from the inside being hastened by aggressive outsiders?

If you know the story you want to write, you can pick cultures with a history that fits your ideas. Similarly, the history of a particular culture can go a long way toward inspiring story lines, events and characters.

Several fascinating cultures are profiled in the following chapter to inspire you to use them or find others more suited to your needs.

RESOURCES

More information is available to writers today than at any other time in human history. In fact, this creates a problem of not knowing just where to start or what to choose.

Despite the vast resources of the World Wide Web, good old-fashioned books are probably still the most accessible resource. Most writers know how valuable bookstores and public libraries can be in finding good source material. You should be careful, however, not to neglect two ends of this spectrum.

Children's books often make great introductions to an unfamiliar subject. So what if a book on the Roman Empire is written at a seventh-grade level? If you don't know anything about the subject to start with, the clear outline, simple prose and pictures will all be refreshingly easy to digest. And fantasy writers might not need much inspiration beyond this.

University libraries are the other end of the spectrum and can provide books of a specialty level that will not generally be found in a public library or mall bookstore. Writer's can explore this venue when greater detail is needed on a specific subject.

Books that focus on specific arts or sciences of a culture can be of use to writers who want protagonists with special backgrounds or skills. For example, a book on Inca record-keeping techniques could be quite instructive to a writer creating a character who is an Inca imperial governor.

Reprints of original epics and texts can be incredibly instructive, of an ideal if not always of a reality. Such texts are of immeasurable value when creating fantasy worlds. For example, the Hindu epics *Mahabarata* and *Ramayana*, Chinese philosophical works like Confucius' *Analects* or Aztec codices.

Periodicals can also be a good source of material. Two of the best are *National Geographic*, which typically features aspects of one or more world cultures in each issue, and *Living History*, which covers historical activities and events from all periods of history.

AFRICA

Africa is now widely considered to be the cradle of humanity, so it is appropriate that some of the oldest and richest human cultures should have originated there.

Many of these cultures veritably demand to be incorporated into the milieux of fantasy worlds. Among these are tribes of pastoral cattle herders in east Africa, forest kingdoms in west Africa, mountain peoples in Ethiopia, and the riverine cultures along the Nile (Blue and White), the Congo and the Zambezi.

One of Africa's greatest cultures, New Kingdom Egypt, is profiled here.

Egyptian (New Kingdom) Culture

What we think of as ancient Egypt lasted nearly four millennia, beginning around 3500 B.C. and continuing until about 30 B.C. Historians divide those thousands of years into ten broad periods and these periods into more than thirty different dynasties.

The New Kingdom, comprised of the eighteenth, nineteenth and twentieth dynasties, is in many ways the most interesting period, and was characterized by dramatic social and political change and by the transformation of Egyptian culture from a simple riverine kingdom into a complex militarized empire.

At the beginning of the sixteenth century B.C., the kings of Egypt were subject to a militarily powerful people called the Hyksos. These people dominated the Nile river valley and occupied the northern part of the country, holding in vassalage the Egyptian nobility. Egyptian kings of the seventeenth dynasty rose up against the Hyksos, leading a war of liberation against them and their native allies and overthrowing them after several years of savage warfare. Amosis became the first king of the eighteenth dynasty (1570–1320 B.C.).

Arts and Sciences. Egypt's great pyramids are what it is best known for architecturally, but they were old when the forefathers of the eighteenth dynasty were driving out the Hyksos. Egypt's last pyramids were completed about one thousand years before the advent of the New Kingdom. New Kingdom architecture is just as significant and even more varied than that of earlier periods.

During this period, the dead were interred not in pyramids, but in smaller, personal tombs. Nonetheless, pharonic tombs were still very elaborate, consisting of chambers excavated from the solid rock of hillsides, their approaches augmented by temple complexes and columned galleries. Walls were decorated with images of mythological and historical events, carved in sunken relief (as opposed to the low-relief figures of earlier periods).

Prior to the overthrow of the Hyksos, Egyptian culture was sophisticated and civilized, but, metallurgically and militarily, it was still in the Stone Age. Their acquisition of Hyksos bronze-working skills brought them up to par technologically with some of the other great cultures of the ancient world. A growing sense of national identity also helped to elevate their position in the international scene of the day.

Pictograms called hieroglyphics were used throughout Egypt for, among other things, record keeping, religious texts and tomb inscriptions.

Government. The pharaoh, a semidivine king wielding absolute power, sat upon the throne of Egypt and served as the ultimate military, secular and religious overlord. Three of the most well-known pharaohs reigned during the New Kingdom: Ramses II, widely identified as the pharaoh of Genesis in the Bible; Tutankhamen, who was laid to rest in the richest royal tomb to survive into the twentieth century; and Hatshepsut, a rare and powerful female pharaoh who ruled for twenty-two years.

As the New Kingdom evolved into a militarized state, a bureaucracy evolved to oversee such things as weapon and equipment manufacturing centers, arsenals, military levy and payroll lists, acquisition and breeding of horses, and the construction of border fortifications.

Military. Three broad arms comprised the Egyptian army during the New Kingdom: Egyptian chariotry and infantry, and auxiliary foreign troops for example, Nubian archers or Canaanite peasant levies.

Prior to and during the early days of the New Kingdom, chariots were rare and highly prized, and often acquired from a defeated enemy force after a battle. Chariots were crewed by two soldiers. The archer was heavily armored in a coat of scales and armed with a composite bow. The driver was lightly armed and had little or no armor but may have had a large shield mounted on one arm. Chariot runners, lightly armored infantrymen, were assigned to chariots and detailed with dispatching the crews of disabled enemy chariots.

The weapons and equipment of infantrymen evolved during the New Kingdom, reaching a characteristic point during the nine-

EGYPTIAN ARMY: Note the archer and chariot driver, and the striped headcloth of the infantryman.

teenth dynasty (1320–1200 B.C.). Such foot soldiers wore the familiar striped headcloth or a simple round helmet, carried large rectangular shields that were rounded on top, and wore armor made of bands of linen across the chest and the nonshield arm. Their wood-and-bronze weapons included hand axes; two-handed, weighted mace axes; spears; throwing sticks; and Khopeshes (heavy, curved swords).

Archers became more important during the New Kingdom, eventually being armed with powerful composite bows in place of simple stave bows. The effectiveness of such troops in battle was greatly enhanced when they were formed in mass. They wore no armor and were kept from close combat with the enemy.

Egypt's borders had traditionally extended only a few miles to either side of the river and along the coast at the mouth of the Nile. During the New Kingdom, Egyptian forces extended these borders into neighboring areas, largely to act as a buffer for the Nilotic homeland. Egyptian armies campaigned south into the Sudan, north into the Levant (modern-day Lebanon), and as far east as the Tigris-Euphrates river valley (in modern-day Iraq).

After the overthrow of the Hyksos, military challenges for the New Kingdom included a long-term war with the Kingdom of Mittani to the north, clashes with the Hittites of Persia to the east and the Libyans to the west, and a major land and sea invasion by the "Sea Peoples," a coalition of eastern Europeans and Asians. Defeated by Ramses II during the twentieth dynasty (1200–1085 B.C.), the remnants of these people settled along the coasts of what is now Israel and became known as the Philistines.

Economy. Egypt's economy was based on intensive agriculture within the lush Nile River valley. Traditionally, farming villages that were clustered around temple or palace complexes, rather than urban areas, were the centers of communal life.

As the militarized society of the New Kingdom developed, fortified palaces, border fortifications, and enclaves of craftsmen specializing in critical skills (e.g., chariot makers, bowyers and fletchers) became increasingly vital.

Egypt also engaged in trade with a wide variety of states, including Somalia and southern Arabia along the Red Sea, and Crete, Phoenicia and Syria in the Mediterranean Sea. And, as a burgeoning imperial power, goods flowed into New Kingdom Egypt from the lands under its control, mostly via specially built coastal and riverine trading vessels. For example, at least three sorts of wood were used for Egyptian war chariots, most of them coming from the Levant, or Lebanon, and many of the spices used for perfumes and embalming were sent from Yemen, in southern Arabia.

Religion. A pantheon of humanlike gods, many of them with animal heads, was worshipped by the ancient Egyptians. Among the most important in the New Kingdom were Amun, god of Thebes; Ra, god of the sun; Set, god of death; and Montu, god of war. The pharaoh was often associated with Amun and Ra, and increasingly with Montu.

Worship of Egyptian gods spread throughout the ancient world, where they were sometimes revered under different names, for example, the goddess Isis was worshipped in Greece as Aphrodite, and later in Rome as Venus.

Egyptian rulers showed devotion to their gods through the construction of massive temple and tomb complexes that required thousands of craftsmen and many years to build. Egyptians believed that properly preserved dead lived on in the afterlife, and the noble and wealthy were embalmed in an elaborate ritual process that lasted several weeks. They also believed that objects buried with the dead could be used by them after death.

One pharaoh, Akhenatan, attempted to impose upon Egypt the worship of a single god, Aten, the sun-disk. His monotheistic reforms did not long survive his death.

During the New Kingdom, the priesthood grew rich and powerful, coming to own a third of the country's arable land. Because they were appointed by the king, however, they could not easily pose a challenge to him.

ASIA

To ancient and medieval Europeans, Asia was a vast, mysterious, fabulous place, full of innumerable foreign kingdoms, peoples and religions. This impression, while not always accurate in specifics, was generally very true.

The largest continent is home to perhaps the greatest variety of cultures, heroes, gods and kingdoms, some of them truly alien to the people of the West. Indeed, Asia is ripe to bursting with rich material for the fantasy writer. Japanese cultural elements have become popularized and familiar, but little is known by most of us about other Asian cultures.

These seem almost uncountable and include the Buddhist kingdoms of Tibet, Indonesia and Cambodia; the Hindu peoples of India; the Muslims of Pakistan and Afghanistan; the nomadic Mongol shamanists of the central Asian steppes and deserts; and the Indo-Sumerian city dwellers of the Indus River valley.

Two Asian cultures, Chinese and Mughal, are profiled here.

Chinese Culture
(Early Imperial Period, 221 B.C.–A.D. 618)

Chinese written history goes back more than three thousand years, and people have lived in China for tens of thousands of years. China's history can be divided into four broad periods: the Age of Conflict (1500–221 B.C.), the early imperial period (221 B.C.-A.D. 618), the Golden Age (A.D. 618–1368) and the late imperial period (A.D. 1368–1911).

In the centuries prior to the Early Imperial Period, China was divided into a dozen warring states. One of them, Qin, defeated the others during the fourth and third centuries B.C., unifying the country in 221 B.C. After this, China was periodically divided by internal conflict and split into as many as three opposing kingdoms, but the ideal of a unified country under a single emperor persisted.

Arts and Sciences. Some of the world's greatest art, literature and architectural wonders were created in China.

Bronze casting was an important art form from about 1000 B.C., and produced beautiful, intricate vessels and implements decorated with abstract designs and animals. Ordinary people never used bronze, however, and such items were reserved for the rituals of the imperial court and temples.

A written language of pictorial figures similar to modern Chinese writing was developed during this period and used for preserving everything from government records to the works of philosophers. This development was accompanied by the invention of bamboo paper around the first century A.D. followed by block printing.

Medicine was advanced by ancient standards, and acupuncture was one of the medical disciplines developed during the early imperial period.

Architectural and engineering accomplishments of the age were extensive. Imperial engineers built bridges and roads, linking the far corners of the country. Among the architectural feats of the period still evident today are the Great Wall and the Grand Canal. During the early imperial period, sections of defensive line in the northwest were connected to form the Great Wall, a fifteen hundred-mile-long barrier intended to hold back the dreaded Xiongnu (Huns). The Grand Canal, flowing one thousand miles from Beijing in the south to Hangchow in the north and linking the Yangtze and Yellow rivers, is still used today.

Chinese cities tended to be symmetrical, walled, laid out on grid-plans of straight streets, and filled with square and rectangular buildings. Buildings were usually of red brick and roofed with green-glazed ceramic tiles.

Government. Imperial Chinese society was structured into a rigid hierarchy, the earthly head of which was the emperor, the "Son of Heaven," who ruled with absolute power. Ministers, officials and a system of bureaucrats assisted the emperor in running the great country, and aristocratic, military and religious factions surrounded him, seeking to forward their own interests and creating continuous court intrigue.

Qin Shihuang was the first emperor of a unified China. He had a reputation for evil and cruelty, but also for efficiency and lawfulness. He instituted standardized weights and measures and built roads throughout the country. Scorning Confucianism, he championed a philosophy called legalism that advocated a system of rewards and punishments for various sorts of behavior. After his death, chaos racked the country for eight years.

The hierarchical nature of Chinese culture was largely based upon the teachings of Kung-Fu-tzu (Confucius), who traveled throughout the warring states of China during the Age of Conflict (1400–221 B.C.) advising kings to rule by setting a good example for their people. His book *Analects* influenced Chinese leaders and scholars for two thouand years. He taught that children were subject to parents, wives subject to husbands and younger people subject to older people.

Military. Unification presented China with different military challenges from those of the warring kingdoms, including quelling uprisings and defending frontiers from foreign invaders. Foremost among the latter were the Xiongnu, against whom several determined military expeditions were led.

Infantry formed the basis of contemporary Chinese armies, augmented by smaller forces of chariotry and cavalry. Forces formed for a special purpose might have a different composition, however; for example, expeditions into the western steppes were made up mostly of cavalry troops. Chariots were typically crewed by three warriors; a spearman, a driver and an archer or crossbowman.

Armor consisted primarily of coats of leather or linen, enhanced with scales or whole plates of bronze or iron for the best equipped troops, and augmented by shields and helmets. Weapons included straight, single-edged swords; crossbows; composite bows; and bamboo-hafted spears.

Economy. The vast majority of Chinese were farmers who worked the valleys of the Yellow and Yangtze rivers. Others were tradesmen, bureaucrats or soldiers who dwelled in towns. The entire country, especially the rich south, paid taxes in the form of grain and manufactured goods to support the government and the army.

Trade was facilitated by the roads, canals and rivers of the empire, and flourished under the stable conditions of a unified government. Among the most important trade routes was the Silk Route, which stretched from Changan in the middle of the country all the way to Persia (modern-day Iran).

Religion. Confucianism, Taoism and Buddhism were three of the main religious or philosophical movements that influenced Chinese history. Their various factions represented them at court, and strove to curry and maintain imperial favor.

Confucianists believed that the earthly bureaucratic hierarchy of the empire was simply an imperfect model of a heavenly hierarchy, and that all people had a divinely ordained duty.

Taosim developed about the same time as Confucianism, but in opposition to it. It was formulated by Lao-Tzu, who in his Tao, or way, said that wise men do not try to change the world, but rather do nothing and seek harmony with nature. Monasticism flourished amongst Taoists, and great monasteries, often supported by pious patrons, were built throughout the country.

Buddhism, an import from India across the Himalayas, brought a pantheon of deities and supernatural beings to augment those of the existing Chinese religions. It too leaned toward monasticism.

Mughal Culture

Hordes of Islamic Turco-Mongol soldiers swept into India in the early sixteenth century, conquering vast territories, subjugating the local Hindu people and establishing one of the most colorful and durable empires ever seen. Established in 1526, the Mughal Empire began to wane in the early 1700s, eventually became a puppet state of the British, and collapsed in 1858. It is possible that no other empire has exceeded the luxuriousness, wealth or absolute power of the Mughals.

The forces that for over a century dominated most of India were descended from Mongols, who had in centuries past settled in Turkey and converted to Islam. Under Babur, a nationless military adventurer descended from both Tamerlane and Genghis Khan, these people conquered Afghanistan in the early sixteenth century. In 1516, Babur made his first raid into India, and in 1526, he invaded in force, deposing the ruling Islamic dynasty and establishing the Mughal empire.

Mughal life revolved around the court and opulent, elaborate, sometimes labyrinthine palaces and **zenanas**, or harem precincts, which were the settings for the intrigues, assassinations and coup d'etats that plagued the Mughals throughout their reign. Mughal emperors, **padishahs**, along with their officials and supporters, had to constantly be on guard against poisoning, strangulation or other forms of assassination.

Arts and Sciences. Although descendants of a people who excelled at destruction rather than creation, the Mughals became great patrons of poetry, painting and architecture.

Tomb architecture is what the Mughals are best remembered for, most notably the Taj Mahal; several other tombs, less well-known outside of India, remain notable sites to this day.

The Mughals were also a very literate people. A well-administered empire, the Mughals employed innumerable scribes and record keepers, leaving behind a detailed, if somewhat narrow record of their reign; for example, women were rarely mentioned at all, and those that rose to positions of power, such as the Nur Mahal, wife of the emperor Jahangir, tended to be vilified for their efforts. The padishahs were multilingual, enjoyed creating poetry and kept detailed memoirs, mostly in Persian.

Poetry was highly regarded and valued cup-companions of the emperor were expected to entertain him with verse. Spontaneous couplets ranked especially high.

Indian miniature painting reached its height under the Mughals, and accurate likenesses of all the emperors and many of their officials survive to this day.

Government. The padishah was an absolute dictator, epitomizing the eastern despot. The earliest Mughal emperors were able military commanders and administrators, and created a stable government and an extensive bureaucracy that allowed the empire to be maintained by the increasingly indolent, less capable emperors that followed them.

By modern standards, the best of them were excessively cruel and authoritarian, routinely torturing to death enemies, and engaging in entertainments that included massive hunts and forcing unarmed men to fight dangerous animals. Invariably, however, the padishahs seemed to have had dual personalities. For example, Shah Jahan apparently murdered two of his brothers on his way to the throne, and rebelled against his father, Jahangir, multiple times. Nonetheless, he was a brilliant intellect who so loved one of his wives that he constructed one of the world's great monuments to passionate romance, the Taj Mahal.

Subadars (provincial governors) controlled the various **suba** (provinces) of the empire, which were divided into **sarkars** (districts) administered by **faujdars**. **Ghatwals** administered small frontier districts.

Military. As befitted a people descended from the Mongols, elite troops of aristocratic cavalrymen were at the heart of the Mughal military system. Cavalry armor and arms included mail, swords, axes, maces, lances and composite bows.

Secondary formations included armored war elephants, matchlockmen and slow, unwieldy artillery trains that tended only to be useful in sieges. Huge, elaborate fortresses housed their troops and watched over the country.

Defense of the empire was a constant concern and necessitated keeping able generals and thousands of soldiers in the border regions. In the north, Afghan tribesmen kept the frontier in a state of almost constant warfare (as they have for so many other conquerors), and Persia periodically attacked, as they did during the reign of Jahangir, capturing the fortified city of Kandahar. In the south, unruly Rajput lords schemed away in their hilltop forts, ever ready to seek personal gain by striking a bargain with a likely pretender to the throne. In the eighteenth century, the powerful Maratha caste arose and began to gnaw away at Mughal territory.

Economy. Mughal government heavily taxed its subjects, taking from the vassal Hindu population a third of its agricultural produce. Trade goods from China, East Africa and the Middle East flowed into Mughal India, and direct trade with European powers began in the sixteenth century. Currency included gold **murhs**, silver **rupees** and gems, notably sapphires and rubies. The complex financial affairs of the empire and the major provinces were overseen by civil officers called **diwans**.

Religion. The Mughals were Muslim, and perhaps more than anything else, this separated them from the subject Hindus, whom they considered pagans. Nonetheless, the Mughals allowed them to worship unmolested, and Akbar, greatest of the padishahs, even tried to unite Hindus and Muslims through a new religion of his own called **Din Ilahi**, Divine Faith.

MESOAMERICA

Mesoamerica, that expanse of land extending north from what are now El Salvador, Honduras, Belize and Guatemala through southern and central Mexico, was home to the most sophisticated pre-Columbian peoples of the New World, among them the Maya, Aztec, Olmec, Mixtec, Toltec and Zapotec.

All the Mesoamerican peoples were products of a shared cultural tradition that included similar art and architecture, agricultural systems and religious beliefs. These people carved their civilizations from the vast rain forests of the Yucatan Peninsula, the rugged mountains of the Pacific coast and the scrublands of central Mexico.

Two Mesoamerican peoples, the Maya and the Aztec, are profiled here. Several others are described briefly in the chronological order of their ascendancy.

Mayan Culture

Mayan culture flourished in the Yucatan Peninsula of southern Mexico beginning around A.D. 300, with more than a dozen of their huge city-states rising up from the steaming rain forests. Many Mayan cities, among them Copán, Palenque and Tikal, were huge by ancient standards and home to as many as fifty thousand people.

Endemic warfare and climatic changes that began around the middle of the ninth century coincided to bring about the decline of Mayan culture. Many cities were abandoned, and the recording of dates on stone tablets ceased, the last in 889. Life shifted to a few rival cities in the north and south of the area once dominated entirely by the Mayan states. These remaining cities held out against various successor peoples for several centuries, but most were conquered by the Spanish conquistadors in the early 1500s. Their final stronghold, Tayasal, fell in 1697.

Arts and Sciences. The Maya were the only New World people to develop a complete written language. Such writing was composed of both pictograms and symbols that represented sounds. By connecting these sound symbols appropriately, the Maya could write any of their spoken words.

Most Mayan books, or codices, were religious texts that Mayan kings believed they could use to predict the future. Hundreds of such bark-paper books were destroyed by the Spanish when they conquered the remaining Maya in the 1520s. Now only a handful of these texts remain.

Mayan astronomers were experts at their craft, gauging the movements of heavenly bodies for religious purposes. They were able to predict eclipses and the movements of the planet Venus.

Government. Mayan society was not unified and individual cities were ruled by their own kings. Such kings were called **ahaw** (lord) or **makina** (great sun lord), and served both as military

A map of Ancient Mesoamerica

commanders and priests. Mayan kings of note, whose names come down to us from monuments and inscriptions, included Shield Jaguar and Bird Jaguar of Yaxchilan and Pacal of Palenque.

Mayan kings served their people by performing critical religious ceremonies that usually involved drawing their own royal blood, which was believed to have special powers. Other duties included human sacrifice to their gods, usually of prisoners captured in war.

Mayan kings led their troops into war and gained prestige for the capture of enemy warriors. However, they ran the risk of being captured themselves and becoming a prime human sacrifice in their turn.

Military. For many years, scientists believed that the Maya were a naturally peaceful people. Evidence has come to light in recent years, however, that a continual need for human sacrifice drove the Maya into constant warfare against each other.

Mayan warriors wore costumes and face paint calculated to terrify their opponents, and went into battle howling and blowing war trumpets. Capturing enemy soldiers rather than slaying them was the primary goal of such conflict, and warriors were respected for the number of enemy they had taken in battle.

The planet Venus was identified with the god of war, and its seasonal appearance marked the annual start of Mayan intercity warfare.

Economy. Most Mayas were farmers, growing corn, squash and beans in forested areas cleared using slash-and-burn agriculture. Such commodities, along with luxury goods and currency in the form of cacao beans, were traded amongst the Maya.

Jade was the most precious material known to the Maya and was used to make ceremonial and religious accoutrements for the nobility and priesthood.

Religion. The Maya believed in dozens of gods who governed the various aspects of nature, and who were able to both create and destroy. The sun god gave warmth and light, but could also bring drought; the rain god brought water, but could also inflict floods; the war god brought victory, but could also impose defeat.

The gods were placated with their favorite foods, notably corn cakes, meat and human blood. Incense made from the sap of the copal tree was burned during offerings to the gods. Rituals also included pageants in which priests dressed like the gods and danced to music.

Prominent among the Mayan gods were Ahaw Kin, the god of the sun, who entered the underworld at night and was transformed into the jaguar god of war; Tlaloc, god of rain, who was worshipped by many other Mesoamerican peoples, including the Aztec; and Yum Kaax, the god of the staple food corn. Many other gods were

THE MAYA: Note the difference in dress between the men and women.

also worshipped, some specific to certain areas or cities; many of them are now nameless, their identities lost to the ages.

Aztec Culture

In the early fourteenth century A.D., the Aztecs were a migratory people who eventually settled on several islands in Lake Texcoco in central Mexico. Here, by 1325, they began building their capital, the city of Tenochtitlán (modern-day Mexico City), which was joined to the mainland by several causeways. From this secure base, the Aztecs began to expand into neighboring lands, seeking farmland, prisoners to sacrifice to their gods, and wealth. They established an empire that lasted some two hundred years.

In 1519, Spanish conquistadors under Hernando Cortés landed on the Mexican coast east of Tenochtitlán, on the day and year it had been predicted the god Quetzalcoatl would appear. Cortés was identified with this deity and was thus able to rule the Aztec through the reigning king, Montezuma II. He ultimately plunged the empire into civil war and left it utterly destroyed by 1525.

Arts and Sciences. The Aztecs had strong engineering abilities and built great cities full of palaces, temples and public areas. Aztec cities did not tend to be walled, and siege warfare was not common. However, Aztec cities were deliberately laid out with convoluted

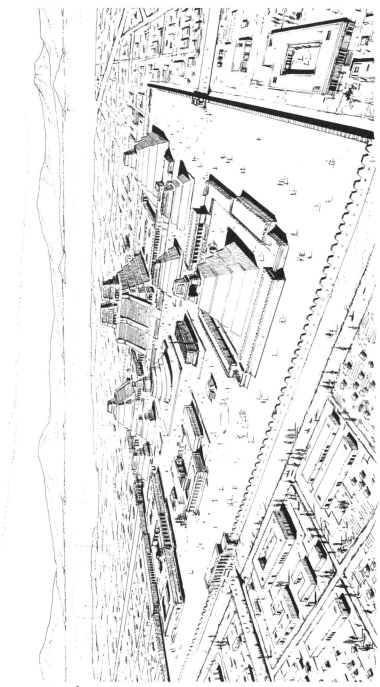

TENOCHTITLÁN: the Aztec capital. Note the precise layout of the city.

street plans that could be used to confuse, trap and ambush invading armies. Temple and palace precincts within cities were often walled citadels, and pyramids and other tall public structures could be used as firing platforms by defending archers. Thus, entering Aztec cities was not hard, but taking or holding them proved to be very difficult (even for the Spanish, who were more than once almost annihilated in brutal street fighting).

Huge pyramids often served as tombs for Aztec rulers, and "god houses," small temples, were built on top of them as a place where the deceased noble or various gods could be honored.

Other prominent public structures included game courts for **hachtli**, a brutal game played with a rubber ball between two teams of warriors (the Maya played a similar game). Such I-shaped courts had walls about eight feet high set with a vertical stone ring through which the ball had to be maneuvered using only elbows, hips and legs.

Aztec astronomers carefully measured time. Time passed in cycles of fifty-two years, and each year was divided into eighteen months of twenty days each, each of these days having its own name. Time was reflected on huge, carved stone calendar wheels, some more than thirteen feet in width.

Government. Head of the Aztec empire was the **tlatoani**, or emperor. Upon the death of an emperor, the army commanders and chief priests chose a successor, usually from among the most qualified members of the royal family. Aztec rulers tended to be wise priests and skilled warlords.

A large staff of soldiers, priests and administrators worked for the emperor and ensured that his commands were carried out, and a bodyguard of two hundred chieftains saw to his personal security.

Military. Aztec methods of warfare were highly stylized but nonetheless brutal. Capture of enemy soldiers was important to the Aztec, who typically had such prisoners killed in ritual combat.

Battles were usually fought between opposing lines of brightly clad Aztec soldiers, with the most experienced soldiers in the front ranks. Levies and veteran soldiers, including knights and shock troops, **cuahchics**, were all identified by distinctive uniforms, and commanded in battle by captains and generals.

Armor for common troops was the **ichcahuipilli**, a heavily quilted cotton vest. A padded cotton body suit, **tlahuizli**, was worn by veteran soldiers. These came in a great variety of colors and

Aztec calendar wheel

patterns, and were determined by experience, status and unit. For example, two elite units were the Eagle Knights and the Jaguar Knights, both of which wore stylized wooden helmets decorated to look like their totem animals. Shields were used by all sorts of troops and were made of wood covered with hide and decorated with colored cloth or feathers.

Aztec weapons were made of wood and stone. Most fearsome of these was the **macahuitl**, a sword-shaped, hardwood club whose edges were armed with rectangular obsidian blades (freshly chipped obsidian is sharper than surgical steel). Another favored weapon was the **tepoztopilli**, a hafted weapon like a spear whose head was armed with pieces of obsidian. Bows, slings and atlatls were also used, the latter to hurl large darts with great velocity.

Economy. The Aztec's primary crop was corn, which was used to make tortillas, their staple food. Because the early island-dwelling Aztecs initially had limited farmland at their disposal, they developed **chinampas**, large floating wicker baskets filled with earth in which they grew plants, including trees.

RITUAL COMBAT: A Jaguar Knight engages a captured enemy soldier.

Merchants called **pochteca** extended Aztec trade throughout Mesoamerica and to the lands beyond (as far north as the Mississippi River valley). They also served as spies, bringing back information about rival cities. Because the Aztec had no beasts of burden and did not use the wheel as a tool, all of the pochteca's wares had to be carried on the backs of porters.

Religion. Aztec gods gave their people what they needed to live but demanded human sacrifices in return. Their chief deity was the sun god Huitzilopochtli, who battled the moon and stars every day but needed human blood for strength and would be defeated without it. Thus, the Aztec believed the world would end if they did not make sacrifices, a belief that made warfare a perpetual way of life. Other important gods included Ixtilton, Huitzilopochtli's lieutenant, and Quetzalcoatl.

Sacrificial victims were frequently treated as honored guests for a time, after which they fought ritual combats or played games of hachtli, often willingly. Survivors were then executed upon the temple altars.

Aztec priests painted their bodies all black and never cut or washed their hair. They often fought on the battlefield as elite warriors.

Clothing. Aztec clothing tended to be simple. Men wore loincloths and decorated capes held in place by a shoulder knot. Women wore knee-length fringed skirts and colorful ponchos. Both sexes wore sandals or went barefoot. The cloth or pattern an Aztec was allowed to wear was determined by his rank, a stricture constantly challenged by the newly wealthy pochteca merchants.

Pendants worn through the nose were popular with men, as were decorative spikes or knobs worn through the skin below the lower lip. Women favored makeup in the form of bright patterns pressed on the face with ceramic stamps.

OTHER MESOAMERICAN CULTURES

Olmec

The Olmec are among the most ancient of the Mesoamerican peoples, becoming fully established by about 1200 B.C. and flourishing until about 400 B.C., when they broke up into smaller communities.

Centered along the southern Gulf coast of what is now Mexico, the Olmec were Mesoamerica's first complex culture, and many other regional peoples ultimately traced their ancestry back to them. Olmec communities were characteristically built in marshy areas on raised clay platforms that included stone paving and drainage systems.

Of all Mesoamerican art, that of the Olmec is perhaps the strangest, and includes colossal carved basalt heads, often as much as ten

OLMEC: Warriors gathered before a carved basalt head.

feet tall and twenty tons in weight, and weird jade depictions of were-jaguars and people with broad, fleshy features (unlike those of other local peoples), many with cleft skulls.

Toltec

The Toltecs migrated into the Valley of Mexico in the seventh century A.D. during the waning of Mayan power and after the collapse of Teotihuacán. They dominated central Mexico from the tenth to the mid-twelfth century A.D., establishing their capital at Tula, the northernmost of any built by a Mesoamerican people.

Droughts weakened the Toltec in the twelfth century, and Tula was overrun by displaced peoples around 1150. Some of the surviving Toltecs fled to the Valley of Mexico, and many Aztecs were later proud to claim a Toltec lineage.

The Toltec had strong contacts with the Maya of Chichen Itza, as evidenced by similarities in art and architecture. They also established trade routes that stretched from what is now Costa Rica to the American Southwest.

Zapotec

Zapotec culture was centered in what is now Oaxaca state in modern-day Mexico on the hilltop capital of Monte Albán, a site founded around 500 B.C.

By about A.D. 300, the Zapotec had developed one of the greatest of the Mesoamerican civilizations, and it flourished until around A.D. 800, when the metropolis of Monte Albán was home to about sixty-six thousand people. After this time, the focus of Zapotec culture shifted to smaller towns and the capital began to decline, but was never completely abandoned.

Mixtec invaders conquered most of the Valley of Oaxaca during the thirteenth and fourteenth centuries, after which the center of Zapotec civilization shifted southward to the Tehuantepec region, where it remained independent until the Spanish conquest.

Zapotec art included the oldest hieroglyphic inscriptions yet found in Mesoamerica, many temples and painted tombs that contained funerary urns in the form of Zapotec gods.

Mixtec

The Mixtec established several city-states in the seventh century A.D. in the mountainous Oaxaca region of southern Mexico. For many centuries, the Mixtec did not intrude much upon the affairs of their neighbors, but in the thirteenth and fourteenth centuries, strengthened by various political alliances and diplomatic marriages, the Mixtec conquered most of the Valley of Oaxaca and displaced the Zapotec. Mixtec soldiers tended to use the atlatl and sling more than other weapons.

The Aztec in their turn conquered most of the Mixtec lands between 1486 and 1519, and later defeated them completely with the help of Zapotec and Spanish allies.

Mixtec artisans were among the most skilled of Mesoamerica, and created turquoise mosaics, gold jewelry, painted manuscripts and stone carvings. Many of the richest archaeological finds from Mexico were fashioned by Mixtec craftsmen.

NORTH AMERICA

Our own continent is home to a great diversity of colorful cultures, some of which are familiar to us, corresponding in part to the popular images we have of Indians. From the wigwam building woodland Indians of the East Coast, to the tipi-dwelling buffalo hunters of the Great Plains, to the whale-hunting totem-pole carvers of the Pacific Northwest, North America provides ample cultural material for the fantasy writer. An added benefit to adapting these cultures is the wealth of resources available, including published literature, historical sites and the living legacy of Indians themselves.

As Indian cultures that predate contact with Europeans are most appropriate to a fantasy setting, writers should be careful to separate indigenous aspects of Indian culture from those that were formed by such contacts. For example, although the Plains Indians are thought of as great equestrians, horses were brought by Spanish explorers and colonists and were unavailable before the seventeenth or eighteenth centuries. Similarly, the familiar tomahawks of the woodland Indians were trade items brought by Europeans. A bit of research in this area can be both instructive and surprising.

Innumerable books on American Indians can provide general leads on the most well-known Indian cultures. One which is not well known is also one of the most exotic, the culture of the Mississippians.

Mississippian Culture

From around A.D. 700 to 1500, a sophisticated people known to us as the Mississippians flourished in the great river valleys of North America, practicing agriculture on an intensive scale and building great cities of earthen mounds and pyramids. In many ways, their culture was similar to those of the great civilizations of Mesoamerica.

Introduction of corn to the region more than two thousand years earlier, in the sixteenth century B.C., allowed the indigenous hunter-gatherers to settle down and practice agriculture in the valleys of the Mississippi, Ohio, Tennessee, Arkansas and Red rivers. The urbanized civilization of the Mississippians evolved from this culture and reached its peak around A.D. 900 during a period of global warming that provided the conditions for even more intensive farming.

Mississippian culture reached its height between A.D. 1100 and 1200, when climactic changes led to widespread drought; this climactic episode lasted until about 1550. These devastating changes led to malnutrition and starvation. This, combined with resulting social chaos and war, a likelihood of diseases or parasitic infestations spawned by overcrowded living conditions, and Old World diseases spreading ahead of European explorers, decimated the native populations and ultimately destroyed the complex Mississippian culture.

Early sixteenth-century French explorers visited some Mississippian cities and contributed to what we know about them. However, when Hernando de Soto ventured up the Mississippi in 1541, all he discovered was ruined cities and abandoned fields. Mississippian culture had disappeared.

Arts and Sciences. Mississippian towns are their most enduring legacy, which in layout were amazingly similar to those of Mesoamerica. Huge earthen mounds, the largest precolonial structures in North America, were the central structures of these towns. Some two dozen flat-topped mounds clustered around a central rectangular plaza. Cahokia, the most prominent Mississippian site, contains more than one hundred mounds, the largest of which is one hundred feet high and contains more than twenty-one million cubic feet of earth. Many mounds were surmounted by temples, and the mausolea of the social elite. Timber longhouses with thatched roofs were also characteristic of Mississippian towns.

The Mississippians had standard units of measurement and a working knowledge of mathematics and astronomy, all of which

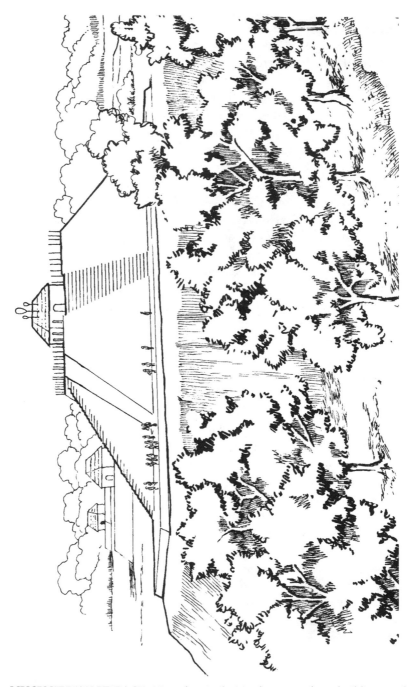

MISSISSIPPIAN VILLAGE: Note the similarities between these buildings and the Aztec and Mayan structures shown earlier.

was applied to the layout of their cities and placement of their mounds. Nonetheless, they did not have a written language.

Government. A stable economic base resulting from the surplus allowed powerful chiefs to consolidate villages into states centered on temple towns, and to levy taxes for public works, like the temple cities. These mound cities served as administrative centers where tribute and grain surplus were brought and food distribution took place.

A complex social order developed, and four distinct castes developed, those of warrior, priest, artisan and farmer.

Military. Collapse of the Mississippian culture led to social chaos and warfare; during the period A.D. 1200–1300, as many as 30 percent of adults may have been killed in warfare. By 1200, all cities and many villages were defended by twelve- to fifteen-foot-tall walls and shooting platforms. Mounds were also pallisaded and used as redoubts. Weaponry included bows and arrows from around A.D. 800; stone-headed axes and clubs were also used.

Economy. Rich alluvial soil, excellent climactic conditions and a new hardy strain of corn produced an annual crop surplus, which allowed village populations to explode from a few hundred to as many as ten or twelve thousand. Diet was nearly 90 percent corn, supplemented with nuts and game.

Labor became specialized, and artisans crafted arrowheads, shell beads and a type of pottery traded up to thousands of miles away.

Trade existed with peoples in Canada, Wisconsin, Virginia, Montana and the Rockies, Ohio, Pennsylvania, Florida and the Gulf Coast, and Mexico. Marine shells, obsidian, jade, mica, quartz, pipestone, copper and silver, and the teeth of alligators, sharks and bears all flowed into Mississippian towns.

The collapse of the agricultural system resulting from climactic changes eventually destroyed Mississippian economy, necessitating a partial return to hunting and gathering.

Religion. The Mississippian mounds were at the center of a complex, widespread religion now referred to as the Southern Cult. It may have had Mesoamerican influences, and was at least in part a death cult; for example, upper-caste dead were left in mortuary houses on central mounds until partially rotted, when they were given elaborate funerals.

Ritual objects found in burial sites and on mounds include disk-shaped gorgets of shell; monolithic axes and maces of dense, polished stone; carved wooden masks; and pottery heads.

Once the agricultural system degenerated, the Mississippian temple cities disappeared, along with state religion.

OCEANIA

Oceania, the island world of the Pacific, is home to a variety of exotic cultures that can be divided into three broad groups. Micronesians, living on the tiny coral atolls of the western Pacific, clad in sea urchin armor and wielding weapons edged with shark teeth; pygmylike Melanesians, dwelling in the mangrove swamps and mountain forests of New Guinea; and Polynesians, inhabiting the islands of Hawaii, Tahiti and New Zealand.

It is a Polynesian culture, the Maori, that is discussed here.

Maori Culture

Around A.D. 900, a Polynesian people arrived at a pair of large, temperate islands far to the south of any known to them. Those islands are today known as New Zealand, and its first human inhabitants as the Maori.

As North Island has a warmer climate that supports agriculture, it became densely settled. South Island is colder, and the Maori there dwelled in smaller groups and lived primarily as hunter-gatherers. Settlements along the coasts were typical, and inland areas were settled where game was initially plentiful. Precolonial Maori population ranged between 100,000 and 250,000.

Maori culture until about A.D. 1350 is referred to as archaic. After that time, many natural resources had been depleted and several game species had been hunted to extinction. From the late fourteenth century onward, warfare increased dramatically, as did the building of fortifications. This is then referred to as the classic period of Maori culture.

Arts and Sciences. Traditional Maori art forms included chants, dances, songs, wood carving and tatooing. Carving was used for meeting houses, great canoes and weapons. Warriors wore tatoos in swirling blue and black patterns on their faces and buttocks.

Poetry and storytelling were also highly regarded amongst the Maori, who were not a literate people but did have a strong oral tradition of myths and legends. Their language is part of the Austronesian family, related to Tahitian and Hawaiian.

Government. Kinship ties were the primary force upon which Maori society was organized. The basic social unit was thus the

whanau, a family group of three or four generations that dwelled together. Several whanau with common ancestry comprised a **hapu**. Such "subtribes" owned valuable assets like canoes and controlled a specific area of land over which it exercised hunting, foraging and fishing rights. Several hapu in their turn made up one of about fifty large tribes, each member of which was descended from a common ancestor, usually a hero with great powers. Within these social units, Maori culture was divided into three social classes: the aristocracy, commoners and slaves captured in war.

Military. By 1350, the Maori were building hill forts called **pa**. These were usually constructed on a piece of high ground or, more dramatically, by terracing the slopes of an extinct volcanic crater; some were also built on level ground or in marshes. Pa were typically composed of ditches, earthen banks surmounted by wooden palisades, and raised fighting platforms from which missile weapons could be hurled. Dwellings, storehouses and sometimes cultivated areas were clustered within the pa around a central open space, or **marae**.

Many warriors went into battle naked, while others wore flax coats, short capes or simple waist-blankets. The most characteristic Maori weapon was the **patu**, a short, broad, tear-shaped club that came in many variations and was made from a variety of materials,

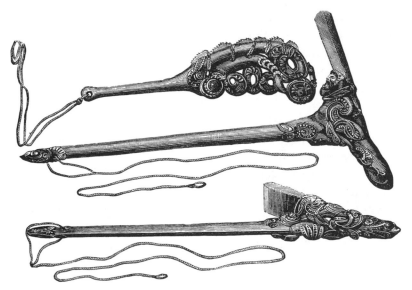

MAORI WEAPONS: (from top to bottom) patu, tewhatewha, taiaha.

including polished black or green stone, wood and whalebone. Other weapons included darts; the **tewhatewha**, a two-handed wooden war club with a beaklike head; and a fighting stick called a **taiaha**, which at a glance might have looked liked a small spear. The Maori were very adaptable in warfare and adopted weapons like shotguns, muskets and hatchets for their wars with the British.

Cannibalism was practiced upon men, women and children killed in the course of warfare. This was done not so much for their value as food but because of a belief that supernatural power could be conveyed by consuming the remains of enemies (relatives were buried with elaborate funerary rites).

Economy. Maori dwelt in villages and practiced small-scale farming, mostly of sweet potatoes. Diet was augmented by fishing, hunting and gathering. Game included at least thirteen species of **moa**, heavy, flightless land birds ranging in size from a few feet to more than three yards in height, and the kiwi, a small bird with rodentlike habits.

Stone of various sorts from throughout New Zealand was traded extensively among tribes, especially obsidian, chert, argillite (for adzes), quartzite, orthoquartzite (for blades) and greywacke. South Island greenstone became a favored stone for status items like ceremonial clubs and ornaments.

Religion. The Maori believed in a pantheon of nature gods, which included major deities like Rangi, god of the sky; Papa, god of the earth; and Tane, god of the forests. Priests, or **tohunga**, consulted major gods prior to important occasions, such as warfare or the construction of a canoe. Commoners were more likely to commune with ancestral spirits or local minor deities, like Maru, a god of war.

Priests communicated with the gods by means of god-sticks, carved wooden images wrapped with a length of cord. Such sticks were thrust into the ground, and the string pulled upon during ritual chants in order to attract the god and petition him.

How **tabu**, or spiritually powerful, someone or something was was very important to the Maori, and very complex and difficult for others to understand. All men were tabu to some extent, based upon factors like their lineage and how many enemies they had defeated (women were tabu only when menstruating or during childbirth), and the status of warriors and priests was measured according to how tabu they were. Great priests and chiefs were so tabu that food they touched could kill commoners eating it and paths traveled by them could not be used by anyone else.

SOUTH AMERICA

South America was home to some fourteen million natives in the years just prior to the arrival of Columbus. The ancestors of these people arrived on the continent around 12,000 B.C., and settled in the lowland jungles of the Amazon River basin, along the shores of the Caribbean and throughout the Andes mountain range. The continent's greatest cultures evolved along its west coast and included the Nazca, Moche and Chimu. Most successful and well-known, of course, were the Inca.

Incan Culture

Largest of the pre-Columbian states, the Inca rose from an obscure tribe to an empire in less than a century. Around A.D. 1300, they settled high in the Andes mountains and built Cuzco, their capital. In 1438, Pachacuti Inca ascended to the throne and began to subdue neighboring peoples; his son Topa continued in his footsteps, conquering the northern Peruvian kingdom of Chimor. Eventually, the Inca empire stretched along two thousand miles of the South American coast, spreading inland an average of about two hundred miles and encompassing a third of the continent's population.

The Inca learned much from other highland peoples, especially the conquered Chimu. When Spanish conquistadors under Francisco Pizarro encountered them in 1522, the Inca empire under Atahualpa was still growing and represented a sociopolitical system that had evolved over five thousand years.

Arts and Sciences. Amazingly, even though they developed an indisputably great civilization, the Inca had very few of the characteristics normally associated with a civilized people. Things they lacked included the wheel and a written language.

Nonetheless, the Inca undertook huge public works and left behind a durable legacy. Massive citadel, temple and fortress complexes, formed of perfectly fitted, irregular blocks of stone weighing several tons each, are the most obvious remnants of Inca engineering ability. Just as impressively, they linked their empire with some twenty-five thousand miles of interconnected mountain and coastal roads, overcoming ridges with tunnels, marshes with causeways, and the rifts and chasms of the Andes with suspension bridges up to seventy-five yards long. These bridges are still built by Peruvian villagers, who construct them in a mere three days using nothing but rope made from twisted grass, anchoring the ends of the bridges in ancient stone sockets carved by Inca craftsmen.

Government. Incan government was pyramidal, a strict hierarchy that ensured government control at all levels of society; at its apex was the Sapa Inca, who wielded absolute authority in political, military and religious matters. The aristocracy consisted mainly of the emperor's relatives, and served as his councilors and provincial governors. Government officials, some of them highly specialized, were all accountable to the Sapa Inca, either directly or through those above them.

A form of record keeping known as **quipus** allowed information to be kept on things such as tax revenue and turnout for public projects or military duty. The quipus, a cord with knots in significant numbers, patterns and colors, was a document that allowed information to be stored and transferred, and was read and interpreted by officials called **Quipucamayoc**.

Couriers, **chasquis**, ran along the roadways to deliver official messages; they ran 6½ minute miles, and in relays could cover 1,250 miles in five days.

Two main weaknesses of Inca government were that there was no clear line of succession to the throne and authority collapsed when the Sapa Inca died.

Military. A standing army of up to ten thousand men formed the core of the Inca military, acting as a cadre for an agrarian militia that could be activated when needed.

Primary Inca weapons were a stone-hurling sling of plaited llama hair and the **macana**, a mace with a star-shaped head of stone or bronze. Other weapons included a double-edged hardwood weapon like a two-handed sword, stone- and bronze-headed axes, and throwing spears with metal or fire-hardened wooden heads. Soldiers' uniforms consisted of their regular clothes, augmented by helmets, quilted cotton coats, shields and slats of iron-hard wood hung from the back of the neck to protect the spine.

Depots of weapons and supplies were set up along the well-maintained Inca road system. The main purpose of this road system was to allow rapid movement of large bodies of troops. Discipline and the ability to quickly move well-supplied armies was one reason

the Inca were able to defeat enemies against which they were superior in neither weapons nor tactics. Battles between the Inca and
their foes were chaotic messes, opening up with volleys of slung
stones, followed by hurled spears and then close combat with
maces, clubs and axes. Inca disorganization in battle, along with
ritualized patterns of campaign and prescribed times for attacks,
made them unable to withstand the brutal efficiency of the
Spaniards.

Defeated but still hostile peoples were relocated to the Inca heart-
land, while loyal subjects were sent as colonists, **mitimaes**, to conquered areas.

Economy. Heavy taxation allowed the Incas to maintain a standing army, fight wars and undertake huge public works projects. A
tax of about 66 percent was levied on produce and manufactured
goods, and the **mit'a**, an obligation to provide labor, was levied on
the masses.

The superior road system also allowed efficient transport of
goods, transported on the backs of llamas and people. Levied goods
were transported to and stored in government supply centers, some
of which were massive; the granaries at Huanuco Pampa could hold
up to thirty-six million liters of grain. Such centers also served as
manufacturing centers for the production of goods such as textiles,
tools or pottery. Such goods were highly standardized throughout
the empire, and show little individual variation.

Religion. The Sapa Inca was believed to descend from the sun
god, and the main state religion was the cult of the solar deity.
Common people were allowed to worship local rocks and streams,
so long as they also propitiated the sun god. Viracocha, the creator
god, was the chief deity and the one worshipped by the aristocracy.

Temples were filled with gold and silver ornaments and statuary,
most of which were melted down and shipped back to Spain as
ingots after the Spanish conquest.

CHAPTER THREE

MAGIC

Allan Maurer and Renee Wright

T he ancient occult sciences retain their power to entrance us even in this age of science and skepticism. In contemporary stories, nailing a few elements of magical lore into the solid timber of realism can provide the essence of a fantasy plot. From the most primitive tribes to the most sophisticated modern city, mankind believes in magic. We mutter spells (knock on wood), curse in holy names, conduct miniature rites (throwing spilled salt over a shoulder). So, too, in all times and places, both professional and amateur wizards, witches, shamans and magicians attempt to discover magic's secrets.

HISTORY

Magic differs from religion primarily in intent: religion is an appeal to the gods; magic attempts to *force* their aid. The nature magic of pagan religion goes back to prehistoric times. The word "magic" probably derived from the Greek word *magein*, the science of the priests of Zoroaster (Assyrian/Babylonian), or from *megas*, Greek for "great." Early Middle Eastern civilizations created a divide between the high magic of the priests and the low magic of the people, which persists to this day. The Chaldeans refined and shaped astrology, oracles practiced from holy temples, and harvest rites became public functions. But less exalted magicians practicing in small towns, the countryside or the neighborhood, offered inexpensive protection against the Evil Eye, explained dreams, foretold the future and sold amulets, talismans and other magic wares.

Ancient Babylonian and Egyptian magic systems were among the earliest known, already thousands of years old when Athens flourished in 400 B.C. or the Caesars reigned in A.D. 1, and many of their secrets are still sought. The mystery religions of ancient Greece and

Rome, themselves descended from the savage primitive rituals of harvest and hunt, degenerated into the magic of the Middle Ages, which the Christian church condemned as witchcraft. At the same time, the Church appropriated pagan holidays and a pantheon of saints, many borrowed from the Olympian collection of ancient gods and goddesses. As religions succeed each other, they often demonize their predecessors. Old Testament Hebrews made demons of hell of Babylonian, Egyptian and other Middle Eastern deities, both male and female. The magician practicing black craft depends upon who tells the story: most of us are familiar with the version of Moses versus the Pharaoh's magicians in Exodus (they turned their staves to snakes; Moses turned his into a bigger snake, which ate theirs). In the Egyptian version, according to witchcraft researcher Margaret Murray, "the wise priest of Egypt defeats the miserable foreign sorcerer whom he had saved from the water when a child."

European magic before the Crusades remained largely a hodge-podge of ancient religions and surviving folk magic. Following the Crusades, oriental theories and practices modeled on those practiced by the Sufis, Byzantines and Moors of Spain created European high magic. Secret societies and secret sorceries flourished, based on Alexandrian Neoplatonic ideas, the Hermetic books and the Hebrew Kabbalah. Basic principles included the Hermetic tablet's injunction: "As above, so below"; the idea that everything in the universe is associated through a series of secret connections between numbers, letters, the heavens, the elements (earth, air, fire, water) etc.; and the conviction that one could magically tap the infinite creative power of the universe. The refined development and application of the magician's imagination played an active role in medieval ritual and high magic.

At all times and places, however, the low magic of necromancers, who called upon the spirits of the dead, invoked hosts of demons and peddled love potions and talismans, coexisted with both established religion and ceremonial high magic. During the medieval era, both deeply superstitious and religious in a way difficult for most people to imagine today, some magicians practiced a black art that was essentially a desecration of Christian rites, symbols, liturgy, biblical passages and holy sites. Muslims who practice black magic do the same things with Islamic religion. These practices survive today, but should not be confused with pagan witchcraft, or Wicca, which are revivals of the ancient world's mystery religions (Rome, Egypt, Babylon, Greece) and have nothing whatsoever to do with Christianity.

The Force

All magic shares certain general features. The concept of **mana**, a magical force in virtually everything, has been called the "mother idea of magic." This idea of a universal force latent in all creation is common to primitive peoples: mana is called **manitou, pokunt** and **wakan** by various American Indian tribes; ancient Peruvians called it **huaca**; in Mexico, it is called **nagualism**; and in Lake Tanganyika, it is called **churinga** or **boolya**. Larry Niven wrote a series of popular novellas speculating that this force, which our mythology and legends suggest was once much more powerful than it now seems, could be used up. He called the first story, *When the Magic Goes Away*. Story ideas lurk everywhere in this material.

The ability to tap this magical force, or mana, is almost always extremely limited. Everywhere, tradition binds magic, ruling its access and use, and magical power traditionally lies in the knowledge of spells and rites. Sometimes it is invested in the person of the wizard. The rules of magic are limited, but it has many classes of practitioner.

Two Worlds

Most magical systems assume there are two worlds. One is the material, everyday, mundane world of reality in which experience and practical knowledge work. The other is a supernatural world, usually accessible only though a medium, the wizard/witch/wise one. Primitive man, for instance, nearly always recognized a natural and supernatural order. He applied knowledge of soils and planting times or where the fish or game were found, but performed magic to ensure good weather and protect himself from accidents.

Magicians attempt to control the unknown: the weather, abundance of crops or hunt animals, the course of a love affair or the outcome of a battle. Magic gives a house sturdiness after it is built with conventional means. Magical rites promote an abundant crop, but seeds are still planted.

PRINCIPLES OF MAGIC

The principles of **sympathy** (homeopathy and contagion) and **antipathy** guide virtually all human magic. They are widely applied in language, actions and even the magician's "inner state" or thoughts.

Sympathetic Magic

Sympathetic magic relies on the ancient idea that if one thing resembles another, the two are magically connected. The two principle types of sympathetic magic are: **homeopathy** (like affects like) and **contagion** (things once in contact, even tenuously, retain a connection even though widely separated).

Sympathetic principles affect all aspects of magic. Words of a spell draw upon this principle. Strong things are mentioned to impart strength; fast things are cited to impart speed. To make a household sleep like the dead, the magician uses grave dirt or the bones of the dead, placing them on the roof or in the home of intended victims. The magician cures "yellow" jaundice by banishing yellow. He paints the patient yellow then washes the color away. He brings in yellow birds then shoos them away. Antipathy is also used. Other colors drive out the yellow; the patient drinks water mixed with the hair of a red bull and sits on the skin of a red bull.

Imitation of successful hunts, fishing expeditions and harvests form the basis of many primitive rituals. African tribal and American Indian dances mimic the animal and the hunter and their interplay. Prehistoric cave paintings in Ariege, France, show a man clothed in a stag's skin with antlers on his head. A prehistoric Egyptian carved slate shows a man disguised as a jackal. Shamans, wizards and magicians throughout time have relied upon animal familiars, vision quest guides and totems.

In planting societies, dancers poked the ground with sticks imitating real planting, a movement you still see some in European country dancing. Ritual movement and dancing played multiple roles in magic ranging from tribal celebrations and occasions to solo dance by shamans.

The sympathetic principle governs performance of rites. If a wizard intends to magically harm a person with his wand or staff by "pointing" in the direction of his enemy, he must emotionally and even intellectually believe and feel he is thrusting the wand as a sword into the enemy's belly and twisting it. He must "act" as if performing an actual stabbing. The similarity of one's actions in a magical rite to the same actions in real life is an important part of making the magic work. Thus, sympathetic relations may involve color, sound, meaning, physical resemblance and the state of the magician's mind and attitude.

Homeopathy. The most common type of sympathetic magic is homeopathy. Homeopathy means like affects like. Some call it imitative magic. A magician might administer a potion that includes animal liver to a patient with liver pain.

Homeopathy is the basis for making an image of an enemy and sticking pins in it to cause him or her pain, discomfort or death, one of the most widely practiced forms of magic. One of the earliest records of this charm is in the trial of women and officers of the harem of Rameses III in Egypt in 1100 B.C.—they made images of the Pharaoh with magical incantations. Familiar to us in the form of the voodoo doll, the practice of making stone, wood, cloth or wax images and puppets in the likeness of enemies was practiced by the ancient Greeks, who inherited much of their magic from the Egyptians and other Middle Eastern regions.

North American Indians draw figures of a person in sand, ashes or clay, then poke the image with a sharp stick, shoot an arrow into it or run a needle through its head or heart. Peruvian Indians mixed fat with grain to form images of people they wanted to harm, then burned the effigy on a road the victim traveled. A Malay version includes nail parings, hair, eyebrows, spittle—enough pieces of the intended victim to represent the whole body—and combines them with bee's comb wax in a figure scorched over a fire for seven nights while saying: "It is not wax that I am scorching/It is the liver, heart and spleen of (victim's name) that I scorch" (from Frazer's *The Golden Bough*).

Making images can work for good as well as evil. In Sumatra, a barren woman holds a wooden doll of a child in her lap to encourage one to grow in her womb. In some cases, the father of a large family recites spells while the woman holds a cotton doll to her breast; in others, a wizard enacts a mock birth with a large stone tied to his stomach.

Homeopathic magic resembles the pretend games of children, often right down to the sincerity of the pretending, which is necessary to make the magic work. Magicians sometimes resort to "tricks" intended to convince others of their power, the belief necessary to working their "real" magic.

Contagion. Contagion is the concept that anything once in contact with something else retains a magically useful connection to that thing even if the two become widely separated. Often contagion combines with imitative and homeopathic principles in spells and rites. A wizard making an image of an enemy would want items once in physical contact with the person: nail clippings, hair, teeth, clothing. Today, superstitious (or careful) people still guard their nail and hair clippings, pulled teeth and intimate apparel. One occult author recalls her mother "keeping a jar full of my nail clippings from infancy on."

Contagion can work to the good of the practitioner, too. Placing an extracted tooth where a mouse or rat could get it would impart the strength of the rodent's teeth to its former owner when gnawed. In many parts of the world, the umbilical cord and the afterbirth are thought to retain such a powerful connection to the child even after removal that what happens to them may determine the child's entire fate. If properly preserved—buried in the sand, for example—the child will be prosperous; if not, he will be doomed. Or to make a child a good climber or hunter, the umbilical cord might be hung from a tree.

Frazer notes the "relation . . . believed to exist between a wounded man and the agent of the wound." Melanesians, for example, keep an arrow that wounded a warrior in cool leaves to combat inflammation. His enemy, meanwhile, knowing he inflicted the wound, drinks hot, burning juices and chews irritating leaves to inflame it. He twangs his taut bow string to pain the wounded enemy. This belief led to the widespread idea that to keep a human or animal wound from a blade or puncture from becoming infected, one must clean and oil the knife, scythe or nail that caused the harm. This idea is based on the notion that blood on the weapon continues a connection with blood in the body.

In the New Hebrides, obtaining a cloth someone used to mop his sweat gave the wizard the power of death over the hapless victim. The magician would wrap the cloth with leaves and twigs of a specific tree and burn them. In Prussia, it was thought that if you couldn't catch a thief, you could snatch a piece of his clothing and make him sick by beating it.

Less tangible connections also offer magicians the power of contagion. In Mecklenburg, Germany, it is believed that driving a nail into a man's footprint will make him lame. A German hunter might drive a coffin nail into an animal's footprint, believing it will hobble the quarry. Many American Indian and African tribes follow similar customs, throwing dirt from an animal's tracks in the air to bring the quarry down, or placing charms on the tracks to magically slow or cripple the beast.

In France, a witchhunter might follow a suspect and drive a knife into her footprint, thinking that if she is a witch, she will not be able to move until the knife is withdrawn. In Bohemia, a peasant girl might plant a marigold in earth she dug from the footprints of a man she loves, hoping love will bloom with the flower. The ancient Greek Pythagoreans recommended smoothing away the impression of your body when you rise from bed as a precaution against magic, so even the most tenuous connection could be magically useful.

Antipathetic Magic

Antipathy is what some anthropolgists call benevolent charms or the white magic that overcomes black. Holy water drives away devils, for example. A sounding bell does the same. A silver bullet slays a werewolf, and a vampire cannot see himself in the mirror because of its silver backing. Red berries or thread, because of their bloody color, counter witchcraft. Garlic repels vampires. Making the sign of the cross or other protective gestures drives off demons as do protective talismans. These examples act in antipathy, or counter to, evil or black magic.

Taboos. Taboos prevent magical contamination. Magic, particularly among primitive peoples, whether African, Polynesian (such as the Maori of the previous chapter) or American Indian, is a highly practical affair. Generally, they are protection against the unknown. Taboos restrict contact between the tabooed person (a king, a woman during childbirth, a warrior before his first battle) and others. They require purification or protective rites, often including bathing, shaving the head, marking of the body by a magician, incense, fire or water.

Touching a king, his clothes or his food is often taboo among primitive peoples. Warriors going to their first (or first several) battles are taboo, often in the same manner as menstrual women are taboo. Rules for both include unapproachable seclusion, taboos against scratching the head or any other part of the body with fingers, sexual abstinence and, minimal handling of food and their containers. The seclusion sometimes requires a man to build a separate hut for a bride in childbirth.

Taboos surround contact with strangers, with both sides performing obligatory rites: fire and incense greet them to drive away evil spirits; the visitor may carry lighted sticks or bark for the same purpose; on returning home, a traveler must bathe and visit a shaman/magician for cleansing, which frequently includes receiving a visible mark on the forehead or otherwise highly visible spot.

Taboos on eating and drinking may be particularly rough on kings, who take extraordinary precautions. The mouth may be a door to the soul, and food, which comes into contact with preparers and may not be completely consumed, may easily be magically (or actually) acted upon. Taboos force eating meals behind locked doors to prevent the soul's escape and being hidden from view, even in public, where, in some primitive societies, a cloth is held up to shield a king taking his meal. Since, by sympathetic contagion, the leftover food one leaves or the dishes one eats from retain a connection to the consumer, leftovers (even bones) are burned, buried or thrown into the sea to prevent sorcerers from obtaining them. A sorcerer keeps his eyes open for such refuse, particularly bones of birds, animals or fish consumed by people. He can concoct deadly charms with them.

A primitive might eat many animals or plants in order to share in their qualities, for example, eating a rabbit to gain speed or an elk to gain strength, but he must not eat others so as not to share them.

Sympathetic and homeopathic principles govern many taboos: boys of a fishing tribe are forbidden to play cat's cradle lest they entangle their hands in fishing nets as adults; warriors may not eat a cock that died while fighting, lest the same happen to them. Women at home during the hunt often face many taboos, such as being forbidden to kill any male animal while the warrior is gone or he may die.

Mourners or others who have contact with: the dead; people leaving and entering houses; women at childbirth as well as menstruation; those who kill another person; hunters and fishers, who must propitiate the animal spirits just as warriors must propitiate the ghosts of their dead enemies, are all heavily tabooed.

WHAT MAGIC DOES

Anthropologist Bronislaw Malinowski (1884–1942), who identified many of these common features, said all magic has one of three functions: to produce, protect or destroy.

Magicians, wizards and so on, accomplish these ends via three elements. They are:

1. Spells, incantations, invocations, enchantments (what is said)
2. Actions taken: rites, procedures, gestures, use of magic tools (what is done)

3. Condition of the practitioner, which requires precise, arduous preparation and might include:
   Purification by fasting
   Meditating in solitude
   Dancing
   Drumming
   Staring into flames
   Inhaling smoke
   Ingesting drugs
   Enduring pain
   Intense sweating

After ritual self-purification, the magician recites the spell, almost always accomplished by an action or rite that is intended to carry the magic to its intended object. Usually continued and unbroken attention to the proper state of mind is necessary for a magician's powers to work. In higher magic, a trained imagination brought to intense concentration may be required.

Let's take a closer look at each of the elements of the magical act:

Spells, Incantations, Invocations, Enchantments

The first element of magic is what is said. Words themselves retain a magical ability to affect us even in our enlightened era. Many people still have difficulty in separating their reactions to words from their reaction to what the words symbolize. Cursing involves invoking the names of deities, saints or devils: holy names or their devilish counterparts, whether in casual speech or magic spells.

The spell is associated so strongly with magic that in some primitive societies, the word for magic and the word for spell are the same. Usually a spell must be spoken exactly, without the slightest deviation from text and with proper pronunciation or intonation. Everywhere, the spoken part of a magic act is of supreme importance.

Spell books, such as the grimmores of the Middle Ages, required debilitating purifications on the magician's part, extreme care in making tools and letter-perfect recitation of enormous lists of words of power, holy names and turgid prose. Among Polynesians, a single slip during the most sacred ritual might cause the death of the practitioner by supernatural causes. Spells are governed by tradition rather than creativity. Altering a spell defuses its magic. Ancient Egyptian magic, **hike**, worked through spoken formulas that had to be recited exactly as proscribed at a particular place and time. Egyptians credited mispronounced words with all instances of magical failure.

The language of spells relates directly to an associated ritual and desired effect. To confer speed to a canoe, for instance, a spell cites birds on the wing, the lightness of a seagull on water, the floating ability of certain woods, onomatopoeic words that sound like speed.

Spells use cryptic, archaic language; lists of ancestral names, holy names, demon names and spirit names; and stories of mythological events, all in precise order and pronunciation, often known only to an elite group of initiates. The difficulties of meeting the stringent requirements for preparation and performance were cited as reasons why magic failed to work. In one of the most moving fantasy short stories of the mid-1970s, Tom Reamy's award-winning "San Diego Lightfoot Sue," a forty-five-year-old woman falls in love with a teenage Kansas lad and wants him to see how she looked at fifteen. The daughter of a witch, she performs a rite that goes wrong. Witnesses see only a green fire that consumes her—virtually the only fantasy element in the story. The archetypal power of this stuff works even in small fictional doses. A single magical idea that spells are dangerous to the magician if not performed properly continues to inspire tales in every medium.

The need for exactness in spells and rites supplies a basis for much humor in modern fantasy with mistakes responsible for all sorts of consequences, from the humorous sort practiced by Samantha's senile aunt on TV's "Bewitched," to the gruesomely macabre. Humor, fantasy and horror often compliment each other in fiction, perhaps because our human reaction to horror and the fantastic is often nervous laughter. In fiction, certain authors always made a living combining humor and horror, and humor and fantasy. At least two twentieth-century cartoonists, Gahan Wilson and Charles Addams, never strayed far from their successful mix of the two. Film and TV scripts combine fantasy, horror and comedy in an almost distinct genre in which the fantasy element—a genie, ghost, witch, magician—serve entirely comical purposes (*Buffy, the Vampire Slayer*; "I Dream of Genie"; *Death Becomes Her*). So don't be overly surprised if the Grim Reaper in your story turns out to have a sense of humor.

Black and White Magic

Magic in all times has served both positive and negative purposes, which are sometimes referred to as white magic and black magic. Magic itself is neutral; it is the application to which it is put that characterizes it. In the case of Christian, Islamic or other religious "black magic," official church rites are often reversed, as in the Black Mass or saying the Lord's Prayer backwards. Necromancy—calling upon the spirits of the dead—is also characterized as black magic.

When one religion succeeds another, as Christianity has pagan worship of multiple gods and goddesses, the priests, wizards or wise men/women of the former (paganism) are characterized as witches and black magicians by the current religion. (Many of the gods and goddesses became Christian saints, and pagan festivals became Catholic holy days.) Hebrew tribes worshiping their God, Yahweh (later Jehovah), did the same to the many Babylonian, Persian, Egyptian and other Middle Eastern deities, going so far as to make devils of former deities such as Baal.

The black magic of the medieval era, with its grimmores and their impossible-to-fulfill requirements, is generally considered silly by modern magicians. But at the same time, magicians practice various high-magic systems imported from the East, where they mix oriental ideas with those surviving from pagan times. (We'll cover this in greater detail later.)

Rituals, Rites and Wrongs

Nearly all spells are accompanied by actions. These "rites" generally require the same exactness on the performer's part as the reciting of spells. The main purpose of a rite is to carry the magic of the spell to its desired object.

Rituals are ceremonial acts for religious or sacred purposes. They have various, frequently overlapping purposes: to placate, propitiate, supplicate, honor, obey or call forth the gods, goddesses, spirits or demons; to initiate passage into adulthood, entrance into a secret society or entrance into a mystical vocation such as magician or shaman (all three may be ecstatic in nature, requiring taking drugs, fasting, lonely ordeals in the wilderness or jungle, pain, sleep deprivation and other means of altering consciousness); to mark transitions or passages; to encourage fertility, healing or cleansing; to protect home, family, children or warriors; to banish wrongdoers.

Elements of Ritual. The elements of ritual vary according to the type of magic practiced. Those required for ritual and ceremonial magic are covered in more detail in that section. Among the common features of ritual in all magic are:

- Reciting holy names, the names of God, spells, chants or prayers
- Dancing and other movement, particularly ritualized postures and gestures
- Costumes, masks, fetishes
- Incense, smoke, candles, fires
- Offerings, sacrifices
- Feasting or fasting
- Purifications
- Use of sacred objects, relics, tools, images, symbols

Ceremonial rituals include making the familiar magic circle, and within it, the triangle of the art. Magicians must remain inside the circle or lose their protection from the entities they summon.

Meditative Magic

Meditation is an element of magic from the shamanism of primitive tribes to the most esoteric ceremonial magic. It is used to cleanse the body, mind and soul, and to connect to the creative force of the universe through altered consciousness. Meditating on the Tree of Life forms an important aspect of Kabbalah.

Some magical systems, such as Hawaiian Huna and Islamic Sufi, actually do their primary work through meditation and associated mental activity—imagination, visualization and concentration. This might be achieved through self-deprivation of food, sleep or company; drumming; drugs; or dancing.

In Sufi practice, whirling is one way to achieve an ecstatic state in which magic of a psychic nature can be performed. Since Sufis who follow pious poverty are called "dervishes"; those who spin their trances are called "whirling dervishes." Fantastic literature and poetry from Rumi to *Arabian Nights* are cited as "quintessential Sufi texts." Since each Sufi adept teaches from his own system, no single Sufi approach to mysticism exists. Orders included not only the Whirling Dervishes, but also the Howling Dervishes, Shaven Dervishes and Silent Dervishes. Islamic black magic works much the same as Christian-inspired black magic: holy objects, places, garments, symbols, rituals and the Koran are desecrated, recited backwards or otherwise profaned for dark magic purposes.

RITUAL AND CEREMONIAL MAGIC

Ritual magic is the performance of ceremony to obtain material and spiritual power. Ceremonial magicians may follow one of two paths. In one path, the magician spends years of study and preparation learning the secrets of the Kabbalah, the Hermetic books or a master's teaching, until he learns to discipline his will and imagination, leave his physical body and work magic on the "astral plane."

This astral plane holds, in hidden planes, worlds of beauty and awesome terror. It is a literal twilight zone containing the highest dreams and darkest nightmares. The shaman travels there in a vision quest or to fight demons making a tribemate ill. The mystic ascends there after disciplining and training his imagination and will. All of the higher occult experiences occur here. The geography of this astral world and means of access to and travel through it supplies the material taught by many esoteric schools of occult science.

The magician ascends the multiple planes by various rituals, but one must be fit to receive these teachings. Magicians map out some areas in this unimaginably vast territory, describing inhabitants, their living space, the language they speak. The student ascends the planes as he rises in grade, and learns the spells, names of guardian angels, smells, colors, and other symbolic aspects of the planes. He learns which demons inhabit the plane, which he defends against with the proper protective spells and rituals.

The simplest method of astral out-of-body travel is through visualization training. The student begins by relaxing, in a prone position and imagining his astral body rising from his physical body. With training, visualization is intensified until the magician's consciousness transfers to the astral "watcher."

Other methods, such as meditating on the paths of the Kabbalistic Tree of Life, follow a specific protocol and traveling unprepared or leaping ahead of one's knowledge is considered dangerous and foolhardy.

Eliphas Levi's volume, *Dogma and Ritual of High Magic* (1856), proved hugely influential on the modern practice of this type of ritual, leading directly to the Order of the Golden Dawn and many other schools of modern ceremonial and ritual magic. The tendency of modern magic, however, has been to bring various systems of magic and occult science together in a synthesis that combines multiple schools. While not true of all modern magicians, many dispense with the more complicated requirements of traditional ceremonial magic in favor of simpler but no less volatile systems.

Following the second path, a ceremonial magician may draw his magic circle, his pentagram of two triangles and call forth deities, spirits, demons and the dead following directions from a grimmore or magic texts such as the medieval *The Key of Solomon*, which names hundreds of Greek, Roman, Egyptian and various other gods, demons and spirits. The paraphernalia required to follow this path and the preparations of the magician are described in arduous detail in spell books. But this concept did not originate in the Middle Ages. Works from the great library of Assurbanipal reveal that grimmores full of spells were common fifteen centuries earlier. Babylonian grimmores included **Utukki limnuli** (evil spirits), **Labartu** (hag-demons) and ceremonial texts such as the **Maklu**, which contained eight tablets of incantations and spells against wizards and witches (making images of their enemies and destroying them is a major element). Another sixteen tablets on exorcism of evil spirits names demons, goblins and ghosts.

This style perhaps reached its highest development when MacGregor Mathers (a Golden Dawn member) translated into English *The Book of the Sacred Magic of Abra-Melin the Mage*, allegedly a fifteenth-century guide but more likely an eighteenth-century work. It did away with most complicated ritual and paraphernalia required by European ceremonial magic. Abramelin magic supposes the material world is created by evil spirits that the magician can control after he attains the help of his guardian angel. (This is an ancient magical idea. The Golden Dawn magicians believed the magician's "guardian angel" was actually his own true self.) Discovering this, the magician can force the spirits—(which may be recognized as materializations of archetypal ideas inside his mind or aspects of himself—to do his bidding. The book includes a large number of magic squares, letter arrangements that represent and empower the magician's wishes. Abramelin magic fascinated Aleister Crowley, who warned that it was extremely dangerous to use without proper preparation.

Both paths may be dangerous to the life and soul of inadequately prepared magicians. One practicing magician says, "It's like a dark force and a good force. The dark force, calling up demons, is quicker, but you pay a toll. It's dangerous and costly to the magician spiritually. The other path, meditating on the Kabbalistic Tree of Life, say, is slower, but still dangerous if you do not do it right."

Both paths also evolved from ideas already old in Egypt when written down in ancient Greece. The occult sciences proceeded from these ancient moorings in sympathetic magic, the study of stars and rites for the Egyptian dead, to the Neoplatonic ideas of Plotinus of Alexandria in A.D. 233, who sought "the ideal reality which exists behind appearances." This idea—similar to Plato's concept of elementary ideas, hence the "Neoplatonic" label—led Plotinus and his followers, Porphyry, Iambilichus and Proclus, into out-of-body magical practice where they encountered gods and demigods, malignant daemons and genii. While in an ecstatic, meditative, out-of-body state achieved through austere living and careful preparation, the Neoplatonists believed evil genii and daemons might pursue and capture them if the philosopher/magicians did not escape by returning to their physical bodies.

Gnostics, who sought **gnosis**, or secret knowledge, further developed and refined Neoplatonic and other oriental magical ideas. Simon the Magus, mentioned in the Acts of the Apostles in the Bible, was a Gnostic magician (and the Bible relates only the canonical Christian version of his story). Gnostics were declared heretical by the Catholic church as it solidified its accepted theology.

The Hermetica

The Hermetica, according to occult tradition, is forty-two books written by various authors, but attributed in a convenient fiction to Hermes Trismegistus, "Thrice Greatest Hermes," a combination of the Greek god and Egyptian god of wisdom, Thoth. The secret knowledge in these works are dense with occult symbolism. Their basic idea suggests that the universe is a whole and is connected via a complicated system of correspondences, which is the import of the statement from the Hermetic work, the Smaragdine Tablet: "As above, so below." Legend says the Hermetic books contain fragments of the magic secrets of ancient Greece and Egypt, which were originally contained on books lost when the library of Alexandria burned, destroying much of the collected knowledge of the ancient world. They include *The Divine Pymander* and the *Vision*, which mix esoteric thought from dynastic Egypt with instructions for the spiritual development of the soul.

Medieval Magic

European high magic kept a low profile after mainstream Christianity conquered the West in the fourth century. The thirty-sixth Canon of the Ecumenical Council at Laodicea in A.D. 364 forbids priests and clerks to become magicians, enchanters or astrologers. It was merely the first of many canons to follow forbidding various magical practices as the Church decided that magic and Christianity were largely incompatible. Most magic practiced in Europe prior to about the twelfth century was the nature religion based on herbs and stones, the moon and stars, and cultural superstition or remnants of the ancient mystery religions. The Church regarded both as witchcraft or black magic.

When the Crusaders returned from the Middle East, they brought with them oriental ideas of theosophy (from the Greek, *theos*, meaning "god" and *sophia*, meaning "wisdom") that claims one can know the nature of the deity absolutely through proper preparation, study and ritual. Magical systems in the Middle East, practiced by the Byzantines, the Moors of Spain and the Arabs, drew upon the Alexandrian Neoplatonic ideas. Paracelsus and Agrippa together virtually outlined medieval high magic principles between them.

Paracelsus (born in 1493 near Zurich) wrote several tomes outlining his complex ideas, which first outlined the astral body concept, established connections between the body and the planets, and preached the importance of the willed imagination. "It is possible," he wrote, "that my spirit, without help of my body, and through an ardent will alone, and without a sword, can stab and wound others. It is also possible that I can bring my adversary into an image and then fold him up and lame him at my pleasure. Resolute imagination is the beginning of all magical operations."

The primary influences of Agrippa were due to the stories told about his own adventurous life. He was born Agrippa von Nettesheim, Henry Cornelius (1486–1535). A German soldier, physician, alchemist, astrologer and magician, Agrippa knew eight languages and traveled Europe widely as a soldier and in service to noble patrons. His defense of magic, *De occulta philosophia* (1531), and the tales surrounding his life (he made enemies freely, particularly among the medieval monks) made him one of the major figures who contributed to the medieval fascination with high magic. Agrippa regarded magic as "the true road to communion with God," linking his mysticism to Neoplatonic ideas and modern magic alike.

POWER ANIMALS

Very early on, mankind recognized the powers of the animals that shared the earth, and the ability to "talk to the animals" became a basic skill of shamans and magicians worldwide. Many tribes, peoples and societies trace their origins to a founding totem animal, often associated with a god, and hold that animal sacred. Animal powers are often invoked through dances imitating their movements and musical instruments imitating their cries.

Acquiring an animal guide or familiar is important in many kinds of magic and spiritualism. The Native American sought his animal spirit guide during a vision quest while alone in the wilderness, or on a spiritual journey assisted by hallucinogenic drugs, such as peyote. Western magicians gained the aid of a familiar through meditation and invocation, wearing masks and practicing shape-shifting.

Alligator or Crocodile: aggression, survival, reason (Egypt)

Ant: group-minded, hard worker, wisdom (Muslim); sacred to harvest goddesses

Ass or Donkey: stubbornness, obstinacy, symbol of opposites; sacred to Greek god Dionysius

Bat: good fortune, great happiness (China), rebirth, guardian of the night, cleanser, guide to past lives

Bear: power, adaptability, knowledge of the healing power of herbs, brings balance and harmony on the astral plane

Beaver: builder, gatherer, concentration, harmony in group work

Bee: purity, queenship, wearer of veils

Boar: courage, protection; fertility; symbol of the Lord of Earth; sacred to the Greek god Adonis, the Hindu god Rudra and the Egyptian god Set

Buffalo or Bison: sacredness, fertility, abundance, symbol of spirit

Bull: fertility, strength; associated with many gods and used in rituals in many religions or cultures including Egyptian (the Apis and Serapis cults), Cretan (the Minos cult), Celtic, Sumerian, Hindu and Mithraic

Butterfly: metamorphosis, carefree, transformer, love (China)

Cat: a strong protector, seer of spirits, independent and self-assured, seeking for hidden information, shape-shifter; sacred to Egyptian goddesses Bast and Pasht

Cow: love, abundance, nurture, contentment; represents goddess in many religions

Coyote: prankster, shape-shifter, illumination, opportunist, insightful, playful

Crane: solitude, independence, intelligence, astral travel to learn deeper mysteries

Crow: trickery, boldness, prophecy, shape-shifter, keeper of the sacred law, omen of change

Deer: see Doe, Stag

Doe or Hind: gentleness, loving-kindness, swiftness, alertness, bearer of messages

Dog: loyalty, companionship, keen hearing and tracking skills, a guard from approaching dangers

Dolphin: kindness, playfulness, link to ocean

Dove: communication through spirit; messenger to spirit world; peace, gentleness, love

Dragonfly: flighty, carefree

Eagle: connection to the Creator, divine spirit, wisdom, swiftness, keen sight

Elephant: confidence, patience, removal of obstacles, ability to learn

Elk: strength, agility, freedom, sensual passion

Ermine: purity

Fish: abundance, prosperity, harmony; loving companions or children

Fox: cunning, provider, intelligence, stealthy, able to make fools of pursuers

Frog: transformation, resurrection (Egypt), link to water element, beginning of new cycle; sacred to Hecate

Goat: wild energies, removal of guilt, independence. Associated with Hindu Agni; Sumerian Marduk; Palestinian Ba'al; Greek Dionysius, Athene and Pan; Norse Thor; Christian Satan

Goose: new beginnings, happy family life

Grasshopper: nobility (ancient Greece)

Hare or Rabbit: alertness, nurturing, hidden teachings, intuitive knowledge, transformation

Hippopotamus: birth of new ideas, righteous anger, protection of the family

Horse: stamina, mobility, strength, companion for astral travel

Hummingbird: messenger, able to stop time, happiness, love

Jackal: seeker of mystical knowledge, explorer of past lives; sacred to Egyptian god Anubis, "Opener of the Way"

Leopard, Panther or Cougar: leadership, courage, swiftness, perseverance, gaining confidence for astral travel

Lion: strength, courage, energy, royalty, family ties

Monkey: ingenuity, clever solutions; sacred in China and Japan; symbol of Egyptian god Thoth

Moose: headstrong, unstoppable strength, longevity, shared joy, wisdom in solitude

Mouse: secrets, shyness, ability to remain inconspicuous, attention to details, stealth, trust, innocence

Otter: finding inner treasure, gaining wisdom, enjoyment of life, a trickster; sacred in ancient Peru and to the Celtic god Cernunnos

Owl: wisdom, truth, patience, keen sight, guide to the underworld, clairvoyance

Peacock: all-seeing awareness, dignity, sacred to the Roman goddess Juno

Pelican: self-sacrifice

Phoenix: resurrection, renewal

Pig: see Sow, Boar

Porcupine: minds own business, trust in spirit, guards privacy; to Native Americans, a symbol of faith and trust

Quail: good luck, courage, victory

Ram: virility, fertility; sacred to Celts and Muslims; symbol of Indian fire god Agni and Phoenician god Baal

Rat: symbol of fertility and wealth in China

Raven: trickster, teacher, hoarder, spirit messenger, change in consciousness, help with divination

Salamander or Lizard: understanding dreams, mental creativity, transformation

Salmon: instinctive, persistent, determined, spiritual knowledge

Scarab: Egyptian beetle, symbol of the sun and creation

Scorpion: keeper of the house of the dead, revenge

Seahorse: confidence, grace

Sheep: timidness, ability to keep your balance; *see also* Ram

Snake: transformation, shrewdness; symbol of rebirth, immortality; associated with many gods

Sow: female pig associated with the Crone goddess, deep earth magic, knowledge of past lives

Spider: creativity, weaver of pattern of life in both ancient Mediterranean and Pueblo Indian mythology

Squirrel: preparing for the future, foresight, warning, changes, spiritual watchdog

Stag: Lord of the underworld, understanding of the cycle of death and rebirth

Stork: carrier of souls, fertility

Swallow: bird of springtime, flowering and love

Swan: grace, balance, innocence; symbol of the Muses and Valkyries

Thunderbird: Native American bird of lightning, bringer of rain and other heavenly gifts

Tiger: swift action, strength and willpower in a difficult situation; associated with gambling, the wind and the elements in the Orient

Turtle: creative source, self-contained, long life, patience, spiritual shield, relaxation

Vulture: carriers and defenders of the dead, prophecy

Whale: wisdom, music, long life, telepathic abilities, provider

Wolf: loyal, successful, leader on the astral plane, hunting and seeking, strong protection

Wren: sacred bird of the Druids, form of the Fairy Queen

Legend said Agrippa always traveled with a familiar in the shape of a large fearsome black dog. He paid his bills with money that looked normal but later turned to worthless shell. Agrippa, it was said, used a magic glass to view distant times and places, once spying his mistress weeping over the absence of another lover. One of the most famous stories says a boarder in his home convinced Agrippa's wife to let him enter the learned man's museum. The boarder found a book of spells and began to read. He ignored a knock on the door and went on reading. Finally, a demon burst through the door and asked why he had been summoned. Terrified, the boarder could not answer and the demon strangled him. Agrippa returned at that moment and, fearing he would be charged with the boarder's murder, persuaded the demon to return him to life. People saw the boarder walk through the marketplace, and after he died when the demon spell wore off, they thought he did so of natural causes. Agrippa's life is a prime example of the power of stories to heighten the power of a magician, for he was actually a relatively harmless alchemist/astrologer with a wide correspondence that accounted for his worldwide knowledge others attributed to his magical familiar.

SECRET SOCIETIES

Rosicrucian Brotherhood

A Rosicrucian Brotherhood published a series of pamphlets in Germany between 1614–1616 claiming to have mystic secrets. Many doubt whether any seventeenth-century Rosicrucian Brotherhood ever existed, but it became fashionable among those who styled themselves magicians to imply they knew Rosicrucian secrets. Modern Rosicrucian groups have only a tenuous link with those of the past. Within the occult community, many believe if such a group existed, then only a few adepts passed on whatever secrets they possessed orally to a few who succeeded them, and so on. Some people who claim to be Rosicrucians say they are doing exactly that.

The nineteenth-century Rosicrucians are particularly interesting. The English Rosicrucians (formed in 1866) included three founding members of the most famous modern magical society, the Hermetic Order of the Golden Dawn, and were mostly occultists.

French Rosicrucians were mostly artists and literary men. The Grand Master of the Rose-Croix in 1885, Josephin Peladan, was a novelist, and the order was important among the Symbolist movement of bohemian poets, painters and magicians. Peladan, who called himself Sar ("King" in Assyrian) Merodack (a character in one of his novels), and his associate Marquis Stanislas de Guaita together created the Ordre Kabbalistique de la Rose-Croix. These two found themselves embroiled in a magical battle with the novelist J.K. Huysmans, author of the novel about decadent French black magic, *La Bas,* and with the Abbé Boullan, a former Catholic priest and magician. Boullan, investigated by the Church for unholy and carnal cures of nuns, murdered a child and practiced sexual mysticism of an unpleasant sort. Stanislas de Guaita stayed with the Abbé in 1886 and left with the text of one of Boullan's magic rituals. Soon afterward, Boullan suffered several heart attacks, which he blamed on sorcery by de Guaita. When Huysmans visited Boullan during work on his novel about magic in nineteenth-century *fin de seicle* Paris, he found him conducting magical rites directed against de Guaita. A letter condemning Boullan to death by "the fluids" arrived while Huysmans was there, and he thought himself under attack by magic as well.

Huysmans returned to Paris and accused de Guaita of magical murder, but was challenged to a duel, apologized and retracted the statement. De Guaita, a decadent, sinister character wrote several lengthy works on magic. His own experiments included heavy drug use—hashish, morphine and cocaine—and he died young and blind.

The Freemasons

Although the Freemasons trace their legendary lineage to the architect of Solomon's temple, who was killed by workmen because he would not reveal the secret "word of God hidden in the temple structure," they were the remnants of a medieval stonemasons guild until the mid-1800s. The secret initiation rite, however, dramatizes the story of Hiram Abiff, the architect skilled in bronze work sent by the King of Tyre to Solomon to work on his temple. Masonic initiates die as Hiram and are reborn as Masons in a ritual drama some trace to the Egyptian mystery school of Isis and Osiris, who also fell to thugs and were resurrected. Followers of the Isis cult were called "the widow's sons," and Masons are the "sons of the widow."

Sufi mystics believe the architects of Solomon's temple were Sufis who incorporated holy words of God as numeric equivalents in its measurements, so an Arabic influence seems likely. The Saxon king Aethelstan (A.D. 894) brought Masonry to England after learning it from Spanish Moors. No one knows why, but the stonemasons guilds, who initially kept the techniques of their craft secret, began admitting "speculative" members. The first important speculative member was Elias Ashmole (1617–1692), an astrologer, kabbalalist, alchemist and Rosicrucian, among other things.

Speculative freemasonry adopted the tools of the craft as symbols (the square, compass, plumb line and level), grades (Entered Apprentice, Fellow Craft, Master Mason), rules of secrecy and member recognition methods from the medieval guilds. Members wear white leather aprons like those builders once wore. Blue and Gold are the ritual colors. Meetings are held in lodges or temples decorated with Masonic symbols and with checkered black-and-white floors, which symbolize man's dual nature. Two important Masonic symbols appear on the back of the U.S. dollar bill: the Great Pyramid of Giza and the all-seeing eye of the great architect associated with Horus, son of Isis and Osiris. Numerous American Founding Fathers were Masons, including John Hancock, George Washington and Benjamin Franklin.

During both the eighteenth and nineteenth centuries, Masonic groups were infused with mysticism by the German Rite of Strict Observance; the French groups were inspired by the Comte de St. Germain, who performed ancient rituals, and the Egyptian rites of Count Cagliostro. The Ancient and Accepted Rite of the Thirty-Third Degree evolved from these. Only Master Masons are allowed to reach for these higher states, which they say leads to "a mystic union with God." The Vatican condemned anyone joining a Masonic Lodge to excommunication in 1917, and the Greek Orthodox church condemned it in 1933, calling it reminiscent of heathen mystery cults.

Levi's Laws of Magic

Despite the increasingly scientific and materialistic world view during the eighteenth-century Age of Reason, the nineteenth century saw a revival of interest in ritual magic. It began with Francis Barrett's *The Magus, or Celestial Intelligence*, published in 1801. The man who virtually created the mindset for modern magic, however, was Eliphas Levi, who penned *Dogma and Ritual of High Magic* in 1956.

Levi outlined what he called the "three fundamental laws of magic." Levi's first law stated that human will was a force as material as steam or a "galvanic current." Levi maintained that all the tools of the magic art—geometrical figures, candles, incense—served only, but necessarily, to concentrate the magician's will.

Levi's second law posits the existence of astral light, a mystic medium like ether scientists once thought existed in the vacuum of space. Some magicians believe they have access to all that ever happened or will happen from the so-called "Akashic Record," in this astral domain. Madame Blavatsky, the famous founder of the Theosophical Society, claimed to "read the astral light" to draw upon the Askashic Record.

Levi's third and most important law updates the medieval and Hermetic idea that correspondences exist between the macrocosm, the universe, and the microcosm, or individual person. The soul of man, Levi said, is the "mirror of the universe."

Levi said anything present in the universe is also present in the person and can be invoked through a knowledge of the correspondences: a force personified as Hermes corresponds to wisdom. The magician can call up this cosmic force into his own soul or call down the force and project it into a magic triangle, where it materializes if a "material basis" such as blood or incense is provided. These personifications of cosmic forces generally are archetypal and include deities, demons and spirits of all times and places.

The Golden Dawn

The Order of the Golden Dawn was founded in 1886–1887 by Dr. William Wynn Westcott, a London coroner, Samuel L.M. Mathers, an "eccentric pseudo-Highlander of no identifiable occupation," and Dr. William Woodman, a physician. The membership and teachings of the Golden Dawn exerted a powerful influence on all of the following magical movements and, indeed, has never been equaled. Its members included not only Crowley and W.B. Yeats, but later, classic fantasy writers Arthur Machen and Algernon Blackwood. Magicians such as Mathers and A.E. Waite reintroduced the tarot to magical practice and, along with Crowley, codified and modernized occult practice, sewing many threads into one complex fabric. The Golden Dawn established a magic school complete with examinations. The Golden Dawn tradition continues in England where two temples survive.

Among other activities, the Golden Dawn added a fourth law to Levi's, that of the trained imagination, which they felt necessary to direct willpower. The Golden Dawn also expanded Levi's correspondences into an elaborate system that, according to the *Encyclopedia of the Unexplained* (edited by Richard Cavendish), connected "every Egyptian, Greek and Roman God, every spirit named in *The Key of Solomon*, and other medieval grimmores, every name in the Jewish and Christian Angellologies, to the twenty-two paths and sefiroth of the Kabalistic Tree of Life. To each of them were attributed colors, animals, precious stones, scents, magical formulae and so on." To evoke the proper force, the magician looks up a table corresponding to it and designs his ritual to fit. Cavendish includes a lush description of a Golden Dawn ceremony following this system in which four magicians stood inside an octagon drawn in orange-yellow chalk. A lamp burning olive oil and snake fat was at each octagon angle. Outside the figure was a triangle where the spirit should appear. Incense of mercury smoldered in a censer. A mercurial "hell-broth" bubbled in a cauldron heated by an alcohol lamp that contained a preserved snake. The mercurial spirit was supposed to form from the mercury smoke. Florence Farr, the magician, spoke:

"Accept of us these magical sacrifices, prepared to give Thee body and form . . . the heat of the magical fire is my will enabling Thee to manifest Thyself in pleasing form before us . . ." and she went on to name which of the magical elements formed which parts of the spirit as another magician threw that element into the cauldron and Farr invoked a magic word. One of the participant's papers included a parchment allegedly consecrated by "being placed on the spirit's head after he materialized."

Many Golden Dawn members freely used various drugs. (Crowley eventually became a heroin addict.) They fought amongst themselves over a variety of matters.

DIVINATION

Foretelling the future always formed a significant part of a magician's job. Reading omens, the stars, the cards, a palm or bumps on a head; casting runes, yarrow stalks, dice, bones, coins or sticks; peering into crystal balls, teacups or animal innards; and talking to spirits, the dead and psychics via telephone hotlines, all have the single purpose of glimpsing the future.

Many of the oldest and most developed branches of the magician's art involve divination, among them astrology, tarot, I-Ching, casting the runes and prophet (psychic) predictions. Signs and portents of the future are everywhere for the knowledgeable and talented oracle—in the air, earth, fire, water, sticks, stones and bones.

Below, we list the best-known and many lessor-known methods of divination with a brief description. Their very number and variety illustrates the importance of this field of magical practice.

Aeromancy: Divination from the air and sky, such as cloud shapes, comets or sky color. Comets in particular inspired prophets of ancient and modern times.

Alectryomancy: A black hen or white gamecock pecks corn grains from a circle of letters forming words or names that the prophet interprets. Recite the alphabet at daybreak, noting those letters that coincide with a rooster crowing.

Aleuromancy: Fortune cookies. Answers to questions rolled in dough and baked. Random choice comes true.

Alomancy: Fortune-telling by salt. Throwing some over your shoulder to avoid bad luck and other modern superstitions are reminders of this ancient practice.

Anthopomancy: Prophecy through human sacrifice.

Arithmancy: Divination through the use of numbers.

Astrology: Divination by the positions of the heavenly bodies.

Augury: Interpreting signs and omens, but also fortune-telling in general.

Austromancy: Divination by reading the direction and force of the winds.

Axiomancy: An axe answers questions by its quivers when hacked into a tree.

Belomancy: Tossing or balancing of arrows.

Bibliomancy: Divination with books opened randomly, and many other methods.

Botanomancy: Burning tree leaves and branches.

Capnomancy: Interpretation of smoke rising from a fire.

Cartomancy: Divination with cards.

Catoptromancy: Turning a mirror to catch lunar rays.

Causimomancy: Studies how objects burn in a fire. An object that burns slowly or not at all indicates good tidings.

Cephalomancy: Reading the head of a donkey, goat or other animal.

Ceraunoscopy: Divination from thunder and lightening.

Ceroscopy: Interpreting the bubbles that form when hot wax is poured in water.

Chiromancy: Divination by reading the lines of the hand. Combined with chirognomy, or reading the shape and structure of the hand, we get modern palmistry.

Cleromancy: Casting lots using stones, sticks or other objects.

Clidomancy: Dangling a key that answers questions by turning one way to say yes, another way to say no. Only one of many forms of **radiesthesia**, where any object on a string or chain may be held between two fingers and questioned. If the dangling object circles, it means yes. If it goes back and forth, it means no. Different movements are sometimes assigned to yes and no, but the principle remains the same.

Crominiomancy: Divination from onion sprouts. (It'll bring tears to your eyes.)

Crystallomancy: Scrying, or crystal gazing.

Cyclomancy: Fortune-telling via a turning wheel.

Dactylomancy: A dangling ring answers questions. Another form of radiesthesia.

Demonomancy: Demon-aided future seeing.

Dendromancy: Studying oak or mistletoe parts for signs.

Geloscopy: Divining the future from laughter. For happy wizards only.

Gyromancy: People walk in a circle and spell the prophecy by marking where they stumble.

Haruspicy (also Hieromancy, Hieroscopy): Prophecy by inspecting the innards of sacrificed animals.

Hippomancy: Interpreting the neighing and hoof stamping of horses.

Hydromancy: Divination by interpreting the color, flow, ripples and other shapes in water. Led to tea reading.

Ichthyomancy: Fishing for clues to the future (examing fish entrails, that is).

Lithomancy: Precious colored stones are spread on a flat surface with the brightest color indicating the future: red—happiness in love; yellow—disaster; purple—sadness; black or grey—misfortune; green—hope realized; blue—good luck. Colored beads may be used.

Margaritomancy: Pearls under a pot (it is said they bounce if a guilty person approaches).

Meteoromancy: Telling the meaning of meteors, which have long been considered potent omens.

Moylbdomancy: Foretells future events by interpretation of hissing molten lead.

Myomancy: Omens made by the sounds or signs of mice.

Oculomancy: Determines events by looking deep into your eyes.

Oinomancy: Like hydromancy, except wine is the liquid examined for future omens.

Oneiromancy: The interpretation of dreams.

Onychomancy: Symbols and signs revealed by sunlight on fingernails.

Oomantia, (also Ooscopy, Ovimancy): Inspecting eggs for omens and signs, a quite ancient divinatory technique.

Ophiomancy: Serpents used for divination.

Ormnithomancy: Birds and their actions tell the tale.

Pegomancy: Spring water and its bubbles are used for divination.

Pessomancy: Signs seen in pebbles.

Phyllorhodomancy: Ancient Greek practice of slapping rose petals against the palm and judging the future by the loudness of the clap.

Psychometry: Obtaining impressions from physical objects.

Pyromancy: Fortune revealed by interpreting flames.

Rhabdomancy: Use of a wand or stick to divine the future. It led to radiesthesia.

Rhapsodomancy: Divination with a book of poetry that is randomly opened; the passage read as an omen or guide.

Sciomancy: Spirits tell the future.

Sideromancy: Studying the shapes of straws burned on a hot iron.

Sortilege: Casting lots (sticks, runes, dice, stones, coins).

Spodomancy: Signs read in cinders, ashes and soot.

Stichomancy: Random opening of a book in hopes the passage will portend the future.

Tephramancy: Burning tree bark and reading the signs in the ashes.

Tiromancy: Examining cheese for omens and signs.

Xylomancy: Divining from the size and shape of pieces of wood randomly collected, or burning the pieces and observing which flame first.

BUILDING YOUR OWN MAGICAL WORLDS

One effective way to create a magical world of your own is to think of yourself as a folklore collector in that world. You will probably not include all of your background material in your actual writing, but even what you do not use will help give your work a solid suspension system—a way to help readers suspend disbelief while they are in your fictional world.

Remember that stories—as legends, mythologies or anecdotes—invest virtually every item and action of a magician's, wizard's or witch's repertoire with meaning and power. The stories themselves are frequently part of a wizard's secret knowledge, which he passes on only to initiates. Other stories are tribal property, but no less holy, honored and valued.

The Handbook of Folklore, by Charlotte Burne, suggests questions folklore collectors ask about any society's magic art. Writers creating fantasy worlds should do the same. For example:

- What are the names for magic users (wizards, witches, charmers, magicians, shamans)?
- Are stories told about famous magicians?
- Are magicians male, female or both?
- What rewards does a magician receive for success?
- Is the magician punished for failure?
- Does the magician do good (white) magic or evil (black) magic or both?
- Are a society's good magicians and evil magicians separate individuals, such as the **sorcheleur** and **desorcheleur** of the Channel Islands?
- How does a magician attain his powers (initiation; instruction; inheritance; preparation through fasting; solitude; trance or drug states; or direct transfer from another magician, deity, demon or spirit)?
- What is the magician's social and/or political status? (In most primitive societies, the magicians are accorded status second only to the chief; however, in some they are accorded respect while alive, but are buried in the hollow of a dead tree or otherwise ignominiously disposed of after death.)
- Do the wizards/magicians form a craft, guild or society?
- Do they assemble secretly and meet with demons or other spirits?
- Are the magicians members of an outcast group, such as Gypsies, or do they belong to the tribe or community?
- Is any country, area, district or people particularly powerful?
- What are a wizard's powers?
- Are a magician's powers general, or specific and limited? Powers the magician/wizard/witch/sorcerer might have:
  Prophecy

Divination
Controlling the weather
Healing
Laying or countering curses
Making amulets, talismans or both
Conducting public and/or private rituals
Exorcising demons
Shape-shifting into animals, spirits, shapes or things
Traveling through the air
Raising or stopping storms
Causing earthquakes
Becoming invisible
Calling up demons or spirits
Talking to demons, spirits, deities or the dead
Kidnapping souls
Transforming men into beasts
Avenging injury
Causing illness or death
Affecting others' bodily functions
Bringing rain to crops, fish to nets or game to hunters
Making a house solid, safe and stable
Giving swiftness to a canoe
Making charms to win a lover, harm an enemy, protect from harm, confer beauty, bring good fortune
Making an arrow, dart, spear, knife or other weapon hit its intended target
Protecting against bad fortune
Providing a bountiful harvest
Inflicting pain or injury
Giving skill in war, games or the hunt
Calling up or repelling spirits or demons
Casting out or exorcizing spirits or demons

- Does the magician have animal familiars? If so, which animals? Is the magician identified with a certain animal? How does the magician acquire an animal familiar or guide?

Magical Rites

Continue to imagine yourself as a folklorist collecting data in your imaginary world, and ask these questions regarding the rites your world's wizards/witches/magicians may conduct:

- What is the what, when, where, how and why in each case?
- Are the rites performed in public or secretly?
- What is their purpose?
- How are the magician and his/her assistants dressed? What apparatus is present?
- What is the meaning and purpose of each item?

Preparations for Rites

- purifying ceremonies (sweat lodge, fasting, meditation, vision quest)
- divining omens
- drawing magic pentagrams or circles

Gestures

- Are gestures used, such as the two-fingered "horns" or the sign of the cross?
- Does the magician dance?
- What symbolic gestures are used, such as tying and untying knots to symbolize binding or loosening?

Sounds Made in Magical Rites

- Chanting, singing, muttering
- Percussion: drums, hollow logs, gourds
- Rattles, bull-roarers, rainsticks
- Flutes, bells, stringed instruments (often one to three strings as in the berimbau or kora)
- Spells, magic words, formulas
- Recited names

Materials Used

- Blood, entrails, eyes, feathers
- Other human or animal body parts
- Roots, herbs, flowers, other vegetable matter
- Air, water, fire
- Iron
- Salt
- Earth
- Wax

At all times, folklorists are cautioned, "Note the colors, numbers, odors in the rites." One national magazine editor told his assistant, "You can always spot amateur stories. There's no smell in them." Scent is often an integral part of magical rites and ceremonies in the following forms and more: incense, herbs, fire, smoke, alchemical reactions, sweat, blood, burning candles.

Magical Practices

The folklorist visiting your world would also want to know which magical practices are used to:

- Kill enemies
- Injure enemies
- Blight crops
- Injure domestic animals
- Harm others' property
- Make themselves or others invisible
- Cause sleep
- Bring luck in games, sports, business, life in general
- Bring success in games, business, travel, love
- Avert evil in travel
- Protect houses, animals, crops; property from theft, sorcery, fire, the weather
- Preserve beauty, loyalty, marital fidelity or wealth

WRITTEN IN THE STARS

"As above, so below" expresses a basic tenet in the world of magic. Astrologers study the movement of stars and planets to determine their relationship to events on our planet. Many stories are written in the stars.

Astrologer and *magician* once meant the same thing in the ancient Middle East, where Chaldean astrologers/magicians guided state affairs. As recently as the Reagan administration, astrologers have been called on for the same services right here in the U.S.

Today, practicing magicians use astrological lore to determine the best times to cast spells and make amulets. For instance, a spell to gain love might be performed on Friday (the day of the week ruled by Venus), when the planet was in a favorable aspect in a favorable sign (Libra, Taurus or Pisces). An amulet made of copper, a metal sacred to Venus, might be used. A spell for prosperity, on the other hand, would best be cast on Thursday (Thor or Jupiter's Day) using tin.

Our current system of astrology derives from the Chaldean and Babylonian systems as revised by Greek, Renaissance, Victorian and

New Age sages. Based on twelve signs associated with constellations on the ecliptic (the path of the sun and moon across the sky), the system organizes a number of correspondences that can prove helpful in designing a fictional character.

Using astrological aspects as the basis for character development, a writer can create conflict within a particular character through an affliction or malefic influence in the chart. A passive Cancer with Gemini rising, for instance, might seem to have a dual personality and suffer from periodic rages, thanks to a poorly aspected moon in Taurus. Other planets might add further complications. Or, simply read the appropriate horoscopes in books or papers.

An author of *Star Trek* novels and her own science fiction series said she learned to characterize by reading Linda Goodman's book, *Sun Signs*, a popular treatment of astrology. The conflicting character traits of those born under astrology's sun signs suggest many a story.

None of this astrological detail needs to reach the page except for how it affects your characters' behavior. Consider creating an astrological chart for each main character to provide a detailed background of character traits and personal preferences. New computer programs make charts easy to cast and can easily determine such significant, but often overlooked aspects as the ''part of fortune.'' Or again, use published horoscopes for this work.

Star-crossed lovers are a prime component of fiction. Water and earth signs are considered poor matches for fire and air signs, and individual charts can place many complications in the most perfect of love stories.

Placing each planet within a chart and its relationship to all the others provides a powerful way to analyze (and design) a personality. Major attention is usually focused on the characters' sun signs, moon signs and rising signs.

Comets and asteroids play important parts both in an astrological chart and in the actual history of a planet. For example, a comet is the source of the destructive ''thread'' that threatens Ann McCaffrey's world of Pern. In the earth's history, the appearance of a comet has traditionally marked an important event—the birth of a hero—or warned of an impending disaster—plagues, famines, wars or the deaths of kings.

Exploring New Worlds

Fantasy writers add an extra element of reality to their works by working out the details of the astrology and astronomy of the worlds they create. J.R.R. Tolkien's work provides an excellent example of the use of the heavens in fantasy fiction. The stars of Elbereth and Earendil serve as visible reminders of the distant past, still remembered by the elves of Middle Earth.

The following are some options in designing the heavens of a fantasy world:

- Use the stars of Earth, either the familiar constellations of the current day, or one of the systems used by other "star-struck" cultures, such as the Mayan, Polynesian, Chinese or Native American.
- Use the stars of Earth, giving them new names, histories, meanings and associations.
- Create a new planetary system and star field for the fantasy world.

Traditional astrology is based upon the stars and planets as observed from our world. In designing the heavens of a fantasy world, consider these elements:

The Primary Star. The primary star is the fantasy world's sun. Determine: its name, color and classification (red giant, white dwarf); its close neighbors (is it a two-star system?); its behavior (periodic sunspots, pulsations); whether the star is seen as the center of the system or the planet itself is considered the "center of the universe."

Other Planets. Planets closer to the primary appear as "morning" and "evening" stars, rising close to dawn and sunset.

"Fixed Lights." Stars seem to remain relatively fixed in position. The brightest stars are usually named and included in constellations that reflect historic or legendary figures and events. Stars can be used to fix specific dates in the year: the Egyptians based their year on Sirius, marking the annual Nile river flood; the Hopi base their ceremonial calendar on the Pleiades.

Satellites or Moons. Besides creating the tides, the Earth's single moon played a determining part in measuring the length of the year. The lunar year varies from twelve to thirteen months before the moon repeats its journey across the star field. More moons would create a more complex situation.

The Length of the Planet's Year. This is the time it takes a planet to circle its star. Our current solar calendar, dividing the year into twelve months of varying length, evolved from the earlier lunar year. Its advantage is that it "fixes" the seasons, so that the same events and weather occur at the same times each year. Many religious calendars remain at least partially oriented to the moon.

The Pole Star(s). The axis of the earth points north and south toward "still" spots that do not rotate as most stars seem to. The North Star (Polaris) is currently the pole star of the northern hemisphere. Because the axis of our planet wobbles, the pole star changes, a phenomenon known as precession of the equinoxes. This precession divides the history of the earth into cosmic ages of about 2,150 years each. We're currently leaving the Age of Pisces for the Age of Aquarius. The earliest horoscopes were most likely cast in the Age of Taurus, some six thousand years ago.

The Galaxy. The Milky Way, our spiral-armed galaxy, appears in the summer sky as a foggy white ribbon. Many cultures associated it with the milk of a moon cow goddess.

Astronomical lore accumulates throughout history, much of it remaining in language as folk sayings or adages. Two examples:

- When two full moons occur in the same month, it's called a "blue moon." This is the origin of the saying, "once in a blue moon."
- The forty days following the helical rising of Sirius, the Dog Star, are called "dog days," usually the hottest days of the year.

Other Astrological Systems

Although our present-day twelve-sign astrological system has deep roots—its based on the Babylonian base twelve numerical system, which was used for all sacred calculations—other systems are possible. Inscriptions indicate that the ancient Babylonians originally recognized eighteen zodiac signs. Some historians contend that the twelve-sign system was originally a thirteen-sign system in some cultures, such as the Celtic/Druid, and was suppressed when solar religions replaced lunar religions in much of the western world. James Vogh, in *Arachne Rising*, suggests Arachne, the Spider, as the missing sign of the zodiac, positioned between Taurus and Gemini and associated with the constellation Auriga. Other cultures have configured the stars differently, seeing different constellations and different truths.

Extensive information on the star systems and astrology of these cultures can be found in anthropological works or, in some cases, current nonfiction books. Here's a brief rundown on the general form of some of the systems developed by other cultures.

Chinese. Chinese astrology placed emphasis of divining the future and determining the proper times to act. The twelve animal signs familiar from restaurant place mats come from a system based on the orbit of Jupiter, which takes about twelve years to orbit the Sun. The twelve signs are the Rat, Ox, Tiger, Rabbit or Cat, Dragon, Snake or Serpent, Horse, Sheep or Goat, Monkey, Cock, Dog and Pig or Boar. Each sign lasts a full year and begins on the second new moon after the winter solstice, which is the generally accepted New Year in Asian countries and usually falls in late January or early February. Works on Chinese astrology delineate the qualities of each sign and compatibility between signs. The much older Chinese system based on the phases of the moon assigns each day to one of twenty-eight named lunar mansions, each regarded as favorable or unfavorable for certain activities. The twenty-eight are grouped into four categories, each with seven mansions: the Green Dragon of spring, beginning with each new moon, followed by the Black Tortoise of winter, the White Tiger of autumn and the Red Bird of summer.

Olmec. Beginning with the Olmec civilization (circa 600 B.C.), Central American societies followed sophisticated astrological systems based on the numbers 13 and 20. Each of twenty signs, called **tonalli** by the Aztec, ruled a single day; another cycle of thirteen ran concurrently, so each day had both a name and a number that provided a key to personality and the analysis of events. Thirteen cycles of twenty days made up the 260-day astrological year. Longer cycles were based on the Jupiter/Saturn 7,200-day cycle (twenty tun, the 360-day civil year), called a **katun**. A creation epoch included 260 katuns, about 5,125 years, one-fifth of a precession cycle. The Harmonic Convergence of 1987 signaled the beginning of the last katun of the fifth (and final) cycle of creation, according to Mesoamerican calculations. Some writer is bound to pick up on this great plot idea for a millennial novel.

Astrological systems can also be based on completely imaginary planets. Uranian astrology, for instance, posits the existence of eight hypothetical "trans-Neptunian" planets: Cupido, Hades, Zeus, Kronos, Appolon, Admetos, Vulcanus and Poseidon.

Other Uses for Astrology

Though today astrology is mostly used for personal prediction, character analysis and relationship compatibility study, other societies have used the study of the stars and planets for a variety of purposes. To:

- answer a question, using a chart cast at the moment the question is asked (horary astrology)
- determine the best time to carry out a particular activity—marriage, planting, beginning journeys, opening businesses (electional astrology)
- predict and guide the course of nations
- predict natural disasters
- predict economic cycles (astroeconomics)
- diagnose and suggest treatment for disease
- choose the best time to plant and harvest crops
- diagnose and treat emotional or behavioral problems (astrotherapy)
- determine the most beneficial place to live (locational astrology)
- predict the weather (astrometeorology)

Besides birth, or natal, charts (cast from the moment a child takes its first breath), other charts can be cast for important occurrences in an individual's life:

- so-called death charts, calculated on the time of a person's death
- decumbiture charts, calculated for the moment one goes to bed at the start of an illness
- conception charts
- compatibility charts, which overlay two natal charts to determine how they will relate, either in love or business

CHAPTER FOUR

WITCHCRAFT AND PAGAN PATHS

Allan Maurer and Renee Wright

Although primitive societies often use the word "witch" for any person in touch with the supernatural, the association in Western culture is usually with people working magic in secret. The Indo-European root word "weik" has to do with religion and magic and is related to another word, "weik," which means to bend or change. Thus a witch was one who could bend or change reality. In Old English, "wicca" was a male witch, "wicce" a female. Although witches today sometimes refer to their order as "the Wise," Old English "witan," which means to know, is unrelated.

The Roman Catholic church tolerated witchcraft and minor sorcery for many hundreds of years, dismissing them as delusion and superstition. The witch trials and burnings began in earnest in the 1300s as witchcraft became associated with heresy and witches were believed to have made a "pact with the devil." Persecution continued until the 1700s and killed an estimated twenty million people, better than half of them women.

HOW TO RECOGNIZE A WITCH

During the Inquisition's five hundred-year-long reign of terror, the accused witch was stripped naked, shaved, then examined for signs of witchcraft. These included:

- The Devil's Mark: Sometimes a scar, mole or birthmark. The mark was variously described as a mole, wart, birthmark, pimple, pockmark, cyst, liver spot, wen, insect bite, ulcer or any other blemish. If nothing was visible on the body, the witch was "pricked" all over in search of the insensitive spot where the devil had given his binding kiss.

- The Witch's Mark: Any protuberance on the body, considered to be a "supernumerary teat" sucked by demons and familiars.

Other signs that someone was a witch that were accepted by the Inquisition included: talking to yourself; talking to animals; keeping a black animal (especially a cat or lamb); being too fond of any animal; spinning around; having freckles, red hair or "unusual" eyes. According to Reginald Scot, a disbeliever, those most likely to be accused were the "old, lame, blear-eyed, pale; wrinkled, poor, sullen, superstitious; lean and deformed; doting, scolds, mad." Any unusual behavior was enough to invite suspicion, especially in the wake of accidents or illness. The Witch of Newberry was executed for surfing on a board in the river.

Failing the discovery of any marks, the accused witch might be subjected to trial by fire, being forced to hold red hot irons (the innocent would not be burned); trial by water, a practice called "swimming the witch" (the innocent sank); or trial by weighing the witch against the weight of a Bible (guilty if the witch weighed less than the massive books of the day).

Today, anthropologists recognize several types of witchcraft. A good discussion of them can be found in Isaac Bonewits, *Real Magic*. He recognizes four types of witchcraft: classical, gothic, family or traditional, and neo-pagan.

CLASSICAL WITCHCRAFT

Classical witchcraft refers to the primitive, so-called "low" magic found among most peoples where adepts cast spells; make potions (and poisons); and practice divination, herbalism and, often, various types of healing and medicine, especially midwifery. It survives today in a variety of shamanic practices around the world.

Shamanism

Shamanism is mostly solo magical work, though shamans usually apprentice and endure many years of training. After an initial vision quest to find an animal familiar, the shaman will continue to go into a trance through various means (solitude, drugs, drumming, dancing) to work his magic. The shaman does much of his magical work on an astral plane not unlike the one ceremonial magicians seek through Hermetic wisdom, meditating on the Kabbalah's Tree of Life, or the other methods discussed in the previous chapter.

This oldest of pagan paths is enjoying a modern revival thanks to the works of Mircea Eliade, Michael Harner (the father of neo-shamanism) and others.

Harner proposes a Shamanic State of Consciousness (SSC) in which the shaman is able to travel into the underworld or into the branches of the World Tree to discover his or her power animal. The shaman enters a trance through one of several methods: rhythmic drumming, chanting, rattling, meditation practices, dancing or swaying or the use of hallucinogens. He then calls upon his power animal to guide and protect him on his journey to the spirit world. Once he arrives there, if he's involved in healing, he battles the offending spirits, or if he is divining, he asks for spiritual assistance.

Many modern shamans are influenced by Carlos Castenada's series of books on Don Juan. The books detail the initiation of Castenada into the shamanistic practices of the desert Native American tribes, including a full description of a peyote ceremony and much "energy work" with the strands of power said to surround every individual and connect him with all others.

Serge King, in his book, *The Urban Shaman*, outlines a shamanism based on the ancient beliefs of Hawaiian **Huna**. The Huna shamans claim the ability to heal instantly, to change the weather and many other seeming miracles through the application of a pragmatic creed. The principles of Huna are:

- Ike: the world is what you think it is
- Kala: there are no limits
- Makia: energy flows where attention goes
- Manawa: now is the moment of power
- Aloha: love is being happy within
- Mana: power comes from within
- Pono: effectiveness is the measure of truth.

Hawaiian Huna teaches meditative and thinking practices that resemble modern neuro-linguistic programming techniques so closely that psychologists and NLP practitioners have studied this Polynesian system.

A **kahuna** is a master who, through proper cleansing of his mind, body and spirit, attains control of psychic powers latent in everyone. He heals by placing one hand on a patient's power spot (base of the spine, top of the spine at the neck, top of the head or some such spot) and another on the troubled body spot. The kahuna keeps his mind connected to both of his hands so that the energy may stream through them. Huna, by and large, is a mental discipline.

Northern Traditions

Norse, Icelandic, Germanic, Teutonic, Frisian, Latvian, Lithuanian and Estonian religious traditions all survive among some groups to the present day. The northern traditions usually give far less emphasis to the goddess and more to the values of the warrior than other pagan traditions. Adepts study shamanism, artistic skills, writing in runes, the martial arts and brewing to achieve goals of honor, honesty, courage and duty to family.

Seidr is the oldest of the Norse traditions and is based on many shamanistic practices. The chorus sings a sacred song that induces a trance in the prophetess, called **volva** or **vala**. Frey and Freya of the Vanir are the principle deities. Adepts reportedly practice sexual magic.

Iceland has the distinction of being the only European country where paganism enjoys equal status with Christianity as the state religion. Iceland's literature preserves much of the mythology of the north, in the prose and poetic eddas, plus various sagas.

Native American Traditions

Each tribe has its own name for the Great Spirit, though beliefs have much in common. In recent years, the language of the Sioux, the last tribe to be conquered, has been adopted as a kind of religious lingua franca. The Sioux revere T'Tanka as the Great Spirit and Watantanka, the Buffalo, as his sacred animal. Most tribes have a great reverence for Mother Earth and are ecologically active.

Important Native American sacred figures include White Buffalo Calf Woman, Thunderbird, Coyote, Raven and Kokopelli. Rituals include the sweat lodge; the pipe ceremony, where tobacco is offered to the four directions; the vision quest, a wilderness experience in which initiates seek their power animal; and the sun dance. Personal talismans, amulets and herbs are often carried in a medicine bag around the neck. Sacred shields depict scenes from the warrior's vision quest.

The Sioux prophet Black Elk foresaw a world in which the peoples of all nations joined in a great hoop around the Tree of Life, but the time of the prophecy's fulfillment has not yet come. His book, *Black Elk Speaks*, outlines his vision and the pipe ritual.

African Traditions

African religions went underground in the slave cultures of the Americas. The African gods acquired the names of Christian saints. Common elements included drumming and dancing to induce trance, blood sacrifice and possession by spirits of the gods, called **loas**. Initiates usually wore white.

Voodoo from Haiti (where it's spelled in the French manner, *vodoun*), incorporates Dahomean, Ibo and Mago tribal influences. Initiates acknowledge a Supreme Being, Gran Met, who is considered remote, but worship a huge pantheon of lesser gods called loas. Principle loas include Danbhalah, the Great Serpent, the oldest of the ancestors; Maitress Erzulie, the moon; her husband Legba (called "Papa"), the sun, who governs all entryways and fences, including the spirit gate; and Baron Samedi, god of death and the graveyard, who wears dark glasses, drinks alcohol and smokes cigars. During ceremonies in the **hounfour**, or "holy of holies," the summoned spirits "mount the horse," possessing their chosen devotee who retains no memory of what happens during the possession.

Santeria developed in the Spanish-speaking areas, especially in Cuba. The African influence comes largely from the Yoruba tribe of Nigeria, whose language is still used in liturgies. **Santeros** and **santeras** join with the high priest, called **babalawo**, in worshipping the **orishas**, ancestor spirits led by Obatala, the oldest ancestor depicted as a white man on a horse, and his wife Oddudua, a black woman usually depicted breastfeeding an infant. (**Orisha** is a popular name for the African traditions in the U.S., especially Santeria. It means "the deities.") Coconuts and herbs play important parts in Santeria. Divination methods include reading a throw of seashells or the meat of a coconut. Babalawos, who are always male, consult the Table of Ifa by throwing sixteen shells onto a straw mat. The pattern of the shells determines each person's orisha, plant, birthstone and animal. The ceiba tree is the cult's most holy plant, thanks to its ability to attract spirits, and water is used to ward off evil spirits.

Macumba came from similar Yoruba roots in Portuguese-speaking Brazil. Some elements of the tribal religions of the Amazon are mixed in as well. The three types of macumba are candomble, umbanda and quimbanda. **Candomble** is very similar to Santeria, except that the priests are often female. The orishas are most often known by the names of their associated saints. The year's biggest ceremony honors Yemanja, goddess of the waters and an aspect of the Virgin Mary, on January first. Over a million celebrants, dressed in white, wade into the surf at dusk and launch small boats loaded with candles, flowers and figures of the Saints out to sea. **Umbanda** is a recent religion mixing elements of the African tradition, especially spirit possession, with elements of Hinduism and Buddhism, and is aimed at spiritual healing of previous incarnations through communication with the spirits. **Quimbanda** is the black magic tradition, calling upon King Exu, the dark lord.

Earth Magic

James Lovelock's book, *The Gaia Hypothesis*, presents the idea that all the living matter on earth, in the air, in the oceans and on land are part of a system that acts as a single, living biosphere controlling things like temperature and the composition of the atmosphere. The goal of many New Age pagans is to awaken Gaia's planetary mind, a concept much used in science fiction.

Traditional Earth magic has always operated from this perspective, studying the powers of Earth as a holistic organism. Earth magicians study dowsing, ley lines, stone circles and sacred sites. Their rituals are intended to correct energy imbalances caused by bad planning. These imbalances are believed to create a "black stream" of energy associated with illness, accidents and poltergeist activity in the area. In China, Earth magic is called **Feng-shui.**

Shinto, the official religion of Japan, also shares many of the concerns of Earth magic. Anything unusual in nature is considered "kami," or divine, and worshiped. Japan is dotted with Miya shrines next to odd rocks and trees. The Japanese "Way of the Gods" is a phallic fertility cult, involving purification rites and ancestor worship. Onogor is the Central Pillar of the Earth; Amaterasu, the sun goddess.

Ritual Magic

Based on the rites of the Golden Dawn, medieval grimmores such as *The Key of Solomon*, and Aleister Crowley's writings, ritual "magick" (Crowley's spelling) tends to be complex with many formal details including robes, tools, temple decorations and verbal formula that must be recited precisely.

Thelemic magick was Crowley's own system of ritual magic, including many sexual rites. It's named for his "abbey" in Thelema,

Sicily. The authorities threw Crowley and his friends out of the country after only a few years.

Enochian magic is ritual with an entirely different pedigree. It's based on a secret language revealed by angels to John Dee, Elizabethan England's greatest magus and alchemist. The language seems to have no antecedents, but the spells that form part of it are said to have exceptional power to summon spirits. Dee and his scryer, Edward Kelley, used the calls or "keys" to invoke angels before scrying in a crystal egg or black obsidian mirror. The Order of the Golden Dawn and Aleister Crowley, who claimed to be Kelley's reincarnation, made use of the calls.

GOTHIC WITCHCRAFT

Gothic witchcraft is the sort confessed to by the witches tried by the Inquisition. Their witchcraft was a form of Christian heresy with many holy Church symbols and practices reversed or defiled, as in the **Black Mass**. Witches were believed to make a pact with the devil. Other elements of Gothic witchcraft: secret meetings at night, orgies, child sacrifice, cannibalism, the desecration of the Eucharist and crucifix, and the "ride by night," usually through the air. Accused witches "confessed" to most of these rites under torture in hopes of a more lenient execution. The charges bore a strong resemblance to accusations brought against heretics throughout the history of Christianity. The Gnostics of the third century A.D., for instance, were accused of the identical set of crimes.

Some perversion of the Christian rites undoubtedly occurred in the Middle Ages and the Renaissance, probably at first by renegade priests who would perform the requiem mass (called the Black Mass at the time) for a person still alive, thus cursing him. It's impossible to discover the extent of these practices and their continuance to the present day, because they quickly made their way into literature, becoming a branch of pornography, especially in France. An outbreak of actual black magic, complete with masses said on the body of a nude woman and child sacrifices, seems to have occurred in 1678 during the reign of Louis XIV, under the patronage of his mistress Madame de Montespan.

Though today most practitioners of "The Craft" follow "the right-hand path" (white magic), but some seek "the left-hand path" of black magic. Most are solitaries, but some belong to organized groups.

Satanism

Anton La Vey's Church of Satan is the present-day descendant of the anti-Christian cults. The press has accused it of blood sacrifices, both animal and human, and sexual orgies, but little has ever actually been proved. La Vey's disciples follow an inverted gospel: "Blessed are the strong for they shall possess the Earth. If a man smite you on one cheek, smash him on the other!"

Other black magic cults prefer the spelling "Shaitan," and follow pre-Christian, often Babylonian or Persian, practices.

FAMILY OR TRADITIONAL WITCHCRAFT

Family or traditional witchcraft involves secret traditions passed down through families, usually from mother to daughter, but sometimes to apprentices. It is a religion of hearth and home, perhaps preserving various domestic rites performed by women in ancient times. Several modern witches, including Sibyl Leek and various Gypsies, claim this traditional form of witchcraft. Typical elements include: worship of Mother Earth, the oak or another tree used to represent the male principle; the use of kitchen implements as tools of magic, such as brooms or cauldrons; the primary practice of agricultural magic, to "work" the weather for the benefit of the crops; and simple divination used for seeing future husbands, children and the like.

Strega is the path of witches following an Italian tradition. They use red chili peppers on their stalks as wands. The peppers are decorated with either a male or female crown. The path is strongly matriarchal and uses much traditional herbal knowledge. Paraphernalia includes a tiny bronze sickle to harvest herbs.

Gypsy Magic

The wandering Gypsies may have set out originally from India. Many of their beliefs and practices derive from rites originally native to the civilization of the Ganges Valley (circa 1000 B.C.). On their travels through Europe, they made their living by fortune-telling. Favorite Gypsy methods of divination include: gazing into a crystal ball, palmistry, reading tea leaves, tarot cards, bumps on the head (phrenology), lines on the face (metoposcopy), dice or dominoes. The apple is often used by Gypsies in rituals, and marriages are solemnized by jumping a broom.

NEO-PAGAN WITCHCRAFT

Although ancient pagan beliefs survive in holiday customs, folk beliefs and popular sayings, there is little evidence of the survival of an organized pagan religion of witchcraft such as Margaret Murray wrote about in her 1921 book, *The Witch Cult of Western Europe*. Neo-pagan witchcraft is a modern development, rising from folklore and literature with only intellectual ties to ancient practices. Influenced by studies of anthropology, the neo-pagans seek to rebuild a culture linked to the earth and its seasons, a link lost in the development of modern civilization. This loss, many believe, depletes our quality of life and endangers the future of our planet. Today, neo-pagan witchcraft falls into three basic categories: Wicca, a revival of ancient goddess worship; revivals of other traditional religions and mystery cults; and New Age neo-paganism, based on modern works of fiction or philosophy.

The Literary Background of Wicca

Charles Leland's *Aradia, or the Gospel of the Witches*, published in 1899, began the modern renaissance of witchcraft. (Aradia was said to be a daughter of Diana and Queen of the Witches.) He claimed to have discovered this manuscript among the peasants of Italy. It contained the secrets of "la Vecchia Religione" or the Old Religion. Though Leland's "discovery" has since been discredited by scholars, Aradia made many contributions to the Wiccan revival, including emphasis on the goddess as its main deity. Most Wiccan paths use some form of the "Charge of the Goddess" found in *Aradia*: "Once a month, and when the Moon is full, Ye shall assemble."

Two works of folklore had special impact on the Wiccan revival. *The Golden Bough* (1922), by Sir James Frazer, explored the widespread existence in pre-Christian times of fertility cults based on the death and rebirth of a god, often seen as both consort and son of the goddess. In 1948, Robert Graves published *The White Goddess*, discussing the ancient and beautiful cult of the earth and moon goddess of many names.

Margaret Murray, folklorist, anthropologist and Egyptologist, had an even greater influence on the development of modern witchcraft. In *The Witch Cult of Western Europe*, she traced witchcraft to a pre-Christian religion centered on a horned deity she identified as Dianus, or the Roman Janus, a two-faced god. As described by

Murray, this was a fertility cult similar to the ones described by Frazer in *The Golden Bough*. The god's death and rebirth reflected the cycle of the seasons and crops. The high priestess of the coven of thirteen members typically took the name of Diana. This "Dianic" cult celebrated eight great **sabbats** during the year, at the solstices and equinoxes, plus four "cross-quarter" days. Lesser **esbat** ceremonies were celebrated at each full moon. Murray believed that this religion originated in Britain, created by a race of "Small People" who later entered European folklore as fairies, elves and pixies. Murray identified at least two of the cross-quarter festivals as preagricultural (May Eve and November Eve), having more to do with the fertility of animals than of crops.

Murray's views, though much criticized by modern anthropologists, especially for her uncritical acceptance of testimony given under torture during the witch trials, hugely influenced a generation of occultists. Gerald Gardner cited her theories as corroboration of his revival of witchcraft.

Wiccan Beliefs

As practiced today, few generalizations can be made about modern Wiccan witchcraft. Unlike traditional ceremonial magic, witchcraft puts little emphasis on the "correct" recitation of incantations or exact pronunciation of names and spells. In fact, neopagan witches are encouraged to use their goddess-given creativity to create new spells, invocations and rituals, which often take the form of poetry or songs. Many books of these rituals have been published, and more continue to be published every year, each giving birth to its own "path." A writer trying to create an authentic witchcraft ritual can feel confident as long as she stays within certain parameters.

Witches meet in covens, usually on the night of the full moon, and are led by a high priestess. Principal gods are the Triple Goddess, known by many names, and her consort, the Horned God of the forests. Their rites celebrate the cycle of the year through the ritual drama of the goddess and her consort, from their courtship and marriage through death and rebirth. Gardnerian and Alexandrian covens traditionally practice their rites "skyclad" (i.e., in the nude) but there are many "robed covens" as well.

The most central belief of all Wiccan groups is the Wiccan Creed (or Rede): "An' it harm none, do what ye will." Attributed to Gerald

Gardner, it puts the Wiccan movement well within the definition of white magic. Gardner probably based it on Aleister Crowley's governing principle, derived from sexual magic: "Do what thou wilt shall be the whole of the Law. Love is the Law, love under will." Related to this is the general Wiccan belief of threefold return: If a spell is cast unjustly, the effects will rebound on the spell-caster in triple strength.

The most common form of spell used in Wicca is candle magic. A candle of an appropriate color—red for love, green for health and prosperity, blue for mental tranquility and so on—is anointed with oil and then burned. The witch then meditates upon the flame, using visualization to imagine the desired outcome.

In recent years, the many groups of practicing Wiccans tried to come to some agreement on beliefs. The Pagan Federation identified three universal beliefs in Wicca: (1) adherence to the Wiccan Creed; (2) love of nature; and (3) a belief in reincarnation.

Common Elements of Wiccan Ritual.

1. A circle is cast and sacred space purified through the use of the elements: fire, earth, air and water.
2. Powers are invoked to guard the circle and aid the rites. These powers of the four directions are variously referred to as Mighty Ones, Lords and Ladies of the Watchtowers, etc.
3. Music, dancing, chanting and/or running in a circle around an altar are used to raise a "cone of power."
4. The coven partakes of a "feast," often of crescent moon-shaped cakes and wine.
5. "Drawing down the moon" is the most typical ceremonial act, though methods of doing so differ considerably. The high priestess "draws down the moon" in some ceremonies. In others, the high priest "draws down the Horned God."

Tools of the Craft

Aleister Crowley identified eight tools or "weapons" of magic. Though Wiccan covens differ in which ones they use, all use some, though meanings attributed to them may vary.

Athame: black-handled, double-edged dagger used for sacred activities

Biolline: white-handled dagger used for carving and other "mundane" activities

SCOURGE: This is a military scourge. A Wiccan scourge would have cords of silk or leather.

Cauldron or Cup: represents element of water, female principle, the womb, the Grail

Censer of incense: used to create a purifying smoke, or smoke in which an apparition can take shape; may be a flat stone, shallow bowl of sand or thurible of brass, ceramic or wood, set on a three-legged tripod or hung from chains

Pentacle: round disk of metal inscribed with a pentagram; represents the element of earth

Scourge: a whip or cat-o'-nine-tails, used to purify but never to draw blood

Sword: represents element of fire

Wand or Stang: represents element of air

The Gardnerian Path

Gerald B. Gardner founded modern witchcraft or Wicca in the 1950s in England, where witchcraft was illegal until 1951. He based it on a combination of influences from traditional witchcraft, folklore literature and his experiences with Aleister Crowley and various ceremonial magic traditions. Gardner, called the "Grand Old Man of Witchcraft," wrote *High Magic's Aid* (1949), a novel containing two initiation ceremonies, plus *Witchcraft Today* (1955) and *The Meaning of Witchcraft* (1959). Citing Margaret Murray, he claimed that Wicca is the surviving remnant of pagan rites from pre-Christian times.

Some Gardnerian covens today claim "apostolic" succession from Gardner's original coven on the Isle of Man. Others are neo-Gardnerians, basing their rites on published accounts of Gardnerian rituals.

Gardner composed "162 Laws of the Craft," contained in the secret *Book of Shadows*, the major text of Gardnerian witches. The main one of these, called the Witch's Law, limits the working of witches to so-called "white magic," as previously mentioned: "An' it harm none, do what you will." Gardner claimed the book was very ancient, inherited by him from his parent coven, but it contains much material authored by Aleister Crowley and sections from Leland's *Aradia*. Initiates swear to keep the book secret and copy their own versions in longhand from their high priestess's or high priest's copy. Though all give an oath never to reveal its contents, various versions and excerpts of the *Book of Shadows* have been published. The mistakes and misinterpretations became so divergent that Doreen Valiente, high priestess of Gardner's coven, co-operated with Janet and Stewart Farrar in publishing what she claims is the correct text in their 1984 book, *The Witches' Way*. Valiente is credited with emphasizing the goddess in Wiccan rites, while downplaying much of the sexual magic derived from Crowley.

Gardnerian witches hold their rites in the nude or skyclad, based on a Celtic belief that nudity provides supernatural protection and, possibly, because of Gardner's own interest in nudism. Adornments traditionally include a girdle, sometimes made of a nine-foot-long braided red yarn used to measure the magic circle. The witches usually wear necklaces, and often other rings and jewels. The high priestess may wear a tiara.

The Horned God is called Cernunnos on the Gardnerian path. The Triple Goddess—Maiden, Mother and Crone—is worshiped under many sacred names. Gardnerian witches avoid using these names in common speech, referring to her as "the Lady" or "Aradia."

A circle is cast using a ritual similar to one found in *The Key of Solomon*, followed by the Charge of the Goddess, often drawn from Leland's novel, *Aradia*.

During rituals, the priestess incarnates the goddess and "draws down" the power of the moon into a nine-foot circle protected by candles and ritual, where the power is raised further through dancing and meditation before being used to work spells and other magic. According to *Harper's Encyclopedia of Mystical and Paranormal Experience*, Gardner identifies eight methods of raising magical power in his *Book of Shadows*: (1) meditation; (2) chants, spells and invocations; (3) trance and astral projection; (4)

incense, wine and drugs; (5) dancing; (6) binding parts of the body with cords; (7) scourging; and (8) ritual sex.

Witches advance through three degrees of initiation: priest or witch; magus or witch queen; and high priest or priestess. After completing the third, called the Great Rite, they are qualified to "hive off" and become the high priest or high priestess of their own coven. The Great Rite is widely believed to be a sacred act of sexual union, either symbolic or actual. Symbolic sexual images pervade Gardnerian ritual as, for instance, when the blade of the athame is dipped into a cup of water or wine.

The Alexandrian Path

Alexander Sanders claimed to have been initiated into witchcraft by his grandmother at the age of seven. Later he began his own system of witchcraft, perhaps after having been refused initiation into a Gardnerian coven, though this rumor has never been documented. However, he took many, if not most, of the elements of his ceremonies from Gardner. The Alexandrian ritual can be found in Stewart Farrar's *What Witches Do*.

Alexandrian witches refer to the goddess and her consort as Aradia and Karnayna. They use a version of the Gardnerian *Book of Shadows*. Elements shared by the Gardnerian and Alexandrian paths include: skyclad ceremonies, ceremonial scourging, anointing with water and wine in "the five-fold kiss," and the use of a ritual password: "Perfect love and perfect trust." Alexandrian ritual adds a unique element to the initiation ceremony: pricking the finger of the initiate so that all pledges are sealed with blood. The Alexandrian path also uses herbal extracts to "condense" ectoplasm, and borrows John Dee's "angelic language" from enochian magic.

The Dianic Path

Dianic covens worship the goddess in a more or less monotheistic way in her three aspects of Maiden-Creatrix, Mother and Old Crone (although the Mother aspect does take a consort in most covens), or as a Triple Creatrix: Moon, Queen of Mysteries; Sunna, Queen of the Stars; and Mother Earth. Rituals emphasize the moon; the myths, lore and mysteries associated with the thirteen lunar months; and the Beth-Luis-Nion tree alphabet of ancient Britain. Robert Graves's *The White Goddess* is their basic reference. Dianic covens are very ecologically concerned and environmentally active.

One branch of the Dianic path is **feminist witchcraft**. On this path, men are excluded from covens. Z. Budapest, who claims a family tradition of witchcraft, is credited with starting the first feminist coven in 1971—the Susan B. Anthony Coven. More recently, Starhawk's writings, especially *The Spiral Dance*, greatly influenced this path. Feminist covens worship both moon and sun goddesses, but more influence than usual is attributed to the sun, under names such as Sunna and Lucina. Matriarchal ideas and institutions predominate.

The Church of Wicca

Though some witches argue that this is not a true Wiccan path, many covens are based on its teachings. Gavin and Yvonne Frost established the School of Wicca and began offering correspondence courses in witchcraft. The lessons combine certain ritual elements of Wicca with a monotheistic belief in an abstract, unknowable god. Students advance through ten levels of the astral plane, called "The Side." The aim is progressive reincarnation into higher levels. Kundalini sex practices, including introitus, are part of the course, but the system is considered antimatriarchal. The Egyptian ankh, symbol of regeneration, and the artificial phallus play important symbolic and ritualistic roles.

Seax Wicca

Raymond Buckland wrote *The Tree*, subtitled *The Complete Book of Saxon Witchcraft*, in 1974. It outlines a ceremonial system based on Saxon mythology and Wiccan ritual. Cerridwen, goddess of the cauldron, heads the list of deities. Se-ax is the Saxon name for the athame. Buckland outlines a complete guide on self-initiation and how to start a coven. He makes no claims of ancient origins for his rites, recommending them on the basis of their effectiveness.

The Fairy Paths

First revived in the early 1970s by Victor Anderson and his student, Gwydion Pendderioen, the path of Fairy Wicca incorporates elements of European folk magic and material from the Gardnerian *Book of Shadows*. Pendderioen later founded Forever Forests, dedicated to the Green Man, aimed at reforestation of the Earth.

Another fairy path honors the Irish fairies, the Tuatha D' Danann. Kisma Stepanich, among others, has published several guides to

Wiccan rites based on Gaelic fairy lore. Dana is their goddess. She receives offerings of warm milk and honey with a pat of butter melted into it. The Fairy Queen, who takes various other names as well, prefers violets, rides often at night, and lives beneath an enchanted mountain where a mortal year passes in a single evening.

Fairy shamans wear a cloak of invisibility made of bird feathers over simple hooded gowns and mantles. They carry staffs or magic wands, often tipped with crystal, a magic bag of tricks and make music on a "musical branch," a rattle made from the branch of a tree and hazelnuts, the symbol of wisdom. Many smoke pipes.

Fairy Wiccans use the usual athame, cup and pentacle in their ceremonies, held inside a fairy ring. Other objects used in spells include the four traditional Gaelic talismans: the Sword of Nuada; the Spear of Lugh, Undry; the Cauldron of the Dagda; and the Great Fal, Stone of Destiny. Those on the fairy path study the Oghans of the alphabet of trees described in Graves' *The White Goddess*.

Spells, many using butter and milk, invoke various fairy spirits and much ritual use is made of herbs and teas. The tradition of "crossing with butter" to mark possessions survives in folklore: people put butter on their cats' feet to keep them from wandering. Other spells are cast using white candles and quartz crystals.

Cows are considered sacred on the fairy path. They represent Dana in her aspect of the white cow. Cows are driven between two fires in a ceremony to insure the fertility of the earth.

Eclectic Paths

The creative bias of Wicca encourages many seekers to combine different elements from other paths with their own individual vision to create new paths. Among them:

George Patterson of Bakersfield, California, began the **Georgian Path**.

Wiccans with Hebrew backgrounds explore their prepatriarchal roots on a path they call **Jewitch**. Rites are held on Fridays, when they light white candles to invite Shekinah, the Sacred Bride, into their homes.

The **Pagan Way** is an open, nature-oriented path that demands no initiation or membership of participants. It sponsors large, public celebrations at the sabbats, and sometimes at the full moon, which incorporate many of the sacred rituals of Wicca without the vows of silence and secrecy imposed upon initiates.

The **Society of the Inner Light**, otherwise known as the Western Mysteries, was founded by Dion Fortune in the 1920s. At first it owed much to the rituals of the Golden Dawn, of which Fortune was an initiate. But after her death, it moved away from pagan influences. Today, it's a mixture of Alexander postural techniques, dianetics and scientology.

Chaos Magick is a product of the 1980s. It combines magical and occult traditions with quantum physics and computer technology. It's creed can be summarized as "Nothing is true. Everything is permitted." Ultimate responsibility is placed on the individual.

In addition, many "solitaries" practice witchcraft outside of a coven, choosing rituals that appeal to them from the immense literature on witchcraft, or designing rituals of their own.

Traditional and Mystery Cult Revivals

A wide variety of traditional religions enjoy a modern revival as people seek to rebuild their links to Earth and its seasons. Based on the newly available folklore studies, various ethnic groups now recreate the religious rites of their forefathers (and mothers). Others feel more drawn to archaic religions examined in archeological works. A swarm of nature-oriented Earth religions, most based on the gods, goddesses and mythology of old, attract adherents.

Rituals typically include the elements found to make effective psychodrama by the ancient masters of Greek tragedy: rhythmic chanting, songs, drums, flutes, pots of flame and smoking torches. Garb invariably includes robes, often color-keyed to the cult member's level of initiation.

Mythology as well as religions provides exceptionally rich fields to mine story ideas. The drama of family strife among the Egyptian pantheon, for instance, has been successfully repeated many times. Osiris is killed by his brother Set, avenged by his son Horus. Shakespeare's *Hamlet* uses the same plot, as does Disney's *The Lion King*. The psychological theories of Carl Jung explain the attraction of these archetypes as stories that can be told again and again.

Druidism

The Druids resumed their rites early, reestablishing the summer solstice festival at Stonehenge in the late 1880s. They follow as closely as possible the Druid practices recorded in literature, including the ritual cutting of mistletoe, and festivals at the solstices and equinoxes. Druid groups are particularly active in ecology projects, reforestation and the protection of sacred sites. Ritual garb includes white robes, torques of precious metals and crowns of oak or other leaves. The National Eisteddfod, the annual Welsh competition of music and poetry, is conducted as a ritual using Druidic symbols.

Ar nDraiocht Fein, established by Isaac Bonewits, represents one path of neo-pagan Druid practice. Initiates are organized in groves named for various sacred trees, and they wear white berets and long white robes. Sacrifices of tree branches, fruits, flowers and vegetables are offered. Symbols include a circle pierced by two parallel lines and a branch sprouting from an oak stump. It is an order of scholars and artists.

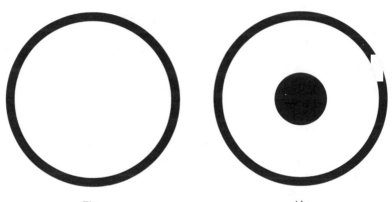

Fire   Air

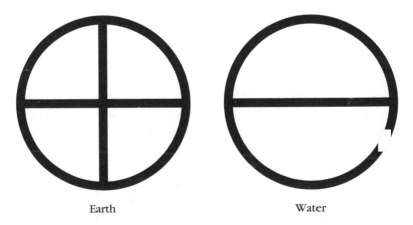

Earth   Water

Symbols of the Four Elements

The **Order of Bards, Ovates and Druids** was organized in 1717, eventually growing to become the largest Druidic order in the United Kingdom and Europe. Initiates achieve the three grades of scholarship by studying healing and divination, in addition to the Arthurian and Grail cycles of myths. Full Druids can form their own groves. The organization is especially active in replanting sacred groves.

The **Reformed Druids of North America** began in 1963 at Carleton College as a humorous protest against mandatory chapel services. A group of faculty and students declared themselves Druids, donned white robes and began holding services in oak groves and on nearby beaches and hills. They recited ancient Welsh and Irish poems, passed the water-of-life (whiskey), and sang hymns to ancient Celtic and Gaulish gods: Danu, the Earth Mother; Be'al, the masculine spirit; Dalon ap Landu, Lord of Groves. Other deities included Grannos of the Healing Springs; Braciaca, god of malt and brewing; Belenos, the sun god; Sirona, goddess of rivers; Taranus, god of thunder and lightning; and Llyr, god of the sea.

The organization named **New Reformed Druids of North America** recognizes many related groups including **Norse Druids**, **Wicca Druids**, **Hassidic Druids**, **Zen Druids**, **Irish Druids** (who conduct their rites in Gaelic) and various other eclectic orders of Druids. Arch-Druid Isaac Bonewits's work *The Druid Chronicles (Evolved)* provides history and liturgy for most of these groups.

Celtic Traditions

The **Pan Celtic** movement is one of the strongest in neo-paganism. Pipes, drums and harps are used in rituals that aim to renew Celtic culture. *Inner Keltia*, the major journal of the Celtic revival, is published in Scotland. Neo-Celts participate in "dressing" sacred wells, believe in the fairy folk, and celebrate great fire festivals at the cross-quarter days. The Celts named the Horned God Kernunnos or Hern the Hunter and identify him as Lord of the Animals and the Great Shaman. His image is found on the Gundestrop cauldron, one of the masterpieces of ancient Celtic art. The winter solstice is often celebrated with dancing in horned costumes.

The Celts begin their year at the feast of Samhain on the eve of November. At the feast of Beltane on May Eve, all fires are extinguished, then relit from Bel's Fire, sacred to the solar-fire god Bel (Balor or Belenus). On May Day, Celts dance around the maypole.

In the **Irish tradition**, harps are considered essential to effective ritual and rituals are often performed in Gaelic. The fire goddess Bridget, goddess of fertility and healing, is honored. Her major festival coincides with Candlemas in early February. Magic is sometimes practiced through plaiting rushes, in which spells are woven into a basket or braid.

The **Welsh** and **Cornish traditions** use the Mabinogeon myth cycle as a source of rituals, poetry and deities. Merlin is a major mage.

The **Bardic path** is an individual one within the Celtic and Druidic traditions. Devotees travel from place to place, reciting mystical poetry, song and mythology.

Neo-Viking Traditions

Asatru, the Scandinavian "belief in the gods," recognizes two pantheons: the early agricultural gods, the Vanir, and the invading warrior gods, the Aesir. Gods include Frey, Odin, Thor and Tir. Goddesses are Frig, Freya and the Norns or Fates. The usual solstice and equinox days are celebrated with rituals, plus the annual festival of Althing and Ragnar's Day, March 28, celebrating the Viking sack of Paris in A.D. 875. The winter solstice was sacred to Odin; the spring equinox or "summer finding" when the color red appears in the ceremonies, was sacred to Thor; the Summer Solstice was sacred to Baldor and a time of great fairs and festivals.

Odinism is a cult of Asatru that recognizes only the Aesir. In the Odinic Rite, established in 1973, an individual takes Odin as his person deity and undergoes a shamanic initiation based on Odin's sacrifice as described in the *Poetic Edda*. To gain knowledge, Odin hung on the world tree Yggdrasil for nine days and nights. You can see him today on the Hanged Man tarot card. The knowledge he gained was the ability to read the runes. Odinists base their conduct on the *Havamal*, Odin's sayings as a lawgiver, and seek to restore the rituals based on the eddas. They are organized in hearths and have a teaching order called the gothar. Larger assemblies, called witans, seek to make the knowledge of Odin more public. The Odinshof is an activist arm of Odinism organized to protect the remaining wild woods of the world through both ritual magic and political activism.

The **Skalkic path** is the Norse equivalent of the Bardic tradition among the Celts.

Mediterranean Traditions

The **Fellowship of Isis**, founded in 1976, seeks closer communion with the Egyptian goddess Isis. The organization, based in the incongruous confines of Clonegal Castle, Ireland, claims thousands of members worldwide, including a large following in Libya, the goddess's traditional homeland. Rituals draw on Egyptian sources and are held on the usual solstice and equinox dates. The Fellowship's values include love, beauty, truth and abundance. It practices total religious tolerance, forbids sacrifice of any kind and discourages asceticism.

The **Church of Aphrodite** also seeks love, beauty and harmony with the goddess. Founded on Long Island in 1938 by Gleb Botkin, son of a doctor who served the last Russian czar, the church has three liturgies, which are performed in front of an altar bearing a reproduction of the Venus de Milo set against purple cloth. Frankincense and myrrh burn on the altar along with nine candles. The planetary sign of Venus stands in place of a cross.

The **Church of the Eternal Source** is a federation of revived Egyptian cults. In the 1960s, Harold Moss began to organize Egyptian costume parties for a club he belonged to in California, the Chesley Donovan Science Fantasy Foundation. Eventually these evolved into recreations of the rituals of the cult of Horus, the Egyptian god Moss felt most drawn to serve. Other people researched and reenacted the cults of Thoth, Osiris, Neith, Isis and Bast. Adepts dress in the Egyptian manner, usually including beautiful jewelry. They study hieroglyphics and books about ancient Egypt, seeking out the best

Norse Runes and Charms

Norse Love Charm

Rune, Mannaz
Symbol for Humanity

translations of the ancient texts. Dates are called by their Egyptian names. Although they have no holy book, they generally recommend Dr. Henri Frankfort's *Ancient Egyptian Religion* as a basic text. Each cult is autonomous and rituals are held separately, but all participate in a large Egyptian New Year's celebration held annually in mid-July at the first rising of Sirius.

NEW AGE NEO-PAGANS

Recent years ushered in a phenomenal growth in neo-pagan paths. Many of them are combinations of elements from many traditional paths, combined with ideas drawn from astrology, Earth religion and science fiction. In fact, science fiction and fantasy are fertile fields for developing religions. Margot Adler notes in *Drawing Down the Moon* that "science fiction and fantasy probably come closer than any other literature to systematically exploring the central concerns of Neo-Pagans and Witches." Persistent rumors in the science fiction community insist that L. Ron Hubbard began scientology on a bet with Isaac Asimov, another science fiction writer.

The Church of All Worlds

Based on Robert Heinlein's *Stranger in a Strange Land*, the Church of All Worlds (CAW) was started by two students in Missouri in 1962. With a group of their friends, they recreated the ceremony of water brotherhood, Atl, from the novel, passing around a goblet of water, "grokking" each other's godhood and repeating the mantra: "Thou art god. Thou art goddess."

Tim Zell proceeded to organize the group into "nests" of celebrants, who advance through nine circles of initiation named for the planets through study that includes long reading lists. They practice a new tribalism, based on the ability to grok a totally empathic understanding of and merging of identity with each other and the earth. Serge King adopts grokking in his *Urban Shamanism*, saying Hawaiian kahunas develop an identical ability.

CAW members are into speed-reading, memory training, karate, yoga, autosuggestion, set theory, logic, survival training, snakes and nudity. Besides Heinlein, Abraham Maslow's theories of self-actualization and the novels of Ayn Rand influenced the group. The CAW emblem is the tiki. CAW has no creed, but its goal is to achieve total telepathic union of all life on earth.

Zell achieved a good deal of notoriety thanks to his winning performances at costume balls (complete with snakes), various DisCons and the 1972 WorldCon. He withdrew from CAW and retired to California to establish a Bene Gesserit shaman training institute, based on Frank Herbert's novel, *Dune*.

Erisian Magic

Erisian magic or Discordianism worships Eris, goddess of chaos and confusion. It began in 1957 when two men in California claimed they were sprinkled with fairy dust in a bowling alley by Eris and inspired to form the Discordian Society, "a new religion disguised as a complicated put-on." The two, Robert Shea and Robert Anton Wilson (who took the name Mordecai the Foul) later wrote a science fiction trilogy about their new religion, the Illuminatus. Sacred symbols are the apple and pentagon. The group, called a cabal, follows the "Sacred Chou," exploring the polarities of humor and seriousness, order and chaos. The system has affinities with Taoism, anarchy and clowning. Rituals are designed as nonviolent, absurdist, revolutionary and surreal experiences, using paradox to expand the perception of reality. One Erisian ritual—the Ancient and Honorable Order of Bill the Cat, lord of the obnoxious and nasty, involving a crude caricature of the circle ritual—is sometimes used by other pagans as a check on egotism, pomposity and taking themselves too seriously.

Feraferia

This system of neo-paganism, begun by astrologer Frederick Adams, incorporates elements of the nudist, vegetarian, naturalist and utopian movements. Its goal is a return to the peaceful existence that existed in a golden age before the beginning of animal husbandry, blood sacrifice and the eating of meat. Adams believed paradises such as Eden, Avalon and the Garden of the Hesperides were distant memories of this utopian existence humans once lived among the trees.

Feraferians worship Kore, the Young Maiden (also known as the Daughter of Demeter), Persephone and the Nameless Bride of Eleusis. She manifests herself in the modern age as Alice in Wonderland, Peter Pan's Wendy, and, to some extent, Lolita and Barbarella.

Festivals use Greek ritual to retell the story of the maiden goddess and her lover in new terms. On May Day, the sun and moon become engaged. On the summer solstice, they marry. Lammas is their honeymoon. At the autumn equinox, they return home to harvest their crops. On Halloween, they prepare for sleep. At Yule, the goddess awakes to find herself alone and pregnant. At Candlemas, the new god moves in her womb, to be born at the spring solstice.

Devotees of Feraferia follow the Hesperian lifestyle, emphasizing organic gardening, tree crops and reforestation projects. They eat a diet of fruit, nuts, berries and leafy vegetables and keep no pets. Areas of interest include ecology, the wilderness, astronomy, astrology and sacred building construction. They build temples in nature oriented to the four directions and positions of the stars and planets in the Henge, or mandala, design.

The **Dancers of the Sacred Circle** are an offshoot of Feraferia.

The Sabean Religious Order

Frederic de Arechaga, who took the name Ordun, composed this cult from Basque, Yoruba, Sumerian and Babylonian sources. The stars are worshiped in a temple of the moon, decorated with columns topped with white elephants. **Sabeans** believe that history, both past and future, is written in the stars and they study astrology, astronomy, herbalism, temple building and the relationship of time and place.

Rituals celebrate the stars and planets in highly choreographed performances incorporating music, dance, art and song, along with elements of mystery plays. Weddings among the Sabeans are called "eclipses" and divination determines the union's duration: a "solar eclipse" lasts for a period of years; a "lunar eclipse" only lasts for a period of months. Margot Adler, in *Drawing Down the Moon*, reports attending a fabulous feast at a solar eclipse celebration where a huge Caesar salad was mixed by hand in a cauldron. All meat eaten is killed in a ritual manner, reminiscent of Kosher rites.

The major Sabean god is Am'n, the "hidden, numberless point," a source either single or plural, neither male nor female, representing total knowledge. Am'n is personified by several goddesses representing the seasons and races of mankind: the red goddess of autumn and the Native Americans, the white goddess of winter and Caucasians, the black goddess of spring and the African peoples, the yellow goddess of summer and the Orient, and the blue goddess, ruler of Leap Year and people living "beyond the earth."

Women are represented by the sun and the metal gold; men by the moon and the color silver.

THE LANGUAGE OF WITCHCRAFT

When writing about magic, archaic terms seem to sound right. Grammatically, thou and thee are singular, you and ye are plural.

Many paths of witchcraft use the greeting "Blessed Be." Spells are sealed with the phrase "So mote it be." The Wiccan passwords are "Perfect love and perfect trust." But, of course, as Gerald Gardner would be the first to tell you, nothing is written in stone. Thus, the following dictionary of terms can be used to help you create your own language for the rites and rituals in your work.

DICTIONARY OF TERMS FROM WITCHCRAFT AND MAGIC

Akasha: All-pervading spirit ether.

Ankh: The mirror of Hathor and Venus, used in Egypt as a symbol of sexual union and the immortality of the gods. The yonic loop portion was painted red; the phallic cross, white. Known as the key of the Nile, a sign of the mystic union of Isis and Osiris, and said to release the annual Nile flood.

Apex: A tall, conical hat, familiar to us as the headgear of Halloween witches; a brimless version served as the cap of Mithra and Frey; later worn by of Rome's high priests, the Pontifex Maximus, and by various elves, gnomes and fairies, clowns, fools and dunces

Athame: Black-handled, double-bladed dagger used by witches to cast circles and other sacred activities. Magnetized at each new moon in certain paths. Name probably comes from "al-dhamme," the sacred knife of a Moorish Andalusian cult of moon worshipers known as the Double-Horned Ones.

Autumn Equinox: A sabbat celebrated on September 21-23; Celtic Mabon, Christian Michaelmass. Days and nights are of equal length. It is the time of the Elusian Mysteries of the goddess Demeter in ancient times. Associated symbols: acorns, hazel branches and brown and green candles. The witches' version of Thanksgiving.

Banishing: This has three uses in witchcraft: the circle is banished at the end of a ritual; an individual may be banished from the coven or from The Craft; and an entity is banished in order to disable a harmful nonmaterial being.

Beltane: Celtic cross-quarter fire festival celebrated on May Eve, April 30-May 1; German Walpurgisnacht. Festival of the Fairy Queen. Marks the beginning of summer. Time of sexual license: "the lusty month of May." Associated symbols: the maypole, flower garlands, wearing of the green. All fires relit from the Beltane fire made with nine kinds of wood.

Biolline: White-handled knife used for carving; carried by a priestess.

Boomerang Effect: The belief of many witches that if you lay a harmful spell against an innocent person, it will return threefold.

Broom: Associated with domestic magic, marriage and midwives in ancient Rome; Gypsy marriages are still solemnized by "jumping the broomstick."

Candlemas: Sabbat cross-quarter celebrated on February 1-2; Celtic Imbolg or Imbolc ("the Womb"). A women's festival honoring Brigit or Brigantia, goddess of fertility, healing and fire. Time of the Lesser Eleusian Mysteries. In Wicca, the most popular time to initiate new witches. Christianized as the purification of the Virgin Mary forty days after the birth of Christ. Associated symbols: red and white candles, plaiting of rushes, divination concerning the length of winter based on the weather (today popularized as Groundhog Day).

Candles: Used extensively in spells; one of the easiest way to cast spells in witchcraft. Usually anointed with oil. Spells may take three days, nine days or one night to cast. Candles were sacred to Juno Lucina, Mother of Light, in Rome; her winter solstice festival of lights still survives in the Swedish tradition of St. Lucy's Day.

Cauldron: Major female symbol of the old pagan world, symbolizing the womb of the goddess, able to assure rebirth or magic power to all who drank from it; frequently watched over by three goddesses, fates or witches.

Chalice (a.k.a. Cup): Drinking from a cup of blood, and later, wine (blood of the earth) represents a major act of communion since earliest times; in pagan (and Jewish) marriage ceremonies, the couple drinks from the same cup to become "one blood." Symbol of water in the tarot deck; later replaced by hearts.

Circle: A primary feminine sign, thought to be protective, drawn in a sacred manner at the beginning of every session of magic or witchcraft.

Cord: Used in witchcraft to tie or bind a spell; often worn as a girdle during rites. Originally sacred to the Egyptian goddess Ma'at, keeper of the law; used in healing amulets in Babylon because of their connection to the umbilicus.

Corn Dolly: Harvest figure made of stalks of grain (called corn in Europe).

Coven: Gathering of witches; originally supposed to contain twelve witches and a devil during the witch trials, mocking Christ and His apostles.

Covenstead: Meeting place of a coven.

The Craft: Name used for the workings of both Freemasonry and Wicca.

Crossroads: Said to be the site of witches' sabbats; sacred to Hecate and Hermes.

Deosil: Clockwise motion.

Elemental: Nonmaterial entities with the nature of one of the four elements: air, earth, fire or water.

Esbat: Celebration at one of the thirteen annual full moons.

Evoking: Summoning entities of a lower order than mankind.

Familiar: An animal or spirit kept to provide psychic support when working spells. The various "Small Peoples" were believed to be the familiars of witches during the witch trials. More frequently, the familiar took the form of an animal, usually a cat or dog, but sometimes a rabbit, goat or other creature. In France, most familiars were frogs, sacred to Hecate; the fleur-de-lis is actually a symbol of three frogs.

Fetch: A male witch who serves as messenger and assistant to the high priest and priestess of a coven; also called the summoner.

Gnome: An earth elemental.

The Grail: Originally the Celtic caldron of regeneration, full of the holy blood of the goddess; later the goal of an immense Quest literature, containing much Celtic imagery mixed with Christian plot lines.

The Great Rite: A ritual merging the polarities of male and female, usually through symbolic or actual sexual activity.

Handfasting: Wiccan or pagan marriage ceremony.

Herm: Phallic pillar with a head of Hermes on top that once guarded nearly every crossroads in Europe; reworked into crosses during the Christian era. Originally a Greek tradition; oddly, the Aztecs had an identical practice in the New World. Travelers frequently made offerings to Hermes and Hecate, gods of the crossroads, and they were honored at festivals called Compitalia.

Hexagram: Six-pointed star, now associated with the Jewish faith, but originally a Tantric symbol of the sexual union of male and female.

Hieros Gamos: Greek for "sacred marriage," the Great Rite (once widespread in the pagan world) by which a man became king through sexual union with the great goddess or her high priestess.

Hiving Off: Establishing a new coven.

Host: The Christian wafer representing the body of Christ in communion; its desecration was the charge in many witch trials.

Incantation: The singing-in of a spell or charm.

Invoking: Summoning an entity of a higher nature than human.

Lammas: Cross-quarter festival celebrated July 31-August 1; Celtic Lugnasad or Lughnassah. The Feast of Bread. "The Games of Lud," god of wisdom. Marks the beginning of the harvest season. First corn harvest and baking of first loaf from new crop. Traditionally the time of temporary "marriages" lasting a year and a day. Associated symbols: corn dollies, sheaves of wheat, grapes, green crowns and candles.

Macrocosm/Microcosm: Principle that states the correspondence between large and small events—as above, so below.

Magus: Male occult adept.

Maiden: Assistant high priestess in a coven.

Maypole: Center of the dance at Beltane when men and women celebrated the fertility of the new season. Origin of square dancing's grand right and left. The pole itself represents the May king's phallus.

Medicine Wheel: Circles, usually marked out with stones, in the American West. Thought to serve the same purpose as megalithic stone circles in Europe. Most have twenty-eight spokes, plus a center stone. Sun dance lodges are still built to the same pattern.

Pentacle: A disk of metal, usually inscribed with a pentagram, placed on an altar to represent Earth.

Pentagram: A five-pointed star, representing the earth and the fivefold path; variously called Solomon's Seal, the Star of Bethlehem, the Druid's Foot and the Witches' Cross (witches "cross themselves" with the symbol). Ancient sign of "gateless" protection used in ritual magic and Wicca, since it's drawn with one continuous line; derived from the apple-core star of the earth. Sacred to Celtic death goddess, Morgan, whose devotees displayed it on a blood-red shield. Sign of the earth element in the tarot suit (today, diamonds).

Poppet: Doll used by witches when casting spells, a very ancient practice dating back to pharonic Egypt.

Prana: Vital force of the cosmos operation on the etheric level.

Ring: Traditional symbol of a bond between giver and wearer, as the peoples of Middle Earth discovered to their despair when they accepted Sauron's rings of power. Other magic rings in literature include those of the Niebelung, and Solomon's magic ring with which he enslaved the demon Asmodeus.

Runes: Letters of an ancient Norse script, used for divination.

Sabbat: Eight annual major festivals, falling at the solstices, equinoxes and four cross-quarter days halfway between.

Salamander: A fire elemental.

Samhain: Sabbat cross-quarter festival, October 31-November 1; All Hallows Eve, Feast of the Dead, Halloween. Marks the beginning of the Celtic year. Feast of Hecate, goddess of the crossroads; Mexican Day of the Dead, when the gates between the worlds of the living and dead open, allowing the ghosts of dead ancestors to visit their descendants. The fairy hills in Ireland also opened on this date. Summerend, the beginning of winter. Associated symbols: black, red, white (the colors of Hecate), cauldron, black robes, masks.

Scourge: Ritual whip, symbolic of firmness; cords sometimes made of silk.

Scrying: Divination by gazing, usually into water, a mirror or ink.

Scythe: Curved blade derived from the crescent of the new moon; a symbol of the great goddess in her devouring aspect; later the tool of Father Time and the Grim Reaper.

Sigil: A symbol used to embody a concept or aspect.

Sistrum: Sacred rattle, originally used in the worship of Egyptian great goddesses, popular at pagan rites today.

Skyclad: Ritual nudity.

Smudging: Purification by smoke; a very ancient practice.

Spiral: Sacred symbol dating to the Neolithic Age, connected with the ideas of death and rebirth. Spiral labyrinths and occuli (double twists resembling eyes) appear on many megalithic monuments, European cathedrals and Native American rock paintings.

Star: Believed in most ancient traditions to be the home of spirits, either of the yet unborn, the dead, angels or gods. Composed of ether, the Greeks' fifth element, said to be lighter, finer and more volatile than fire. The goddess is identified with the morning star (Venus) under many names: Astarte, Venus, Ishtar, Esther, Stella Maris. Lucifer (Son of Morning) and Christ both have associations with the morning star, as well.

Summer Solstice: Midsummer Eve, Celtic Litha, celebrated June 21-23 on the night before the longest day of the year. Christianized as St. John's Day. Traditionally a festival of fire when bonfires burned on the hills all night. Associated symbol: wheel covered with flowers.

Swastika: Ancient religious symbol of the four corners of the world. Arms pointing clockwise make it a masculine, solar symbol (used by the Nazis as their major symbol); arms that point counterclockwise indicate a feminine, lunar symbol.

Sword: Symbol of fire, virility and power. Most heroes of myth had magic swords forged in fairyland or by smiths of the underworld. At the hero's death, his sword went with him to the grave on a final journey over water or was thrown into water. In parts of pagan Europe, his sword was often a man's only possession; all else—the fields, flocks and household—belonged to the woman. Sign of the Doom suit and the element fire in the tarot deck. (Later became spades, thanks to the Spanish word for sword, *espada*.)

Sylph: An air elemental.

Talisman: Like an amulet, but worn for a specific purpose.

Triangle: Upright, symbolizes the male essence; reversed, the Yoni Yantra, symbolizing the genital area of the Threefold Goddess. Triangular cakes baked for sacred rituals by Egyptians, Jews (for Purim) and Scots (for Samhain).

Undine: A water elemental.

Vernal or Spring Equinox: A sabbat celebrated on March 21-23; Germanic Ostrara, became Christian Easter. Marks the beginning of spring, when days and nights are of equal length. The return of Persephone from the underworld. Associated sacred symbols:

hare, egg, lily, the color white, doe, bow and arrow, silver and green candles.

Wand: A magical rod of power representing the element of air, used in witches' rites; made of wood, bone, ivory or amber, often tipped with crystals and decorated with ribbons and magic stones. Used in love magic. A symbol of mercy. Dionysus (Bacchus) carried a wand made of a fennel stalk topped with a pinecone. Fairy wands are tipped with stars. The sign of air in the tarot deck; later became clubs.

Wiccaning: The pagan equivalent of Christening.

Widdershins: A counterclockwise direction.

Winter Solstice: Germanic Yule, December 21-23. Shortest day of the year. Odin honored at a great feast. Time of the Roman Saturnalia, celebrating the birth of the Unconquered Sun; a time of gaming, exchanging presents, sexual license and reversed social roles. Associated symbols: red and green candles, holly, mistletoe, ivy, oak logs, pinecones.

Wotan's Cross: A cross inside a circle given various symbolic meanings in paganism: the earth and the four directions; the sun embraced by heaven; the union of the rose (feminine) with the cross (male) in cabalistic symbolism.

HERBS, PLANTS AND ESSENCES USED IN WITCHCRAFT

Acacia: sacred to Diana; used to commune with spirits
Angelica: sacred to Sophia; restores harmony
Cinnamon: attracts lovers, health and luck
Irish Moss: place under your rug for the "luck of the Irish"
Laurel: good luck; worn by victors
Mandrake: hold the root as you conjure to strengthen spells
Myrtle: sacred to Artemis
Patchouli: sacred to Pan
Rose: sacred to Diana
Rosemary: offers protection; worn by pagan warriors into battle
Vervain: sacred to Venus; used to banish evil
Violet: sacred to the Fairy Queen
Witches Broom: purifies water

CHAPTER FIVE

COMMERCE, TRADE AND LAW IN CONTEMPORARY FANTASY

Sherrilyn Kenyon

I t is a common misconception that the Middle Ages was broken into three factions: those who worked, those who fought and those who prayed. As with any broad generalization, this doesn't even begin to scratch the surface of the complex infrastructure and relationships of peasant, lord and priest, especially since these three often overlapped with such occupations as warrior-priests or peasant soldiers, or my personal favorites, the peasants who became lords and the lords who were forced to work.

In the fantasy genre, these relationships can be even more blurred or more rigid depending on the author. In R.R. Mallory's short story, "Sword Song," warriors are literally one with their weapons. Anne Lesley Groell uses aristocratic ladies as guild assassins in her novels *Bridge of Valor* and *Anvil of the Sun.* In a brilliant blending of medieval feudalism with fantasy, Kinley MacGregor's *Pale Moon Rising* shows us a magic-based society where vassals swear alliegance to the Mage-Lord and his underlings.

Similarly, when it comes to law in fantasy, the author is High Judge. However, the laws and punishments should be consistent within that world, unless the capriciousness or injustice of the person in charge is something you wish to illustrate.

Even though you and your imagination are the only limitations in fantasy, it still helps to understand the basic classes and positions held by medieval men and women. The following list should aid you in creating a unique world tailored to your story.

COMMERCE

Throughout most of the Middle Ages, a peasant wasn't tied to the land (serfs were, but even they could escape). In the early part of the period, a peasant could escape his status by either becoming a fighter or becoming an apprentice to a trade—and on a much smaller scale, even a member of the church. There were, of course, other members of the lower class—Gypsies, peddlers, vagabonds, prostitutes and the like. What generally segregated these people from their middle-class counterparts was a lack of land and money.

In the Middle Ages, the possession of land was the only real value a person had. Serfs who were bound to the land were infinitely richer than those who were cast off their lands, even though those without land were able to travel about.

These vagabonds were seen as disease carriers or thieves. Unfortunately, destitution often casued them to become those very things. A woman without money usually turned to prostitution where she contracted numerous diseases, and both men and women who were denied jobs turned to theft.

With so many villages and even towns xenophobic, most people couldn't find work once they left their lands. The only way to circumvent this was to go somewhere they had family who could vouch for them, or to carry a letter of reference from their previous clergy member or lord.

The idea of the cutpurse or thief took on a noble air with some of the troubadours who were many times vagabonds themselves and who often tried to dignify the homeless wanderer. However, it must be noted that most minstrels were nobility who had dropped out, or were forced out of their traditional place in society.

Lower Class

Acrobats/Jugglers: These performers traveled about the countryside in search of either an inn, tavern, fair, castle or court where they could perform. Since they could go long periods of time without finding a place to perform, many of them turned to theft and other crimes to make ends meet.

Adamist: A gardener or tiller of any field.

Adamite: Term for a nudist, usually a poor pilgrim or hermit who was doing penance for something.

Alchemists: Charged with turning common items into gold, alchemists had a tenuous place in society. Often the brunt of superstition and hostility, they were left alone and ridiculed, except in extreme times when they might be singled out as warlocks and punished by extreme measures.

Artists: Commissioned to paint portraits of various people, they had a reputation for seduction, thievery and other crimes. Though looked down upon by most of society, they were left alone unless they committed punishable crimes.

Barber: One who cut hair, but also let blood to cure infections.

Bard: A musician or minstrel who usually sung only of heroic deeds. Like acrobats, they traveled in search of donations to live on. Many bards and minstrels were nobles who either dropped out or were forced out of their noble status.

Bear Baiters: Much like a modern rodeo clown or matador, these intrepid spirits would bait bears and run from them for the amusement of their patrons.

Beggar: Usually a mentally or physically handicapped person who was unable to work. They either begged in the street or frequented alms houses and hospitals so that they could eat. However, it was also a common occupation for those who didn't want to work; these people were seen as frauds and, if caught, could be severely punished.

Chamber Maid: Usually of the peasant class, these were young women who went to work in either a middle- or upper-class household as cleaning servants.

Chambrieres: Women who tended cows.

Champion: A man or knight who hired himself out as a stand-in for trials by combat. Some were permanently retained by nobles or towns, and in some cases, several were retained to participate for both the accuser and the accused. Of course, this profession was considered the lowest of the low, and the shame of a father being a champion was passed on to his children, who were sometimes not allowed to own property. It was also a highly dangerous occupation, since most of the time the champion shared whatever punishment was dealt to the accused.

Churl (a.k.a *Serf):* The lowest class of peasantry. As early as the ninth century, it was also used alternatively for husband. (Never say medieval folk didn't have a sense of humor.)

Comandarreses: Women who hired out other women as servants or wet nurses.

Comedians: Just like their modern counterparts, these individuals traveled around telling jokes for profit. They would sometimes be forced to commit crimes in order to survive, or they would tell a joke that didn't meet with the tastes of their host. In such cases, the punishment could be quite severe.

Dancers: Male or female, they traveled about in search of arenas in which to perform. They were often condemned by the Church, but the lay society enjoyed seeing them. The best engagements were found around festivals, holidays and celebrations.

Dwarves: People short in stature who often hired themselves out as oddities, jesters or fools.

Dyer: One who dyed cloth. They were looked down upon by everyone and were easy to spot due to their dye-stained fingers. Most were male, but some females also plied this trade.

Fishmonger: One who dealt in fish. Though profitable, for an obvious reason it wasn't a very prestigious trade.

Fishwife: A woman who sold fish.

Fools: Most were similar to comedians, the primary difference being that these were people who were a permanent member of a nobleman's entourage. They often made scathing political commentaries masked with their humor.

Footpad: One who robbed on foot, usually on a road or highway.

Fortune-tellers: Though they were often part of the Gypsy clan, there were others, some even born of noble households, who were able to read tarot cards, palms, bones, stones, runes, tea leaves, crystal balls and mirrors. Their readings took up much time and were usually very detailed. The common form of payment was silver. The Church completely banned such practices and called for death as a punishment. Lay courts, however, held more to the old Roman laws and they made a determination between beneficial and malevolent diviners. Beneficial practitioners were often left alone or fined; those judged malevolent were put to death. In times of famine or pestilence, a local priest or friar could single out fortune-tellers and use them for scapegoats. They then would be hanged or stoned to death by the very people they had once helped.

Freebooter: A thief or pirate, most often with a devil-may-care attitude.

Friar: Often seen by the local priests as competition for local charity and giving, friars had a raunchy reputation as purveyors of sin. They preferred to frequent towns and most especially taverns, and were infamous for performing forbidden ceremonies such as secret weddings, last rites for those to whom it had been denied, and so forth.

Gypsies: Though not part of the Middle Ages until the mid-fifteenth century, Gypsies are undeniably a part of fantasy. Medieval Gypsies were feared and often met with horrible deaths and punishments from both the Church and lay courts. Seen as purveyors of sin and sorcery, they were ranked with Jews and generally avoided.

Heretic: This was a term applied to many different types of people. Heretics were witches, political enemies or anyone who contradicted the Church. For those found guilty of it, the penalty was almost always death. However, it should be noted that there were large groups of heretics that were allowed to live in peace, even though the Church condemned them. It was only when these groups began to threaten local church or lay officials that they became objects of persecution.

Imp: One who grafted feathers on hawks or falcons to aid them in flight. Also, a devil-child.

Jongleurs/Minstrels: Traveling musicians who essentially sang for their supper. Their songs could be heroic, religious or bawdy depending on the needs or wants of their audience. They were often from noble families, but were either left to their own accord or were second-born sons with no inheritance. Though women were rare, there were a few who chose this career. Many of these ended up pursuing criminal activities to make ends meet.

Kidnapper: A popular occupation in the high and late Middle Ages. These were often common born thugs who grabbed travelers off the roads, or they were hired by someone to go into another person's home and kidnap them. The punishment for this crime was death.

Mercenary: This term could be applied to low- or high-born men who rented out their military service for a fee. Many mercenaries banded together and sold their services as a group or traveling army. They also had reputations for turning on the very people who hired them, or of keeping the spoils of war for themselves.

Midwife: A woman who was in charge of delivering babies (a task that was too tedious for a doctor to bother with). Midwives usually passed their craft down from mother to daughter and were most often of peasant stock. Many also attended to other female health issues and diseases. Their cures were often more humane than those of their so-called learned colleagues. When some of their cures proved more beneficial, some of their unscrupulous

and jealous male counterparts would call them witches or
heretics.

Mimes: Actors and actresses. Condemned by the Church, mimes
could be male or female if they were a traveling band who performed for taverns, inns, courts, castles and fairs. If they were
involved with the Church, however, they were exclusively male.

Oracles: One through whom the gods speak. A mainstay of fantasy,
these are revered religious figures who are often sanctified or at
least tolerated by the Church. They are usually hermits or other
people who have withdrawn from society and must be sought
out by those in need of their help.

Pardoner: Men licensed by the Church to sell indulgences, or absolution, for sins. Many of these men were so corrupt (and a large
number unlicensed) that the pardoner was often considered a
criminal. Thus the epithet "penny-preacher" was born, indicating that anyone could buy absolution for a penny.

Pawnbroker: Worked the same way as the modern pawnbroker,
although they could also be loan sharks. Although they could be
fined if caught, they were most often viewed as a despicable but
necessary part of society.

Peasant: Simply means a rural laborer. They could be free or tied
to the land where they worked. Those who were free often sold
themselves out for other types of labor or took a second job as a
peddlar or household servant. In the worst of times, they would
also sell their children and even spouses. Once slavery was
banned, they abandoned offspring in lean times. Most countries
allowed them to regain their children later if they came upon
good times and could repay the people who had kept the child
during those years.

Peddlar: A traveling vendor, usually male but at times female, who
roamed the countryside. Though most were common born, they
were often entrusted to carry messages and such during times of
war. Despite such activities, they were tolerated by all nobles and
royals as a necessary and vital part of the economy.

Penitent: Someone (male or female) who was repenting their sins.
They were often found as pilgrims or just rootless wanderers
clothed in rags (or nothing at all), with ashes smeared on their
bodies.

Pilgrims: Men and women who were traveling to a holy shrine.
Many of these people tended to fall to the wayside and used their

PEASANT GIRL: The bouquet and headdress of wheat and wild flowers may indicate that this girl is dressed for a celebration.

©1998, Chivalry Sports, Inc.

pilgrimage as a cover for a variety of crimes. Also, some women would be robbed or would otherwise find themselves without enough money for the trip. Most of these women turned to prostitution. So many pilgrims were victims of crimes that they began traveling in large groups, such as the group of pilgrims in Chaucer's *Canterbury Tales.*

Poacher: A man or woman who illegally killed game. Most of the time, poaching was an act of desperation. If caught, the punishment was blinding, amputation or death.

Prostitutes: Though usually a tolerated crime, when lawgivers decided to punish women who sold their bodies, they chose a variety of means. Punishments ranged from merely cropping the prostitute's hair or shaving her head to abysmal types of death.

Serf: A man or woman who lived off a section of land and had to make a labor payment to the landowner for the privilege of living there. They could easily find themselves homeless if the land was sold or given over to the Church. With little or no money of their own, they often became vagabonds.

Shepherd: Tended sheep.

Skald: A minstrel-poet similar to a bard and usually of Danish origin.

Slave: A man or woman owned by another person. Most slaves in the Middle Ages were used as prostitutes or by artisans who needed many servants or laborers for their particular trade. Females tended to be used primarily for household tasks, and men for apprentice/journeyman type work or other heavy menial labor tasks.

Soothsayers: For some reason in fantasy and classical literature, soothsayers tend to be blind in one or both eyes. They are usually elderly, bedraggled and dirty. They can be meddlesome, and often put in their two cents without being asked. Though they can be punished by a nobleman who doesn't want to hear the truth they speak, they are often left alone and deemed addlepates. Those who appreciate their words pay them with either food or with copper coins.

Spinner (a.k.a *Spinster):* Usually a position held by women, spinners spun fibers into threads and threads into textiles.

Stew-holder: One who ran a brothel. Stew-holders were charged with having their prostitutes examined on a monthly basis to ensure their health. If they were found to be selling girls or boys who were disease carriers, their penalties could be harsh. Overall, they were left alone, but in times of censure, they could be run out of town, tarred or killed.

Swineherd: One who tended pigs and hogs.

Thieves: A generic term for people who took what didn't belong to them. The punishment for theft depended on what was stolen and from whom. Thieves suffered amputation, branding, blinding or death.

Tinker: One who repaired or made metal items. They were usually travelers, but some had shops.

Usurer: One who loaned money for profit. Denounced by the Church and hated by everyone, usurers were often ostracized by society. It was tolerated as a necessity.

Wet Nurse: A woman who sold her breast milk. Usually, they were women whose own child had died, but there were a number of cases of them being new mothers who hired themselves out to motherless infants or to wealthy women who didn't have the time, inclination or nutrient-rich milk to feed their own infant.

Wolf's Head: An outlaw. In Old English, it meant one who was to
be hunted down like a wolf.

Woodcutter: One who chopped wood for a living or to subsidize
their income.

Middle Class

Almoner: One who collects and dispenses alms to the poor. He or
she is usually employed by a wealthy or middle-class household,
and it is his or her duty to gather table scraps and see them
dispensed after every meal. The title can also be given to a member of the church who fulfills this position on a regular basis.

Apprentice: These were either boys or girls who were indentured
to a trade between the ages of five and seven. The actual time of
their servitude was worked out when they were apprenticed, but
the average length was seven years, at which time they became
a journeyman or journeywoman and entered a guild.

Armorer: One who made armor (steel, iron or leather) or chain
mail.

Arrow-smith: One who made arrow heads.

Avener: In charge of a stable.

Bailiff: Overseer of the manor. Same as a steward or sheriff, he
could be charged with managing household affairs, or with over-
seeing local laws and courts.

Beekeeper: Usually a man who kept the bees and sold their honey
and honeycomb.

Blacksmith: One who worked with iron or black metal.

Brewer/Brewster: Brewed ale and the like.

Burgher: A citizen of a town.

Capper: One who made caps.

Chandler: Maker of candles.

Clockmaker: The first mechanical clock of the Middle Ages appears
around 1271 and portable clocks appear in the early fourteenth
century.

Clothier: Maker of clothes.

Cobbler: Repaired shoes.

Cooper: Maker and repairer of wooden vessels such as barrels, baskets, tubs, pails, etc.

Constable: Chief military officer of the household. In the absence
of the lord or king, he would lead forces to protect the castle or
country.

Confectioner: Maker of sweets.

Cordwainer: A shoemaker.

Cutler: A knife maker.

Daserii/Deiciers: Dicemaker.

Draper: Cloth dealer.

Fletcher: One who made or dealt in bows and arrows, or an archer.

Fullers: One who cleaned or thickened cloth.

Glassblower: Maker of glass and glass products.

Glover: Maker of gloves.

Goldsmith: One who designed and made gold products.

Groom: A stablehand.

Hayward: In charge of maintaining fences and enclosures and, at times, tor herding stray cattle.

Herald: Heralds had a variety of roles. They were charged with assigning, designing and identifying coats of arms. In their original and simplest forms, they were merely messengers sent to deliver letters and missives.

Housecarl: Royal bodyguard.

Jewelers: Makers and sellers of jewelry.

Knave: A boy who served in the lowest capacity in a household. A lowly servant.

Knight: In its pure form, a servant or boy. It didn't become synonymous with a military person until the twelfth century.

Leech: A monk appointed to care or bleed the sick, so named after the animals they sometimes used.

Marshal: A farrier, or one who was entrusted with the military affairs of a royal household.

Man-at-Arms: Soldier.

Mercer: A man who dealt in silks and velvets. Merceress is the female counterpart.

Merchant: One who bought or sold goods.

Miller: One who ground corn. Corn in medieval England was a generic term for any kind grain or seed.

Monk: A member of a commune of other men sworn to poverty and celibacy. The practice of those two things varied greatly from individual to individual.

Physician: A trained doctor who tended the sick. They attended and taught at the universities and were paid more than surgeons. Many of the better physicians were retained by the wealthy.

Poulterer: One who dealt in poultry.

MIDDLE CLASS: This woman's dress may indicate that she is an innkeeper or tavern owner.

©1998, Chivalry Sports, Inc.

Prefect: Govenor or overseer in a variety of offices. Could govern a city, town, village or manor.

Prelate: A bishop or archbishop usually of noble birth, but sometimes rising from a wealthy middle-class family.

Priest: One who performed public religious ceremonies.

Scribe: Can mean a variety of things. One who interpreted the law. A clerk or secretary, or one who translated or copied manuscripts.

Scholar: A university student. They were infamous for their licentiousness, purveyors of confidence scams and as wastrels (good-for-nothings).

Seneschal: Could be a steward, or a govenor of a city, or a member of a high noble household who oversaw judicial matters.

Shepster: Dressmaker.

Sheriff: Oversaw the local court and was the chief administrator of the shire laws.

Spurrier: One who made spurs.

Squire: A servant or a youth of noble birth who assisted a knight.

Steward: Overseer of the castle and demesne lands (land possessed
by an individual, usually a lord).

Surgeon: The practical doctor. The surgeon was responsible for
bleeding, as well as for pulling teeth and other more grisly responsibilities that were too common for physicians to bother with.

Tailor: One who cut cloth.

Tavern/Innkeeper: One who ran or owned a tavern or inn.

Vintner: Maker of wine.

Weaving/Weaver: One who wove cloth; usually a woman, but there
were also men in the industry.

Upper Class

Abbot, Abbat: In charge of a monastery. Usually a man of noble
birth.

Abbess, Abbadisse, Abbas: In charge of a nunnery or convent. Usually a woman of noble birth.

Archbishop: Highest ranking bishop. Almost always a man of noble
birth.

Baintighearnas: Ladyship (Scottish Gaelic).

Banneret: A military commander who led knights under his own
emblem or banner.

Baron: Tenant-in-chief who holds lands from the king or an
overlord.

Baroness: Wife or widow of a baron.

Baronet: Nobles who don't have a title, but are members of the
House of Lords.

Bishop: Director of a diocese. Usually of noble birth.

Cardinal: Member of the Pope's council. There are three ranks of
cardinal: Cardinal Bishop, Cardinal Priest and Cardinal Deacon.

Ceann-feadhna: Chieftain (Scottish Gaelic).

Chieftain: Ruler of a clan.

Countess: Wife or widow of an earl.

Duchess: Wife or widow of a duke.

Duke: Title for relatives of the royal family.

Earl/Eorl: Highest of the nobility (not of the royalty).

Jarl: A Norse or Danish chief or underking.

Jarless: The wife of a jarl.

Kim: Ruler or chief (Celtic term).

King: Ruler of a kingdom. Referred to as Your Grace or Sire.

UPPER CLASS: This woman's fine apparel denotes her wealthy status.

©1998, Chivalry Sports, Inc.

Knight: In the early part of the Middle Ages, they were seen as low-born thugs (even if they came from a noble family). It wasn't until the eleventh century that they began to gain respectability. And by the twelfth, they were almost always of noble family with noble lineage (either real or fabricated). Supposedly held to a higher standard of conduct, most knights tended to forget their vows and held the view that might makes right. Knights were the cavalry of the army or, in more modern terms, they were tanks. A fully armed knight was virtually indestructible, at least in the early part of the period. As time went on, special weapons were designed to neutralize them such as cannons, handguns and estocs (thin knives designed to slip between the plates or rings of metal).

Knight-Errant: Wandering knight in search of adventure.

Lady: A courtesy title given to any female of noble birth. If she was single and had no property of her own, her name was styled Lady *First Name*, for example, Lady Alice. If she was married or widowed, she could be called Lady Alice, or Lady *Her Lands/Castle* (Lady Nottingham or Lady of Nottingham).

Laird: Scottish term for a leader or nobleman who held lands directly from the king. He was usually styled as *The Clan Name* (The MacDougal).

Lairdess: Wife of a laird.

Lairdie: A petty laird.

Lord: A courtesy title given to any male of noble birth whether he had land or not. If he was without land, he was simply Lord *First Name*, for example Lord Stephen. If he had land, he could be Lord Stephen or Lord *His Land/Castle* (Lord Nottingham or Lord of Nottingham).

Miles: Attached to the end of a knight's name as a designation of his status (French term).

Mother Superior: Title of an abbess.

Pope: Head of the Catholic church. Almost all came from noble families (or, at the very least, extremely wealthy middle class).

Prince: Son of a king, or husband of a queen. In conversations, he was called Your Highness.

LAIRDESS: The wife of a Scottish laird.

©1998, Chivalry Sports, Inc.

Princess: Daughter of a king or wife of a prince. She was referred to as Your Highness.

Queen: Wife of the king or a female ruler. She was referred to as Your Grace or Your Royal Grace. If she had children and/or if the king was dead, she would be called Queen-Mother. If the king were alive, she was properly called Queen-Consort. The basic title Queen meant a woman who ruled in her own right.

Sir: Title attached to the name of a knight, clerk or scribe.

Tighearnas: Lordship (Scottish Gaelic).

PUNISHMENTS

Amputation: The removal of a body part, the exact one to be determined by the judge. Usually it was something that had to do with the crime, for example, a thief lost his hand, or a Peeping Tom lost an eye. However, this was not always the case, and any body part could be removed, for example, testicles, breasts, tongues or ears. It is interesting to note that at one point in the Middle Ages, this was such a common punishment that people who had accidently lost body parts such as eyes, ears and/or limbs would carry certified notes that assured people that they were the victims of an unfortunate accident or battle rather than criminals.

Banishment: This was used for treason or just about any crime when the judge or king didn't want a convicted person hanging around their territory. Banishment was most often used with noblemen and women, but could also be used for those in lesser positions. The duration of the banishment would depend on the crime and position of the convict. At one point, it became quite fashionable to force people to take pilgrimages to specific holy shrines, or to force them to walk from shrine to shrine until the saints forgave them for their crime. Just how did one know when the saints had forgiven them? The chains they were forced to wear supposedly fell from their arms or legs. It was often reported as a type of advertisement for shrines just how many prisoners had gained their freedom while visiting such and such church or relic.

Beheading: Reserved for capital crimes, it was accomplished by a variety of means, the most common of which was with the convicted person's head being placed on a stool or block and an axe being used to strike off their head. In other cases, a sword was used to whack off the head of the convicted felon while they knelt before their executioner. Some countries had laws that only allowed so many strokes to complete the deed. If the person survived, they were set free, but more often than not, it resulted in a long, painful death for the convicted while they slowly bled to death from their wounds. It was also customary for the head to be placed on a pike and publicly displayed for a designated amount of time.

Blinding: Prescribed for various crimes, including robbery, rape and so on. It involved having one or both eyes gouged out.

Boiling: A person was placed inside a large cauldron and literally boiled alive.

Branding: This involved having a red-hot iron placed against the naked skin. In some countries there were specific designs to designate what crime had caused the brand to be given.

Burning: This is most often associated with heresy and witchcraft, though it should be noted that it wasn't the usual punishment in the Middle Ages for witchcraft. Hanging had that dubious honor. It was, however, used for various crimes such as treason, rape and abduction.

Cucking Stool or Ducking Stool: A punishment chair used to confine a person for public humiliation where they were either set in the town square or led through town. Also used for dunking in water. Usually reserved for prostitutes, witches, heretics, scolds, disorderly women or fraudulent trades people.

Dungeon: A room where the accused was kept in a near-naked or naked state and forced to live on three morsels of bread and three draughts of stagnant water. The accused was always denied light, and some of them were kept inside with a board and weight placed on their chest.

Embowelling, Disembowelling (most commonly referred to as Drawn or Drawing): The removing of organs. This was usually performed on people who were awake and very concious of what was being done to them.

Excommunication: This was the trump card of the Church and was used for all manner of crimes, petty and large. It meant that the person couldn't attend mass, or have any sort of benediction from the Church. In the later Middle Ages, one couldn't marry while under this, nor could one receive last rites or confess their sins.

Fine: Most punishments could be commuted to a fee penalty, which meant that the rich seldom paid physically for their crimes. Those who couldn't scrape together enough money, or those accused of the severe crimes that couldn't be commuted to fines, suffered the full torture of the court.

Flagellation: Flogging. This was used for most any crime and as a way to induce confessions. The exact whip took on a variety of forms, from just a simple leather whip to one laced with shards of glass or steel spikes.

Garrotting: This involved having the convicted person strangled with a cord by an executioner. It was the chosen means of Spanish execution, but can also be found in other countries.

Hamstringing: This involved cutting a convicted person's hamstrings, thus crippling them. It was used commonly for robbery and prostitution, and as a means of compelling testimony.

Hanging: One of the most common forms of execution. It was usually done at a crossroads in order to gain the widest audience. Those executed were often left hanging until their bodies decomposed.

Hung, Drawn and Quartered: The convicted felon was hung until they were barely alive (in the event they passed out, they were revived), then they were disembowelled and what remained of their body was cut into four pieces and buried in four parts of the city, town or village.

Impaling: This was performed either with a red-hot poker or stake being driven through the rectum. In some cases, the convicted was placed on a greased pole and they struggled to remain above the stake as long as they could. Invariably, they would lose their fight and be impaled. Again, it was customary to leave those impaled on public display.

Imprisonment: Imprisonment wasn't used through much of the Middle Ages, but in time it did become more and more fashionable. It should be noted that many of those imprisoned were usually political hostages who were too valuable to kill, more than they were people who had actually committed crimes. Where a person was imprisoned would depend on who they were and why they were being detained. Many political hostages were kept in lush towers with servants and some of the lesser noble, rich or middle class were kept half naked in dungeons. (This was also a method of keeping rich Jews until their relatives could pay ransom).

Iron Boot: Fit to cover either the leg and foot, or just the foot, it allowed wood or metal wedges to be hammered into specific places of the feet of those being questioned. It was a favored device of the Inquisition.

Judicial Duel or Trial by Combat: Fought on foot or on horseback, it involved numerous weapons. The choice of weapon would depend on local custom, which would stipulate it was the accusers choice or a predetermined choice decided by the accused's social status and/or alleged crime. Not only could the accuser or accused demand a trial by combat, but they could also challenge any witness who testified. Throughout most of the Middle Ages, women, physically infirmed people, children and clerics were not banned from participating, and there are several cases of them having to take arms against trained men. Although it should be noted that most courts did allow them to choose a champion to fight in their stead. There were also champions for hire, but it was a dangerous occupation since, for most of the Middle Ages, the champion shared whatever punishment the accused was given, for example, death, amputation or dismemberment.

Ordeal by Boiling Water: The defendant was ordered to fast and pray for three days. When the day arrived, a mass was held and a priest oversaw the event. A single ordeal was used by those accused of minor offenses. In this the accused had to plunge his hand up to the wrist and, in some cases, retrieve a stone or ring from a kettle of boiling water. In the event of a triple ordeal (used for more serious offenses), the accused had to plunge his arm up to the elbow. The wound was then bound and sealed with the judge's signet. After three days, the wound was examined and if it bore no sign of burns or scalding, the defendant was released. If the burn was evident, then the accused was convicted.

Ordeal by Cold Water: The accused was bound by both hands and feet. A piece of rope with a knot was attached to his or her midsection, and the accused was lowered into the water. If the accused and the knot floated, then they were adjudged guilty. But if the accused and the knot sank, they were innocent.

Ordeal by Fire: The three-day preparation was identical to an ordeal by boiling water. After three days, a woman who was suspected of adultery was forced to place her naked foot against six, nine or twelve red-hot ploughshares. In other cases, the accused was blindfolded and made to walk across the red-hot ploughshares.

However, the most common form of punishment in an ordeal by fire was for the accused to walk nine feet while carrying a red-hot lump of iron. For minor offenses, the hot iron weighed a pound, but for treason, secret murder, counterfeiting, robbery or any other felony, the weight was three pounds. Upon completion, the wounds were wrapped for three days and then examined. If the wound was still intact, they were guilty. If no wound was evident, they were innocent.

Oubliette: A tight-fitting hole that allowed those imprisoned in it to neither sit nor stand, forcing them to endure an uncomfortable position of complete torture. There are two arguments for the name, which is obviously derived from the French verb *oublier*, meaning "to forget." One argument is that it was a place to put someone you wanted to forget; the other is that those put inside an oubliette would quickly forget their sanity.

Outlawry: This was used to punish those who fled before they could be tried. What it meant was that the accused was no longer entitled to the benefits of the law, and anyone who came across that person should hunt them down like a wolf. A standard fee of five shillings would be paid to the outlaw's killer, and anyone could kill an outlaw with immunity. Any lands owned by the outlaw would be forfeited.

Pilgrimage: Due to the high cost of imprisoning someone, this became a fashionable way to get rid of the undesirables. They were condemned for a certain time to walk from shrine to shrine. If the crime was severe, they would be forced to pilgrimage until they died. The only reprieve from this life sentence was if one of the saints took pity and the convict's chains miraculously fell from him. Since this didn't happen very often (to say the least), the propensity to hand out this type of sentence made the roads very dangerous for everyday people and other pilgrims. This is the reason that group pilgrimages and caravans became very popular.

Pillory: This had two forms. One was simply stocks placed on a pillar for better display. The other consisted of manacles and an iron circle around the neck that held the person to a pillar. It was used for any number of crimes, including adultery, perjury, public drunkenness, spousal abuse and others. It allowed the convict to be ridiculed, abused and molested by anyone passing by. This made female convicts particularly susceptible to rape.

Pulled Apart: This was used for more severe crimes, including abduction (which was called raptus or rape regardless of whether the woman was physically violated), treason, murder and other such larger crimes. It usually consisted of a person having each of their limbs tied to separate horses. The horses were then whipped into a run, resulting in the person being pulled apart limb from limb.

Pulley (a.k.a. *Squassation*): Another popular implement of the Inquisition. The victim of this torture had his hands tied above his head, and his feet were tied to the floor or the bottom of a frame. A set of weights was then attached to the ropes holding his hands and then dropped suddenly. This would disjoint the arms and/or legs of the victim.

Quartered: The person was cut into four pieces and buried in four sections of the town. The thinking behind this practice was that on Judgment Day, the person wouldn't be whole and would therefore be denied entrance into Paradise.

Rack: An iron or wooden frame where victims were placed for interrogation. Pulleys would allow the victim to be stretched to unbearable degrees. It was another favorite of the Inquisition.

Sanctuary: Any criminal, regardless of his deed or sentence, was given sanctuary by the Church if he could make it to Holy Ground. Any person who violated this code by dragging the felon out was excommunicated.

Stocks: Essentially, a thick board with a large hole in the center and two smaller holes on the left and right. A cut bisected the board lengthwise through the center of the holes, allowing the top to be raised and a convict's head and hands inserted. The top was then brought back down and locked into place, securing the convict. Sometimes holes for the feet were also included. This was commonly used for any crime, especially misdemeanors. Like the pillory, it placed the convict on public display for ridicule, abuse and molestation by the citizenry.

Water Torture: The accused was either dunked into water repeatedly or had a large amount of water poured over his face.

Wergild (a.k.a. *Wergeld*): In England, the amount of money owed a victim's family by a murderer. The amount was on a fixed scale relative to the victim's social position. In tribes where money was scarce, the payment was made in cattle or other livestock.

TRADE AND BARTER

Though it is a common belief that everyone in the Dark Ages bartered, this has been proven false. Archeologists have uncovered proof that a monetary system remained in place throughout the entire medieval period, even in the early centuries after the collapse of Rome. Those with enough coins were always able to buy luxury items and the collection of coins was quite prevalent. Wages continued to be paid.

However, those who were poor did barter. In fact, this helped found the whole feudal world, wherein one traded work for protection or some similar service. Of course, this is a gross oversimplification; even in the earliest times, those who had coins could pay instead of work.

Peasants were allowed to work their land as long as they either provided their landowner with a certain amount of work or a certain amount of their produce or, in some cases, both. Whatever was left over was either sold or traded for what they needed. Many peasants also took on side jobs as servants or peddlers to make ends meet. One common way to earn extra money was in rounding up hawks and falcons that had escaped mews or jesses and returning them to their lords, who often paid a tidy reward.

Some peasants were lucky enough to escape their poverty by becoming members of the Church (though most were banned from high office) or by entering apprenticeships. However, it should be noted that most apprenticeships went to those of the merchant class. Apprentices usually began their training between the ages of five and seven. Their parents negotiated a contract with their master for how long the apprentice would serve and be trained in a particular trade.

Most tradesman chose to have their children trained in the same profession, though there are some cases of them choosing complimentary trades. For example, a dressmaker might have a daughter or son trained as a silk weaver or capper.

Many women were employed as sellers and laborers, but their pay was usually substantially lower than their male counterparts. Most women tended to work for family members, and those who were apprenticed seldom went to work for themselves.

Most women married another in their profession and went to work in his store. Though some women did attain high rank in the guilds, almost all women were banned from holding office or voting on guild matters. However, it should be noted that if a guild member died, his wife could continue to run his shop until the day she remarried.

Fairs and markets were important aspects of both guild life and medieval life in general. Some fairs were biannual or annual events, while others ran continuously. Merchants, entertainers and the like would gather in a designated area and sell goods and services to their patrons. These fairs were also good places for thieves, prostitutes and cutpurses to make money.

If the market was set in a town, then where a person set up his shop was usually highly regulated. Tanners, butchers, fishmongers and others who had smelly or distasteful jobs tended to be segregated out of the other districts and usually located downwind of the town. One area might be set up for clothiers and those selling textiles, while another area would be all the metalworking trades. And, of course, those of ill-repute would be confined to their own district.

The key to fantasy world-building is that the layout of the story, the monetary system, the laws, et al are completely up to you, the writer. However, these elements must make sense, or the reader will become frustrated or confused by the gaps in your logic. For this reason, you may want to chose a real setting such as medieval England or ancient Rome and alter it to fit your needs and ideas.

CHAPTER SIX

FANTASY RACES

Andrew P. Miller and Daniel Clark

A ny attempt to survey the multitude of races that exist in legend and imaginative literature is open to criticism of being incomplete in some areas and too inclusive in others. The obvious dilemma is the question of how one defines a "race" in fantastic literature and legend. In reference to humans, the term race is fraught with political and cultural implications; in general, it refers to similarities and differences in certain physical characteristics like skin color, facial form or eye shape. Political and cultural affinity factor into the debate as well and are sometimes more important than an individual's particular genetic heritage. But humans as a group are far more similar in appearance than the groups that populate the landscape of the imagination. Bushmen and Celts are virtually indistinguishable in comparison to the differences between merfolk and trolls. But just as with defining human races, there are considerations beyond the physical that enter into the issue. It's not just a question of which arbitrary physical features to consider since the differences in these imaginative beings are long established; it's really a question of what distinguishes a fantastic *race* from a fantastic *creature*.

The terms race and creature suggest differences, and one difference is in total population in a group. It's easy to see that a unique being like the Hawaiian shark man is a creature and not a race. Or that rare beings like the rocs are creatures and do not constitute a race. But there is a qualitative difference between the way groups of beings, like elves and giant squids, are portrayed in fantastic stories that has to do with a metaphysical hierarchy. It's not merely a question of humanoid shape; elves are obviously patterned on humans—often they are more diminutive and more beautiful than the average human—and giant squids are patterned on their smaller counterparts in the real animal kingdom, but what about the Yahoos and Houyhnhnms of Jonathan Swift's *Gulliver's Travels*? The Houyhnhnms, outwardly equine in shape, have a complex society, and appreciate art and intellectual pursuits, whereas the Yahoos, outwardly human in shape, have no language and live in packs in the forest like wild dogs. Obviously, similarity to a human shape is not the most important factor in determining the difference in race and creature.

As *Gulliver's Travels* points out, we must not be too anthropomorphically bigoted when we determine where various groups rank on the Great Chain of Being in fantastic stories. Instead, we tend to be prejudiced by the nonphysical attributes and values of humans. For our purposes in this chapter—and this seems to hold generally true for the body of fantastic literature and legend—we define race using the following criteria:

- Physical Similarity: This one is pretty obvious. Elves look like elves, dwarves like dwarves.
- Population: It can't be a unique being and still be called a member of a race. Now there can be exceptions to this; Tolkien, at the end of *The Trilogy of the Ring* suggests that the fantastic races are slowly dying out and humans replacing them. A writer could create a scenario in which a being is the last of his or her kind, but the implication is that there once were many more.
- Procreation: The ability to create offspring. This also implies gender, sexual relationships, children and familial groups.
- Reason: Call it intellect, intelligence, thought, rationality, sentience, awareness. Members of a race, by virtue of not being creatures or animals, are capable of forethought, of being motivated by needs and desires that are not purely physical.
- Culture: Call it culture, call it society, call it politics. A culture is constituted of beings with common beliefs, values, traditions, art and language—all things that involve needs separate from the purely physical and that arise from social and political relationships.

Of the five criteria, the latter two seem to be the most crucial in determining whether a fantastic being is a creature or a member of a race. To return to the example from *Gulliver's Travels*, the Houyhnhnms clearly qualify as a race—one that embodies what we would normally consider to be all the best virtues of humans. The Yahoos, however human in appearance, are merely animals to be controlled and used for their brute strength as draft animals.

The technique that Swift employs, that of elevation, is one way of doing something new or unusual in the fantasy genre. Stories of the fantastic are so old that it is often difficult for a writer to do something unique in such well-worn territory. By elevating horses and reducing humans, Swift makes a striking social statement about human society. Richard Adams employs elevation beautifully with rabbits in *Watership Down* and *Tales From Watership Down*. The rabbits have a complex social structure, politics, art and even religion and myth. But both writers are using mundane creatures, not fantastic ones. The irony is that the fantastic races—elves, dwarves, giants and the like—have become morbidly clichéd in fantastic literature. Many writers have dealt with this problem by using elevation as Swift and Adams did, or by employing humor or parody. In some cases, writers have adapted fantastic races to fit into contemporary or science fiction settings. Other times writers adapt an existing legendary race into a new race. In the rest of this chapter, we hope to help writers overcome this problem by offering some different perspectives on the "standard" races, suggesting some techniques for avoiding the cliché, and proposing new arenas from which to draw inspiration.

DWARVES

In physical appearance, **dwarves** are short in stature, much shorter than humans, and sometimes they are misshapen, with heads or shoulders disproportionally larger than a human's. They tend to be bearded, and are identified with the underworld, whether as their home or as a place they frequent (since dwarves are quite often miners). In Norse mythology, dwarves lived in the caves of Nidavellir. The dwarves in Norse mythology were also exquisite craftsmen, often making magical items. The dwarves Brokk and Eitri made such treasures as Mjollnir, the hammer of Thor that always returned to his hand; Gullinbursti, a boar with golden bristles that could travel over air, sea and earth; and Draupnir, the gold armband that on every ninth night, produced eight more rings just like it. This is similar to the fairy tale of Rumplestiltskin, who could spin straw into gold. Dwarves usually have reputations for being helpful, though they could wreak revenge on hapless mortals who wronged them.

Tolkien (with the possible exception of Disney's seven dwarves) again provides the standard by which dwarves have been seen in fantasy literature. Tolkien's dwarves are drawn from the Norse legends as well. The dwarves of Middle Earth were workers of metals and stone. At the height of their glory, they crafted magical and mechanical wonders and lived in a mountain stronghold complete with secret doors that couldn't be distinguished from the side of the mountain. Physically, the dwarves were short, stocky and had beards of different colors, including, at least in one case, blue! Middle Earth dwarves also had a tendency to sing; when Bilbo Baggins first meets dwarves in *The Hobbit*, they make up a song about him. Tolkien's dwarves could also be fierce warriors.

In his Discworld novels, Terry Pratchett uses parody to play on several clichés about dwarves, particularly those established by Tolkien. In their native lands, Pratchett's dwarves are miners and usually dwell in subterranean caverns. This goes along with many old ideas of dwarves. Pratchett's dwarves seem fairly typical, even to the description of the dwarves as being short humanoids with heavy beards. Of course, both sexes have heavy beards and sometimes even the dwarves can't tell each other apart. But Pratchett's dwarves also move into the city, particularly the unique city of Ankh-Morpork. In the city, the dwarves tend to adopt barbarian names and pretend to be sword-carrying warriors. They have dwarf restaurants specializing in various rat dishes. Like Tolkien's dwarves, Pratchett's dwarves have a penchant for song. In fact, they gather at night in low-ceilinged dwarf bars to sing their songs, all of which have the same words: "Gold, gold, gold, gold. . . . " Additionally, Pratchett's dwarves have also turned the culinary arts into a military art; a good loaf of dwarf bread can be used as a cudgel, shield or projectile weapon.

ELVES

One of the most common fantasy races in legend and literature is the race of **elves**. They appear in a variety of fairy tales such as "The Shoemaker and the Elves," and have different appearances according to different legends. Many elves are portrayed as tall and bewitchingly beautiful, but they are sometimes classed among the more general "little people" or fairies and are small in size. (This is the image of the pointy-eared elf, usually dressed in forest green.)

In whatever form, elves tend to have magical abilities. Some elves are considered to be benevolent spirits, such as "Light Elves," while others are considered malevolent, or "Dark Elves." In the Norse myths and stories told in the *Elder Edda* and other works, light elves lived in Alfheim, a realm near Asgard and Vanaheim, the lands where the Norse gods lived. Dark elves lived in Svartalfheim, a realm somewhere below Midgard, or Earth. Norse dark elves had little distinction from Norse dwarves. In fairy tales, many elves seem to be amoral. They like playing tricks and having fun and don't particularly care about the consequences.

In fantasy literature, J.R.R. Tolkien drew upon such legends, particularly the Norse legends, setting the standard (and the eventual cliché) for the depiction of noble light elves. Tolkien's elves were tall, elegant, with an unearthly beauty. When the elf-lord Glorfindel was first seen by the hobbit Frodo in *The Fellowship of the Ring*, "it appeared that a white light was shining through the form and raiment of [Glorfindel] as if through a veil." The elves of Middle Earth were artisans, scholars and musicians, and had taught men language and other skills. They controlled power and magic and were a force for good; an elven blade was anathema to dark forces. Elven horses were faster than other horses and never let a rider fall. Most of the elves were magnificent and benevolent beings who looked out for the well-being of all in Middle Earth. However, in *The Hobbit*, Bilbo and company run into a group of elves that sang from the trees whom the dwarves considered foolish. In later books on Middle Earth, the elves were defined into specific subgroups, explaining the differences between them.

Andre Norton, in her classic Witch World series, adapts the legends of the elves differently. One of the countries of the Witch World is Escore, whose most powerful native is Dahuan, Lady of the Green Silences. The Lady has many magical abilities and her form constantly shifts. While she can leave the Valley of Green Silences, her power is definitely tied to the land and she is powerless when away from it. Norton adapted elves and fairies and threw in a dose of nymphs as well to create Dahuan. Perhaps, since Norton was well read in fairy tales, this Lady of the Green Silences was an adaptation of the Green Ladies, tree elves that could be found in certain trees (much like nymphs). Like the Green Ladies, Dahuan had power over trees as do her **Green People of the Valley**. Unlike

Dahuan, however, Green Ladies had dark purposes in many English folktales.

In *Stalking the Unicorn*, Mike Resnick does two things to make his elves noncliché. First, he puts the elves in a modern, urban setting, even if it isn't quite an urban setting we're used to. Resnick's elves live in an alternate Manhattan, one that exists out of the corner of the eye where they drive colored elephants through the streets in lieu of cabs. Resnick also uses parody to make fun of the elf cliché. In that book, John Justin Mallory, a Manhattan detective, is hired by Murgensturm, an elf, to find a unicorn. Murgensturm is indeed green with pointy ears but he has some other unusual characteristics, not the least of which is his almost insatiable sexual appetite. Mallory and Murgensturm square off against a demon and a treacherous leprechaun named Flypaper Gillespie. The whole book takes a humorous look at many fantasy races.

FAIRIES

The term **fairy** (sometimes spelled faery) tends to be a general designation that applies to a wide variety of beings known alternately as the **little people** or the **fair folk**. Fairies have different shapes and can appear to mortals in different forms, usually that of a beautiful male or female. Some fairies are small, winged and female (like Tinkerbell), while others are closer to human stature. Fairies have a variety of abilities, one of the most powerful being that of the "glamour," which allows them to fool humans with illusions. Fairies have their own sense of what is proper and polite, and the smallest slight can result in a fairy punishment on a hapless mortal.

Fairies usually are found living in mounds or fairy hills, which are occasionally accessible to mortals. In most legends, time flows differently in the fairy realm—one hour there may equal a year in our world! Mortals who partake of fairy food are usually stranded forever in the lands of fairy, for mortal food will never again sustain them. Fairies do have some dealings with mortals, particularly in the custom of the changeling. Fairies will steal human children and leave one of their own or a doll in exchange for the child. Morgan le Fey, of Arthurian legend, was supposed to be part fairy.

Shakespeare's *A Midsummer Night's Dream* is an early literary use of the fairy. In Shakespeare's play, Oberon and Titania are king and queen of the fairies. They also mettle in mortal affairs. These ideas of Shakespeare's were recently updated by Neil Gaiman in the comic book *The Sandman*. In the comic book, Morpheus, the personification of Dream, makes a pact with Shakespeare. He will give Shakespeare ideas in exchange for two plays, one of which is *A Midsummer Night's Dream*. Dream commissions this play as entertainment for King Auberon and Queen Titania. The court of fairy arrives on earth to see Shakespeare's play, and members of fairy appear throughout the comic book series.

Gaiman also takes readers through the world of fairy in the comic book limited series, *The Books of Magic*. In the first limited series, Tim Hunter is destined to become the world's greatest magician. As such, he is taken on journeys to be shown magic. One of these journeys is to the realm of fairy, where he goes to the fairy market and is offered his heart's desire for a year of his life. He also meets Queen Titania, who tries to trap the young boy into being her servant for the rest of his life.

The Books of Magic was continued as an ongoing series by John Ney Reiber. The fairies, especially Titania and Auberon, play major roles throughout the series. Tim Hunter has many interactions with the fairy, especially since Titania claims to be his mother and the authors keep developing this as a subplot. He also has an adventure in which he has to save Auberon from an enchantment after the fairy king journeys to earth. In a later story line, Tim's girlfriend Molly finds herself trapped in fairy and becomes the rival of a vengeful Titania. Molly eats a berry grown in fairy and ceases to be human. After their appearances in *The Books of Magic*, Titania and Auberon were featured in their own limited comic book series called *The Book of Faery*. That series detailed the mortal origins of the fairy queen and how she became both queen and mother.

Throughout these series, the authors take a look at the race of fairy and incorporate the legends into the story lines and mythos that they are creating. By creating political and personal intrigues as well as giving individual fairies personalities, they breathe new life into the little people. It should also be noted that both authors use other myths and folklore in their writings, and blend them with contemporary themes and story lines.

Julian May's *Saga of Pliocene Exile* does something completely different with the fairy race; her series is a time travel story. In the future era of the Great Milieu, people who do not fit in with the galactic society can choose to be exiled back into Earth's Pliocene era by a one-way time machine. The story focuses on a group that chooses such a path. However, once they arrive in the past, they find Earth inhabited by the **Tanu**, an extraterrestrial race that has been exiled to Earth from their own galaxy. The Tanu are beautiful, exceptionally tall humanoids who wear golden torques around their necks to amplify their latent psychic abilities. The Tanu possess such powers as telekinesis, telepathy, mental coercion and illusion casting. Their illusions—**glamours**—can bewitch or bedevil the average human. In fact, the Tanu keep most of the humans as slaves or servants this way.

The descriptions of the Tanu match legends of the fairy found in many European mythologies. For example, May uses the notion of the fairy rade in her story. According to European legend, the fairy rade was an elegant procession of the best of fairy bedecked in their fineries and jewels. May's version is the flying hunt, during which the Tanu hunt Pliocene creatures, using their telekinetic powers to fly and their illusion-casting powers to make themselves beautiful. According to May's account, the Tanu *are* the origin of the legends of the fairy rade and all fairy legends.

GIANTS

Giants have appeared in various forms and mythologies throughout the world. In Greek mythology, the **Titans** were the children of Gaea, Mother Earth, and Uranus, the Heavenly Sky. They were of gigantic stature and each Titan governed a certain realm, such as Oceanus over the ocean. Cronus led them but was eventually dethroned by his children, led by the god Zeus. Gaea also gave birth to other giants such as the one-eyed **Cyclopes** and giants that had one hundred arms and fifty heads. (The multiheaded giants had been imprisoned by their father and the Titans never released them after Cronus came to power. Because of this, they helped Zeus and the gods defeat the Titans.) Another race of giants sprang from Uranus's blood when he was killed by Cronus. They were also defeated by the gods. Antaeus was a giant who was building a temple out of skulls. As long as he touched the earth, he was unbeatable. Hercules held him in the air and strangled him.

Norse mythology has even more stories about giants. The **rock** and **frost giants** lived in Jotunheim and often battled the gods; at Ragnarok, the giants were to rise up against the gods to aid in the destruction of the world. The thunder god Thor was the chief enemy of the giants. However, some gods, like Freyr, married giants. Loki, god of mischief, also wedded a giantess and produced three terrible offspring: the monstrous Fenris Wolf; Jorgumund the Midgard Serpent; and Hel, the goddess of the dead. Several individual giants held importance. Ymir was the first giant, the father of the frost giants, and was formed from fire and ice. Odin and his brothers killed Ymir and created the world from his body. Surt (or Surtur) was the giant who ruled over Muspel, the land of fire. At Ragnarok, he will set fire to the world. Utgard-Loki was a king of the frost giants. Skilled in magic and trickery, he beguiled Loki and Thor into degrading contests while they were in his realm.

Giants also appear briefly in the book of Genesis: "There were giants in the earth in those days. . . . " And, of course, Goliath was the giant slain by David. Fairy tales have their giants as well, with "Jack and the Beanstalk" being one of the best known. Giants, as they most often appear, are malevolent creatures who seldom bear goodwill toward humans. They may possess magical abilities and often hoard magical items and treasure.

Stephen Donaldson, in his *Chronicles of Thomas Covenant: The Unbeliever*, uses giants effectively as a race, though they are not the villains. They are denizens of the Land, the world that Donaldson creates. They help Thomas Covenant in his journeys, particularly when he sets off to find the One Tree. The giants are a seafaring race who travel in stone ships. They have names that reflect their occupations, such as Saltheart Foamfollower. These giants are a noble and majestic race who stand as allies with the forces of good against the evil Lord Foul.

GOBLINS AND ORCS

Goblins appear in many folk and fairy tales as mischievous creatures, bewitching and tormenting men. Goblins in folk tales often wear caps and are depicted as misshapen and bowed little people. They are associated with the earth, live among tree roots and cracks in rocks, and are meddlesome but not usually dangerous.

Tolkien's goblins are more extreme than the mischief-making sprites of legend. His goblins infest the tunnels and mountains of Middle Earth. Like dwarves, they can make things and dig tunnels. Unlike dwarves, the things they make are seldom beautiful and are usually dangerous. The goblins and dwarves were ancient enemies, most likely because they inhabited the same areas. Tolkien's goblins are misshapen and quick, or at least quicker than dwarves, and can manipulate rock. When they attack Bilbo and the dwarves in *The Hobbit*, they appear out of a crack in the cave wall and then seal it behind them as they leave. Tolkien's goblins are also more dangerous to human, dwarf and hobbit, perfectly willing to take their enemies' lives. Tolkien also used the goblin race as a basis for his orcs.

Orcs had been mentioned in folklore before Tolkien, but the term "orc" was usually given to sea beasts or sea serpents with sharp teeth that preyed on whales (the term becoming orca). Tolkien changed the orc into a type of goblin, keeping the sharp teeth and giving them broad faces and slanting eyes. Tolkien's orcs live underground, battling dwarves for caves, and can only come out at night or when the sun doesn't shine, for most of them cannot stand the sun's rays. They were the evil servants of Sauron, the Dark Lord in Tolkien's world.

Like she did with the fairy, Julian May adapts the goblin legend to fit her science fiction universe. The Tanu's enemies are the **Firvulag**, or the little people. The Firvulag come in many different shapes and sizes, and their different appearances are reminiscent of goblins, kobolds, trolls and occasionally giants. The Firvulag also possess a wide variety of psychic abilities, though they usually don't possess the power of their Tanu cousins. Chief among their psychic abilities is the power to cast illusions. The Firvulag are often referred to as the shape-changers because of they are adept at illusion. They engage the Tanu in ritualistic battles.

Actually, both groups are part of the same "bimorphic" race and had arrived on earth together in their space ship. May even throws in the legendary fairy anathema to iron in her creation of her exotic races: both the Tanu and the Firvulag are vulnerable to the metal. She gives this a genetic rationale instead of a magical one.

HALF-LINGS AND HYBRIDS

Hobbits, Tolkien's most famous creation, are adaptations. Tolkien calls them **half-lings**, and they resemble various little people from legend. They range from about two to four feet high, averaging about three feet. In Middle Earth, this is smaller than dwarves. They seldom wear shoes since they have tough soles like leather and curly hair covering the tops of their feet. The most common color for their hair is brown. When they wish, they can move almost silently through the forest. They wear brightly colored clothes and enjoy drinking tea and smoking pipes. They frequently live in comfortable holes tunneled into hills, although they eventually move into small cottages.

Half-lings started appearing in other works as well, sometimes resembling hobbits and sometimes as creatures that were half human and half some other creature, basically hybrids between the human race and a fantastic race. In Terry Brooks's *The Sword of Shannara*, for example, the hero Shea is a **half elf**.

MERFOLK

Water-breathing races have appeared in a variety of legends. The Greeks had their sea nymphs, the Nereids. Triton, the son of Poseidon and the Nereid Amphitrite, had the tail of a fish. In fact, his name became a generic term to describe men with the body of a man and the tail of a fish. More commonly, these legends developed into the tales of **mermaids** and **mermen**, whose chief characteristic as a race is their half-fish forms and their ability to live underwater but not on land. Mermaids sometimes had a reputation for mischief if not disaster. Though some mermaids gave up their tails to join men on land, there are also stories of mermaids dragging mortal men beneath the waves to join them. Other times, mermaids caused shipwrecks, especially if one had fallen in love with a sailor. Hans Christian Anderson's "Little Mermaid" is probably the most famous tale of merfolk. In his classic story, the little mermaid trades her voice for legs and the chance to win a mortal husband. Of course, the original tale does not have the happy ending the Disney version put on it.

Andre Norton offers a different spin on water-breathing races. Living in the Witch World's Escore are the **Krogan**, who dwell in the waters of their world. They are mostly human in appearance with some noticeable differences. The Krogan have webbed feet and hands, pale glistening skin and gills in their necks. They possess their own type of magic as well. They may not have the tails of fishes, but their water-dwelling habitats suggest the legends of the merfolk and possibly those of river gods, naiads and other water-dwelling spirits.

TROLLS

Similar to giants, **trolls** are popular bad guys in legends. When Thor was not fighting giants, he was often off fighting trolls. Trolls are often large in size though not as large as giants. They are associated with rocks and being rocklike in both durability and intelligence. According to some legends, trolls turn to stone if they are struck by sunlight. Trolls usually live in caves or mountains, though sometimes they dwell under bridges and accost innocent goats.

J.R.R. Tolkien provides a variety of trolls. In *The Hobbit*, Bilbo and the dwarves encounter three trolls in the woods. These trolls have heavy faces, tree-trunk-sized legs and vulgar mouths. They are named William, Bert and Tom and plan on eating the dwarves, a race the trolls despise. Luckily, Tolkien's trolls have the legendary weakness to sunlight and the group tricks them into arguing until dawn, at which point they are turned to stone. In the later tales of Middle Earth, trolls are the servants of evil, scaled creatures with skin as hard as rock. Sauron, the Dark Lord, changed them for this purpose.

Robert Asprin, in his Myth Adventures series, updates the cliché through humor and parody. The series' hero is Skeeve, an apprentice magician. One of his companions is the beautiful Tananda. She has gold skin and green hair, and hails from the dimension of Trollia, where the men are trolls and the women are trollops. Besides working with the pun, Asprin also works with the stereotypes. Tananda may be built like a brick castle, but she is smart, witty and a competent assassin. Her brother, Chumley, is first introduced as the gigantic, dull-witted "Big Crunch" with "scraggly hair, long-rubbery limbs, and a misshapen face." He picks up Skeeve and says, "Crunch likes little persons. Crunch likes little persons better than Big Macs." But he soon drops the cliché troll persona to show an eloquent, thoughtful, shy, caring person beneath the troll's frightening outer appearance. Chumley is also a vegetarian.

Terry Pratchett also plays with the idea of trolls. Instead of turning to rock when exposed to sunlight, Pratchett's trolls are already made of rock. More specifically, they are silicon life-forms with rock bodies, diamond teeth and an appetite for minerals (and only occasionally people). Pratchett's trolls are mostly slow-witted (since they have rocks for brains), but some manage to go beyond that, especially when they move to the city. There, Chryophase the Troll is one of the leaders of the Ankh-Morpork crime syndicate.

In Pratchett's world, like Tolkien's, dwarves and trolls are natural enemies. They often tussle when they come into contact with each other in the city. However, in *Men at Arms*, a satire of modern human times, he has members of both races join the Ankh-Morpork

City Watch in an affirmative action campaign, which had been partially brought on by the Silicon Anti-Defamation League. The outcome is both hilarious, touching and fresh.

MINOR RACES

Other races appear with less frequency in legends and literature. **Gnomes** are similar to dwarves, though are usually depicted as having more human proportions than often misshapen dwarves. Like dwarves, gnomes generally live underground.

Mike Resnick plays with this idea in *Stalking the Unicorn*. His gnomes also live underground in the subways. The Gnomes of the Subway congregrate at subway stops and eat subway tokens.

In his three books *Truckers*, *Diggers* and *Wings* (collected as the *Bromeliad* by the Science Fiction Book Club), Terry Pratchett uses science fiction to update the gnome legends. Pratchett's **Nomes** look exactly like humans but are only four inches tall (much like Lilliputians). They have very short life spans (usually not living past their teens) but live accelerated lives, at least to humans. One group of Nomes makes its way into the Arnold Brothers store in London and meets the store Nomes. The store Nomes had thought themselves unique in the universe and, of course, the universe is the store. The Nomes had built a culture around the store including kingdoms and fiefdoms based on departments such as the Duke de Haberdasheri, Lord Protector of the Up Escalator and Knight of the Counter, and the Abbott of Stationeri. Eventually, they discover that they are not native to Earth and find their lost spaceship.

In Greek mythology, **centaurs** were half horse and half man. They were human from the waist up and a horse from the waist down. They were usually shown to be barbaric and savage, though the centaur Chiron tutored many of the great heroes of Greek mythology. Centaurs seemed particularly vulnerable to excesses of wine and found human women attractive. At the wedding of the King of Lapithae, a centaur got drunk and tried to abduct the bride. The hero Theseus, best known for killing the Minotaur, saved the bride by slaying the centaur. The centaur Nessus was responsible for the death of Hercules; when his wife, Deianira, suspected the hero of being unfaithful to her, she poisoned him with the centaur's blood.

In contemporary fantasy, Piers Anthony uses the centaurs as a race in his humorous Xanth series. He plays on both the belligerent aspects of the race as well as Chiron's tutorial scholarly activities. When the magician Dor goes back in time, he has to convince the somewhat savage centaurs to continue building a castle for the king. Later in the series, the young Dor is tutored by the centaur Cherie. He also recruits a centaur magician and scholar named Arnolde to help him travel into the mundane world (i.e., the world as we know it). In the "present" time frame of the series, centaurs are the scholars and poets of Xanth.

NON-WESTERN RACES

Most fantasy novels feature magical races from Western or European mythologies and folktales. But of course, Europe does not have a monopoly on legendary races. Such races can be found in the folktales, myths and stories of other cultures as well.

For instance, Hawaii has its own race of little people called the **menehune**, and these little people resemble many of the fairy folk of Europe. The menehune were small in size, described as dwarves. They had supernatural abilities such as the ability to shape and cut rock with greater skill than any human hands could ever achieve. Most of their work was accomplished overnight, and never done during the day, such as building a great irrigation ditch that stretched for miles. They could also vanish into thin air. The king of the menehune sounds much like a leprechaun. In one tale, he was described as being dressed head to foot in brilliant green with a crown of emeralds. The menehune made deals with humans and instead of being paid in cream or honey, they were paid off in fish. At one time, the number of menehune was so vast that a line of them stretched for miles.

Other types of fairylike creatures appear across the world. Hindus knew of a type of fairy called **asparas**, whom they believed lived in fig trees. Also called sky dancers, their appearance to mortals at turning points in their lives (such as weddings) was a blessing. Appearing to dying men on battlefields, they conveyed hope in the afterlife instead of fear. On occasion, asparas would use their charms to distract scholars from learning things they shouldn't know.

Other fairylike beings appear in Eastern and Pacific myths as well. In Thailand, the **phi** resemble fairies and inhabit natural places like trees and waterfalls. Like European fairies, they could demonstrate both good- or ill-will towards humans. Sometimes beautiful and sometimes bewitching, fairies appear throughout

Pacific mythology. In Japan, they are the **tennin** and **yosei**; among the Maori, they are the **patupaiarehe**; in Java, they are called **apsari**.

Other mischievous and dangerous little people are also known in these cultures. The **Ponaturi** are wicked shape-changing sea fairies that battle Maori heroes. The **tipua** are other wicked shape-changing spirits known to the Maori. If the setting was right, a fantasy author could make these beings into a viable fantasy race instead of the more cliché fairies of Western culture.

Some Native American legends have their mythical races too. In an Algonquian legend, the god-hero Glooskap encounters a giant named Winter. Winter casts a spell of cold over Glooskap and the god slumbers for six months before the spell wears off. When he awakens, he travels southward and eventually comes to a land blooming with flowers. There he spots beautiful little people dancing. These little people are called the Elves of Light. Glooskap snatches Summer, their queen, and takes her with him to once more encounter Winter. Summer's warmth and power eventually melt the coldhearted giant. Another Algonquian legend tells of the fairy wives, named Weasel, that were married to Marten.

The Iroquois also have stories of giants made of stone who planned to attack the Iroquois but were defeated by the god of the west wind. Little people, according to the Iroquois, made all the beautiful things on earth and helped to protect humans from monsters.

CREATED RACES

Many authors create their own races through the methods of adaptation and elevation. As previously mentioned, Andre Norton adapted elves and merfolk. She also adapted the legends of werefolk for two separate races, the Gray Ones and the Were Riders. The **Gray Ones** are intelligent, fierce fighters that are half men and half wolves. They are also capable of magic, particularly as a group. The **Were Riders** are native to the land of Arvon. These men have the ability to alter their shapes to look like specific beasts such as boars, horses and snowcats. Each Were Rider has his own animal form, usually reflective of his personality. The Were Riders have their own codes, customs and magic adapted from various folklores.

Norton also uses adaptation and elevation for a race of horselike creatures known as the **Keplians**. When they first appear in the series, they are evil creatures. Beautiful black steeds, they trick inno-cents into climbing on their backs and then carry them away to their evil master. The Keplian is an adaptation of the kelpie, or water horse, a legendary creature that had similar abilities. Later, in *Key of the Keplian*, she elevates the Keplians into a race. The dark horses become creatures of light and allies to those who fight against evil. They even create their own haven and code of conduct.

Norton adapts/elevates other creatures into races as well: **Flan-nans** are bird/human hybrids; **Renthans** are intelligent creatures similar to antelope or deer; the **Vrang** have bird bodies and lizard heads. There are also the intelligent **Lizard folk**. All of these races communicate telepathically with each other and their human allies.

Mercedes Lackcy does similar things in her Valdemar series. Valdemar is in many ways reflective of the Witch World. She has several races that are her versions of Norton's earlier creations: the lizardlike **hertasi**; the antelopelike **dyheli**; and the birdlike **terv-ardi**. The large wolfen **kyree** fall into a similar category. These races, for the most part, play minor roles in the world of Valdemar. Of more importance, however, is the author's elevation of the **gryphon** into a race. (Norton has gryphons in the Witch World as well, but not as a race.) Lackey's gryphons were created by Urtho, a great mage. He used several types of birds as models, such as eagles and falcons. Lackey is very precise in talking about bird types, probably because she helps rehabilitate different types of raptors. For instance, gryphons, like many Earth raptors, must mate in flight and can only concieve when magic is added to the coupling. Lack-ey's gryphons co-exist with human and nonhuman species, and help with guard duty, politics and city planning. The gryphons also have their own mages and are in every way the equals of their human colleagues.

David Weber in *Oath of Swords* creates the world of Norfressa, a land with five races of Man. Four of these are familiar to fantasy readers: humans, elves, dwarves and half-lings. Weber's elves are immortal and withdrawn. His dwarves are rich, but the one we actually see in the book is a merchant and not a miner. The half-lings have curved horns erupting from their foreheads. Some of the half-lings, the Purple Lords, are arrogant aristocrats who enjoy hav-ing a stranglehold on the main water route, while others are rough-and-tough sailors.

But the fifth race is different. The **Hradani** look like humans except for their ears, which are foxlike and tufted. Hradani are also larger in stature than most humans, some topping seven feet tall. But Weber creates more in the race than just pointy ears. The Hradani are tribalistic and tend to the savage and barbaric side. They trust few outside their own clans and are mistrusted if not despised by the other races of Man. Birthrates are low and Hradrani women are considered precious; rape is the worst crime imaginable. But what really distinguishes the Hradani is the Rage, a state of mind that can engulf a Hradani and make him almost unstoppable. Pain and wounds don't matter, only killing. The Rage was inflicted upon the race by wizards hoping to use the Hradani as a weapon. Instead, the Rage shields the Hradani from most spells and magic, thus making them immune to the magicians. Weber adapted the stories of Berserkers in order to create an entire race of Man for his novel.

INDIVIDUALIZATION AND CHARACTERIZATION

Although there are several ways of creating or adapting new races and new outlooks on races, one of the surest ways of bringing a race to life is by creating an individual from that race and making him a fully developed character.

For example, Asprin introduces trolls by presenting Chumley as a real person. Asprin demonstrates Chumley's intelligence and his big heart through his interaction with the other characters. Pratchett does the same for the troll Detritus. Though slow-witted, the troll develops a friendship with his co-worker, the dwarf Cuddy. Pratchett's dwarves also come alive through Carrot, the six-foot adopted dwarf, and Corporal Littlebottom, a female dwarf who also joins the Guard. Norton's Dahuan brings the Green People to full realization as Orsya of the Krogan does for that race. Gaiman and Reiber make Titania a complete character with wants, desires and secrets. Lackey's gryphon Skandrannon's love of adventure, his vanity and his devotion to his family make him as human as anyone. To be a successful dwarf, troll, fairy, elf, gryphon or whatever, the character must come alive. That is one of the true keys to breathing new life into a clichéd race.

CHAPTER SEVEN

CREATURES OF MYTH AND LEGEND

Andrew P. Miller and Daniel Clark

Writers of fantasy, horror and science fiction are often looking for obstacles for their heroes. And what better obstacle than a nightmarish monster carved from the fears and imagination of the ages? Myths and legends from around the world provide us with a wealth of creatures to use in our stories. What you'll find here is a brief survey of fantastic creatures from around the world. Not all of these are monsters, but all are strange, wonderous and fabulous creations and their stories are waiting to be continued in the hands of the skilled author.

ALPHABETICAL LISTING OF CREATURES

Banshee: In Irish legend, the banshee is a female spirit that voices her strange wail when a death is imminent. Banshees are usually attached to a specific family and wail when a member of that family is near death. Banshees have streaming hair and red eyes from weeping. Some accounts only give them one nostril. In Scottish legend, the equivalent is the **Little Washer of Sorrow**. In this case, the female spirit appears at the side of a stream washing the clothes of the soon to be departed.

Bunyips: Making its home in the waterways of Australia, the bunyips are often described as having a crocodile's tail with the rest of its body resembling either a bandicoot, an emu or a man. They can have manes or heads covered with weeds, and their feet are turned backwards. One constant in the tales of bunyips is the fact that the bunyip's cry can be heard as a terrifying booming noise coming from the swamps. Bunyips devour people, preferring women and children.

Chimera: A child of Typhon and Echidna, the Chimera had the head of a lion, a goat's body and a snake's tail. Her breath was a deadly blast of fire. The hero Bellerophon killed the Chimera with arrows while flying above it on the back of Pegasus.

Coyote: In the mythology of the Plains, Southwestern, Great Basin and central Californian North American Indian tribes, Coyote is primarily a trickster figure, and for many of these tribes, he is also the creator or culture hero. Coyote stories often involve other animal characters such as Badger or Raven or Wolf, and they are all presented as behaving and talking like human beings; sometimes they are represented as looking like men with animal heads. As the culture hero, Coyote is responsible for giving to humans the knowledge of fire, weapons, arts and crafts, or the sun. Sometimes Coyote is presented as a foolish character, easily duped by others. At times, he is also presented as lewd or mischievious.

Cyclopes: The Cyclopes are giants who have one eye in the center of their foreheads. The first Cyclopes were said to be children of Gaea, Mother Earth and Uranus, the Heavenly Sky. They helped the Greek god Hephaestus in his forge. Polyphemus, the cannibalistic Cyclops who menaced Odysseus in *The Odyssey*, herded sheep and was a son of the sea god, Poseidon.

*Djinn (*a.k.a. *Genie, Jinni, Djinni, Djin):* In Arabian and Eastern legends, the djinn are spirits capable of great magical feats. They can be either benevolent or malevolent to human beings. Magicians can conjure and control these spirits to do their bidding. Djinns are commonly bound into rings and jewelry, or in the most famous case, Aladdin's lamp. Related to djinns are peris and efrits. A **peri** is usually a much more benevolent spirit, often giving directions and help to humans. They opposed evil djinns. **Efrits** were almost always evil and dangerous spirits.

Dragons: Dragons appear in various mythologies and legends. The Greek monster **Echidna** was supposed to be half dragon. In Babylonian myth, **Tiamat** was the great she-dragon that battled the god Marduk. In Norse mythology, **Fafnir** kept guard over his hoard until killed by Sigurd. The hero Beowulf was eventually killed by a dragon. In English tales, St. George killed a dragon and rescued a young virgin.

The most familiar form of the western dragon is a great flying reptile. It has large batlike wings, a serpentine tail, sharp claws or talons and lots of teeth. These dragons usually breathe fire and some have a penchant for virgins. Often, like Fafnir, they are known to hoard gold and jewels. Dragons are hard to kill but almost always have one vulnerable spot for the hero to find.

Oriental dragons: These differ from their western counterparts. In China, dragons are more benevolent creatures of great power, often counted peers of the gods. They are usually associated with the elements, particularly water. Each river and stream has a dragon or dragon-king associated with it. Their features vary, often being an amalgam of various animals. They often have heads of camels, antlers of deer, eyes of a hare, scales of a fish and talons of eagles. Although they are quite often wingless, they sometimes have bat wings. Chief of the Chinese dragons is **Lung**, who controls wind and rains, monsoons and hails. The **Great Chien-Tang** is another important Chinese dragon who commands all river dragons.

Japanese dragons are similar to Chinese dragons in appearance and function. There are dragons representing the four elements and a dragon rules each sea.

Fantastic Horses: In many myths, the sun is pulled through the sky by fiery horses. **Papillon** is the fiery steed of the faery queen Morgana. The Valkyrie rode great flying war horses onto battlefields to choose the heroically slain. Others include **Al Borak**, the horse that carried Mohammed up to heaven; the man-eating horses that belonged to King Diomedes in Greek mythology; and **Sleipnir**, the eight-legged horse of the Norse god Odin.

Feng Huang: The feng huang or "red birds" are the Chinese equivalent of the **phoenix**. They are rare and beautiful birds that are extraordinarily long-lived. With the unicorn, the tortoise and the dragon, the feng huang is one of the four spiritual animals of Chinese lore. Legend says that the Chinese musical scale came from the song of the feng huang. "Feng" designates the male of the species and "huang" the female. The feng huang have bright coloring like peacocks and pheasants, but have curling tails and long claws. The rainbow plumage of the feng huang represents undying love—one of the five basic cardinal virtues—because of the devotion between the feng and the huang. Stories say that the chariot of the immortal Jade Emperor is pulled by feng huang and that they live in the Vermilion Hills, a borderland of sorts between worlds. The feng huang's appearances in legend are rare and coincide with times of prosperity. The feng huang's departure brings calamity and it is said that the feng huang will reappear again only when China is at peace.

Goliath: In the Old Testament of the Bible, Goliath was the Philistine warrior who challenged King Saul of Israel and his army to send forth a warrior to engage in man-to-man combat in order to decide the war between the Isrealites and the Phillistines. David, a boy who tended sheep for the army, was strong in his faith in God and took up the challenge, defeating the heavily armed Goliath with only his sling and some stones. David then killed Goliath and cut off his head with Goliath's own sword. David's success in battle was a testament to his faith in the Hebrew god and to his worthiness to be ruler of the people of Israel.

"Goliath" is often used as a term to refer to an individual or party that is so large and powerful that it seems impossible to defeat, but which may be brought down by a smaller, more clever and more faithful challenger.

Golem: The golem was created by a Jewish rabbi in the city of Prague. The Jews who lived in the ghettos of Prague were being persecuted. The golem was constructed as a means of protection. Made of clay, it was given life when the rabbi wrote the word *shem* ("name") on a piece of parchment and put it in its mouth. He also wrote *emet* ("truth") on its forehead. The golem was strong and defended the Jews. However, the city began to fear its own creation, so the rabbi destroyed the golem by changing the word *emet* to *met*, which means death.

Gorgons: Sisters to the Graeae, the Gorgons were three in number: the immortals **Stheno** and **Euryale**, and the more famous and mortal **Medusa**. These women were said to have wings and sometimes claws, but their most outstanding feature was that they had snakes for hair. The Gorgons' looks could turn people into stone. The Greek hero Perseus slew Medusa with a magic sickle after watching her reflection in a shield. Pegasus is said to have sprung from her blood.

The Graeae: Sisters to the Gorgons, the Graeae were three gray women with but one eye and one tooth, which they passed back and forth. According to some accounts, Perseus snatched the eye and tooth and wouldn't give them back until the Graeae told him the secrets of the Gorgons.

Grendel: The monster of *Beowulf* is described only as a gruesome creature that hunts the Danish moors. He is "descended from the race of Cain" and bears Cain's mark. He is humanoid in shape, nearly gigantic in stature and incredibly strong and fierce. Only Beowulf's great strength is Grendel's undoing when he rips the monster's arm off. Grendel nearly bleeds to death in the marsh before Beowulf beheds him on his deathbed. Beowulf must also confront and slay Grendel's mother as she seeks revenge. (John Gardner's *Grendel* retells the story from the monster's perspective, making him an almost sympathetic, tragic character.)

Harpies: Usually portrayed as creatures with the head and breasts of a woman and the body of a large bird, harpies are known for their foul smell that ruins anything they come near. Called the **Hounds of Zeus**, they were sent by Zeus to punish the prophet Phineas. Whenever Phineas went to eat, the harpies descended, fouling the food. Two of the Argonauts, sons of the North Wind, defeated the harpies.

Hell Hounds: Various myths speak of fearsome canines inhabiting the underworlds. Most famous is probably **Cerberus**, the three-headed, snake-tailed hound that guards the way to Hades. Cerberus was fierce but could be overcome by brute strength as when Hercules subdued him, or lulled by song as when Orpheus entered the underworld. **Garm** was the hound of Hel in Norse mythology.

Hippocampus: A hippocampus is half horse and half fish; the name itself means "sea horse." They have the head and forelegs of a horse, but the legs end in powerful webbed fins and their mane is a fin. Their long, horselike bodies end in a fish-tail. In Greek mythology, the sea chariot of Poseidon is drawn by hippocampi. For mer folk, the hippocampi are steeds prized for their ability to travel swiftly through the seas.

Hippogriff (a.k.a. *Hippogriffin*): The hippogriff was the offspring of a gryphon—a half eagle/half lion—and a mare, and was considered by medieval writers to be a natural, nonmagical beast. It had the body of a horse and the forelegs, claws, wings and beak of a gryphon, which were basically identical to those of an eagle. The hippogriff is often associated with the sun, the gryphons and horses of Apollo's chariot, and the **Pegasus**. The hippogriff's story is told in *Orlando Furioso* by Ariosto, most episodes of which are derived from Greek and other legends. The hippogriff was originally tamed by a magician named Atlantes who lived in a castle in the Pyrenees where Rogero, the magician's foster son, was kept prisoner. Eventually Rogero escaped and took the hippogriff as his mount. In one adventure, it was ridden by Rogero as he tried to save a damsel from sacrifice to a sea beast, an episode that greatly resembled one of Perseus's adventures.

The hippogriff eventually passed into the hands of one of Charlemagne's knights, who then learned from Saint John how to defeat the pagan Africans. In the end, the hippogriff was set free into the mountains and never seen again.

Hoop Snake: A creature of American folklore, the hoop snake puts the end of its own tail in its mouth and rolls across the ground. The hoop snake can move so rapidly that it cannot be outrun, and the only way to escape it is to jump though the hoop it makes, which so confuses the hoop snake that it just rolls on and cannot turn back.

The hoop snake may be related to the **uroboros**, a symbol of eternity and cosmic unity in Greek and Egyptian art. The uroboros depicted a snake with the end of its tail in its mouth, drawn in the shape of a circle. The **Midgard Serpent**, which in Norse mythology encircles the world by holding its tail in its mouth, is a type of uroboros.

Hydra: The Hydra was a child of Echidna and Typhon. Dwelling in the swamps of Lerna, this deadly poisonous, nine-headed creature had one head that was immortal. Whenever any head was struck off, two more took its place. Hercules killed the monster by using a torch to sear the necks so that no new heads would spring up. He buried the immortal head under a rock.

Incubi and Succubi: These spirits or demons visit people in the night for sexual intercourse. **Incubi** are male spirits that visit women during their dreams. Incubi can impregnate mortal women; one child from such a union was Merlin. **Succubi** are hideous females that trick sleeping males into intercourse. The succubi seem to be related to **Lilith**, the first wife of Adam. Expelled from Eden, Lilith became the mother of demons. She is also said to visit men in the night, looking for semen so that she can bring forth more of her brood.

Jabberwock: "The Jabberwock with eyes of flame" is a creation of Lewis Carroll and appears in the poem "Jabberwocky" in the book *Through the Looking Glass and What Alice Found There*.

It also has "jaws that bite" and "claws the catch" and "burble[s]" when it walks. It apparently lives near the "jubjub bird" and the "frumious bandersnatch" (also Carroll's inventions). The young hero of the poem dispatches the Jabberwock with a "vorpal blade" that goes "snicker-snack."

Jersey Devil: Stories of the Jersey Devil come from the Pine Barrens of New Jersey, a surprisingly isolated and sparsely populated region. No one is quite sure when stories of the Jersey Devil originated; some believe they began only 150 years ago, while some say they precede colonial times.

The most popular version of the Jersey Devil's origin says that in about 1735, a woman named Leeds, who was the mother of eleven children, discovered she was to have a twelfth child and cried out in frustration that she was sick of children and that this one could be the Devil—and, as it turns out, it was. Another story says that the Jersey Devil was born in 1850 as the result of a Gypsy's curse on a young girl. In both stories, the monster escaped into the woods shortly after its birth and still lives there.

The Jersey Devil is said to have a head like a horse or ram; large, batlike wings; and a long, serpentine body. Occasionally, there are outbreaks of stories about the Jersey Devil, the largest during the week of January 16–23, 1909. Eyewitness accounts are documented in newspapers of the time, most of them reporting eerie sounds coming from the direction of the Delaware river and a strange glowing creature flying through the sky. The hoofprints of a strange animal were reported in odd locations, such as on the roofs of houses or near chicken coops.

Kappa: In Japanese legends, the Kappa is a type of water demon that likes to drown its human victims. The Kappa has a skinny body with a large, bowl-like head filled with water. It also has a tortoise shell on its back and smells of rotten fish. Besides drowning its victims, it eats them as well. However, it is not an intelligent demon and can be fooled quite easily. A person confronted by the Kappa needs only to bow politely from the waist. The Kappa will return the bow, spilling the dangerous water from the top of its head, and will be powerless to drown its victims until it has reclaimed the water. By that time, the person can escape.

The Kappa is also appeased by the gift of a cucumber. The cucumber has to have a person's name and age cut into it. If the person throws this cucumber into the water, the Kappa will re-member the gift and the person will be safe from its clutches.

*Kelpie (*a.k.a. *Water Horse):* This Scottish water spirit, can be either mischievous or deadly. It has several forms, including that of a hairy man and a beautiful horse. As a horse, it lures men to ride it. Then the rider finds himself unable to get off and the kelpie returns to its watery home. Depending on the nature of the kel-pie, the man either merely gets dunked or he is drowned. In some cases, he may be eaten. River kelpies usually only dunked their victims. The **Each-Uisge**, found in lochs, was the more danger-ous and lethal. (In Ireland, the **aughisky** are water horses of saltwater streams and lochs. They are also man-eaters.) In horse form, a kelpie can be identified by its backward hoofprints. Kel-pies can be controlled with the use of a bridle, but it is not a good idea to use one for long since it also has the power to inflict curses.

Kelpies can also take on the shape of handsome men to lure women into their domain. In this form, the kelpie can be identi-fied by shells and seaweed in its hair.

Kraken: The kraken is a sea monster so huge, according to legend, that it can be mistaken for an island. This enormous size accounts perhaps for the ambiguous description of it. Sometimes confused with the giant octopus, the kraken is said to be tentacled, but little else can be said authoritatively. Sailors can easily be swept from ships, and the ships themselves crushed by the monster. In calm seas, sailors look for the bubbling and boiling waters that indicate the kraken is surfacing. Some legends have it that there are *two* kraken, created when the world was made and existing for as long as the world exists.

Lamia: The first lamia was one of the many conquests of Zeus. Hera, Zeus's jealous wife, cursed Lamia and gave her a monstrous form: a woman's head, a snake's body, cloven hooves and a lion's tale. Hera also killed Lamia's children. Lamia then went about killing children in revenge. She eventually had other children known as lamiae. In some accounts, these daughters had monstrous forms similar to their mother's. In other accounts, they were beautiful young women. The accounts agree though that Lamia's children sucked the blood from their victims and are thus similar to **vam-pires**. Lamia is related to Lilith in that both are cursed women responsible for a demon brood.

Leprechauns: Probably the most famous of Irish fairies, **leprechauns** are little people that are usually shoemakers. They can be identified by their hats, breeches and big-buckled shoes. Leprechauns are also wealthy and known to hide pots of gold and other treasure, though they part with the secret of their stash only if tricked. Exceptionally clever and tricky, very few mortals ever get the best of a leprechaun.

Leviathan: In the generic sense, "leviathan" refers to any huge sea-animal, but in the Old Testament it is used in several places to refer to a specific monster or monsters. In Job, the creature is depicted as a fierce monster with nearly impenetrable scales and terrible teeth. In Isaiah, the Leviathan is called the "coiling serpent" and the "gliding serpent." Psalm 74 refers to a "monster in the waters." But in Psalm 104, however, the leviathan is described as "frolicking" in the sea apparently a different sort of creature. Some scholars have speculated the crocodile may be the basis of the Leviathan of Job and Psalm 74, and that Psalm 104 may be referring to a whale. In most uses, however, the Bible creates an image of a fierce mysterious creature that is an adversary of God.

Lorelei: A water spirit of German legends, the Lorelei is known for both her beautiful appearance and her beautiful song. In fact, like the Greek sirens, the Lorelei's song is nearly irresistible and lures men to their doom. The creature takes its name from the large rock of the same name in the Rhine River, upon which it sits and sings.

Manticore: A creature associated with India, a manticore has the head of a man, the body of a lion and a tail like a scorpion's (although some accounts describe the tail as a spiked ball). It has three rows of teeth and can shoot the spikes from its tail like arrows. A manticore is a savage beast with a voracious appetite and often preys on people.

The Minotaur: Unlike centaurs, the Minotaur was a unique monster, half man and half bull. He was the son of Queen Pasiphaë of Crete and a bull. The sea god Poseidon gave the bull to King Minos to use as a sacrifice, but Minos liked the bull and preferred to keep it for himself. Angered by this, Poseidon made Pasiphaë fall in love with the bull. She had Daedalus, the master inventor, build her a wooden cow with which she could court the bull. When the Minotaur was born, Minos had Daedalus build the labyrinth to hold him. Minos also had the city-state of Athens pay a tribute of seven maids and seven youths to him, to be sent to the Minotaur. Eventually, the Athenian prince and hero, Theseus, came to Crete. With the help of Ariadne, Minos's daughter, he killed the Minotaur while it slept.

The Minotaur has been depicted in several ways. The most common is a human with a bull's head. The second is closer to a centaur, with a human torso and horned head atop a bull's body.

Monstrous Wolves: Gigantic or monstrous wolves appear in a variety of folktales and myths. In Norse mythology, **Fenris** or **Fenrir Wolf** was the son of the god Loki and a giantess. His siblings were Hel and the Midgard Serpent. Besides being of gigantic form, **Fenris** was incredibly strong. The gods feared him and tried to chain him but he broke all of their chains. Finally, the gods had the dwarves forge a magic chain called Gleipnir that was exceptionally thin but exceptionally strong. Fenris would only agree to be bound by it if one of the gods placed his hand in the monster's mouth. The war god Tyr did. The chain would not break and Tyr lost his hand. At Ragnarok, the twilight of the gods, Fenris finally breaks his chain and kills Odin. Fenris is then killed by Odin's son, Vidar.

Also in Norse mythology, giant wolves chase the sun and the moon across the heavens. They occasionally catch them, causing eclipses. Odin also kept two wolves called **Geri the Ravenous** and **Freki the Greedy**.

Naga: The naga originated in Indian myth, but can be found in legends throughout southeast Asia. It is a semidivine and semi-human creature in the form of a snake; both more powerful and wealthy than humankind, nagas dwell in lands under the earth or beneath the rivers and seas. But nagas are inferior to human-kind because they have no soul and therefore can achieve no enlightenment. Nagas have seven heads, hooded like cobras, and resemble the Hydra. Like the Hydra, nagas are associated with water, particularly rainfall and all the good and bad connected with droughts and floods.

In early legends, nagas withhold water from the earth and must be slain to end droughts. In others, villains seeking to destroy or imprison nagas must be defeated in order to prevent drought. In Buddhist legend, Buddha's superior spiritual and moral power persuades the nagas to relinquish the rains during the proper season and in the proper quantity. In another Buddhist legend, the boddhisattva (the "Buddha-to-be") chooses to be reincarnated as a naga and discovers how terrible it is to live without a soul. This and other stories show a close relationship between Buddha and the nagas, and he is often depicted seated on and protected by a naga.

Nemean Lion: The Nemean Lion was gigantic and ferocious. His hide was so tough that swords and arrows bounced off of him. Hercules eventually killed the beast by strangling it. Hercules then wore the lion's pelt as protection.

Nymphs: Nymphs are spirits or personifications of natural objects such as trees, rivers, streams and mountains. They are represented as beautiful maidens. In Greek mythology, **dryads** and **hamadryads** are spirits of trees. Dryads live in forests and hamadryads have connections to specific trees. Their lives were as long as the trees in which they lived. **Oreads** are the nymphs of the mountains. **Naiads** are water nymphs, inhabiting streams and rivers. The **Nereids**, fifty in number, were sea nymphs and the daughters of the sea god Nereus.

The Phoenix: The phoenix is closely associated with legends of the sun and appears often as a symbol of immortality, rebirth and power. According to legend, the phoenix lived in an eastern paradise of eternal springtime where there was no hunger and no night. The phoenix was larger and more graceful than the eagle; its head, breast and back were scarlet, its eyes were sea-blue, its feet purple and its iridescent wings were many colors. The phoenix did not eat grass or prey on other animals; it consumed the very air.

The phoenix lived there for exactly a thousand years; at the end of its lifetime, it left paradise and flew west until it reached Arabia. There it gathered perfumes and spices, which it took to the coasts of Phoenicia where it built a nest in the tallest of palm trees. It then began to sing its death song, a song so beautiful that even the sun god was said to stop in his tracks. Then the sun went on, and the phoenix' nest caught fire from the sparks of the sun, burning the bird and its nest to ashes from which the new phoenix rose.

The new bird then took the ashes of the old nest to Heliopolis, the City of the Sun, in Egypt and placed them on the altar of the sun temple. As the phoenix flew east, it was joined by all the other birds of the world—even predator and prey—which flew in peace as they accompanied the phoenix to the border of paradise.

Different legends give different life spans for the phoenix: some say 350 or 500 years, some 7,006, others 1,460 and still others but a day. The phoenix has been a powerful symbol in many cultures; it was used by Christians to represent Christ and the Resurrection; the Romans used it in the fourth century to represent the promise of the rebirth of the Roman Empire; and the phoenix was used in a symbol for Joan of Arc after her death. The phoenix appears in Chinese legend as the feng huang, a beautiful and musical bird more like a peacock than an eagle and appears in Japanese legend as Ho-ho, which is often used to symbolize the royal family.

Puca (a.k.a. Pooka, Puck, Pwca): Puca are English woodland faeries with diminutive human forms, known for mischeviousness and trickster-like qualities. Though the puca are often depicted as **satyr-like**, they are not known for lasciviousness. In Britain, puca became known as **puck** and eventually **Robin Goodfellow** came to be known by that name. He was a shape-shifter and preferred the company of animals, though he liked humans who appreciated and acknowledged his existence and persecuted those who scorned their lovers.

In Wales, puca are called **pwca** and are considered to be ill-tempered and ugly, often quarrelling among themselves. In German and Scandinavian countries, the puca are goat-bodied creatures called **kornblockes**. They are said to help grow grain and corn, but will steal or spoil it if given a reason.

Satyrs and Fauns: Half goat and half man, **satyrs** bound through the woodlands of mythical Greece, usually in pursuit of nymphs. Mostly human in appearance, satyrs have goat legs and hooves and small horns on their heads. The Greek god **Pan** also had the same physical characteristics. Some accounts say that **fauns** are the Roman version of satyrs, while other versions say that fauns are half deer and half man, and have much gentler natures than satyrs. They are named after the Roman god **Faunus** who later became identified with Pan.

Ruhk (a.k.a. Roc): The ruhk, giant birds known in the Middle and Far East, come from Arabic legend and are described in the

Arabian Nights stories as being so large that they blot out the sun when they fly. One of their eggs is as large as 148 chicken eggs and they feed elephants to their young. When they fly, the beating of their wings creates wind storms and lightning. In some Arabic legends, the ruhk never land on earth except on Mount Qaf, which the Arabs considered to be the *axis mundi*. In other legends, the ruhk live on certain islands in the Indian Ocean, but they often fly to India, Arabia and Africa to find food.

In the Arabian Nights stories, Sinbad has more than one adventure involving ruhk. In one story, Sinbad, marooned on an island, discovers a ruhk egg. He waits until the ruhk lands, then ties himself to the ruhk's enormous, tree-trunk-sized leg, thereby escaping the island when the ruhk goes in search of food. In another adventure, Sinbad and his sailors discover a young ruhk hatchling and kill and feast on it. When the parents of the bird return, the sailors flee to the sea and the two ruhk drop boulders on the ships, sinking them.

The ruhk appear to be similar to another giant bird of Arabic lore: the **anka**. Allah is said to have created the anka to kill and eat most of the wild animals of Palestine so that the Israelites could move into the country. Allah forgot to remove the bird, however, and it went on ravaging the countryside, making large parts of that country barren and uninhabitable.

Sasquatch: "Sasquatch" is an Indian word made popular in the 1930s by the stories of J.W. Burns, a British Columbian writer. Burns used the name for one of his characters, a giant Indian who lived in the wilderness. The character was quite popular and the name was used by a hotel and an annual festival in Harrison, B.C. The local celebration drew the attention of others who reported having seen a large, furry, humanoid creature, which soon was given the name Sasquatch. Most accounts of the Sasquatch are of a single creature, glimpsed only for a few seconds as it moved through the woods. When a bulldozer operator named Jerry Crew found a large, human-shaped footprint in Northern California and made a plaster cast of it, the creature who made it was dubbed **Bigfoot**, and the names Sasquatch and Bigfoot have become synonymous. By almost all accounts, the creature is described as larger than a man, covered with dark fur and very shy of human contact. One man reported being captured by a band of Sasquatch, and a group of miners near St. Helens claimed that their camp was attacked by "giant apes" throwing rocks after one of the miners shot an "ape" earlier in the day. Such stories of violent aggressive behavior by a Sasquatch are very rare.

Scylla and Charybdis: There are two main versions of the story of Scylla in Greek mythology and for each, the details vary widely. In one account, Scylla is a young woman whom the fisherman-turned-sea-god Glaucus spies and falls in love with. She refuses him because his mermanlike body is repellent to her. Glaucus seeks the help of Circe, asking for a love potion to turn Scylla's heart. As he tells his story, Circe falls in love with Glaucus, but he remains devoted to Scylla. In her anger, Circe prepares a poison for Scylla and pours it in the bay where she bathes. The potion turns her into a horrible creature that is rooted to the rocks on shore. In some accounts of this version, Scylla is a water sprite and she is the daughter of Phorcys and Crataeis, Typhon and Echidna, or Poseidon, and Glaucus is only a fisherman.

In the other main version of Scylla's story, she is seduced by her father Poseidon. When Amphitrite, Poseidon's wife finds out, she goes to Circe for help in punishing Scylla, which Circe does with the potion that turns her into a monster. Some descriptions have Scylla-the-monster with both the heads of serpents and fierce dogs; in others, she has twelve legs and dog heads on long serpentlike necks. All accounts consistently describe Scylla as turned into a hateful monster seeking to destroy anything that comes within her reach.

Today, Scylla is the name of a great rock that juts out of the sea between the tip of Italy and Sicily.

Charybdis is more mysterious in origin: in some accounts, she is a monster that lives under a rock on the Sicilian side of the strait. She traps sailors by creating a gigantic whirlpool, which sucks their ships under water. In other accounts, she is the whirlpool itself.

Sea Lion: The sea lion belongs to a class of part-lions like the Chimera and manticore, but is also associated with water- and merfolk. The sea lion has the front part of a lion—the forelimbs and claws, the maned head—and the hind parts of a large silvery fish. The sea lions live in packs along rocky seacoasts where they hunt for schools of fish or shipwrecked sailors. Their powerful jaws and claws make them very dangerous when angered, and their powerful tails and webbed forelimbs make them very fast in the water. Their bellowing roars can be heard even underwater. It was said that sailors could hear the packs of sea lions bellowing in hunger as the ships approached rocks and dangerous coastal areas.

Selkies and Roanes: **Selkies** are English sea fairies while **roanes** are Scottish. Normally, selkies and roanes have seal forms. Both can, however, shed their skins to reveal human bodies. They particularly like to become human to dance the night away. Humans can capture selkies, particularly female selkies, to be their wives if they can steal the selkie's or roane's skin away from her. The captured fairy may make a good wife but will always long for the sea and will return if she ever finds her skin. Selkies are also reported to be more hot-tempered than roanes and can cause storms if angered.

Shark Man: Similar to a werewolf, the Hawaiian shark man is capable of changing back and forth between man and shark. As a shark, he possesses all the attributes of the animal and usually preys upon members of his village. The most famous shark man was **Nanaue**. The son of a mortal woman and a shark god, Nanaue had a shark's mouth on his back. When he entered water, he changed into a shark, but he was vulnerable if he could not get to water. When he was found out, he fled to another village and was eventually trapped by fisherman, cut into small bits and burned.

Sirens: In some accounts, sirens are said to have the bodies of birds and the heads of women. Other sources say no description can be found since no one survives them. The chief characteristic of the sirens is their song, which no man can resist. Ancient sailors who heard the sirens were lured to their doom. The Greek hero Odysseus had his men stop up their ears, then had the crew tie him to the mast. Even so, their song nearly drove Odysseus mad. In another tale, Orpheus used his superior vocal skills to get the Argonauts past the rocks where the sirens lived.

Sphinx: Creatures known as sphinxes appear in a variety of cultures, particularly Egypt, Greece and Babylon. Sphinxes are generally known to have the bodies of lions, the wings of eagles, and the face and chest of humans. The monument of the Sphinx at Giza is supposed to represent Horus, the sun god. The Greek sphinx was a child of Typhon and Echidna and plagued the city of Thebes. She asked everyone her riddle, and those that could not answer, she devoured. Her riddle was, "What walks on four legs in the morning, two legs in the afternoon, and three legs in the evening?" Finally, Oedipus answered the riddle with the answer of "man." A man crawls on all fours as a baby, walks upright as an adult and uses a cane in old age. The sphinx supposedly killed herself in fury at having been thwarted.

The Stymphalian Birds: These birds lived along the shores of Lake Stymphalus in ancient Greece. They were about the size of cranes and had beaks and talons of bronze. Some accounts say they could shoot their bronze feathers like arrows. As one of his labors, Hercules had to rid the lake of the birds. With the help of the goddess Athena, he drove them into the air and shot them with arrows.

Tengu: The tengu of the Japanese Shinto religion are strange half-man, half-bird creatures. In some accounts, they have the body of men and faces of birds, and carry large fans of feathers. In others, they look like men with wings, bird-claws for feet and beaklike noses. They are mischievous creatures and are often credited, or blamed, for teaching humans how to use weapons of war. Sometimes, a tengu will possess a human, causing the victim to show great skill in battle. When the tengu spirit is driven out, the victim has no memory of what happened.

As creatures of the Shinto religion, tengu were fierce enemies of the Buddhists in the Middle Ages. They often tried to tempt, fool or carry off Buddhist priests and set fire to Buddhist temples. The Buddhists forbade the worship of the tengu and even had a mythical place called the "tengu road," an area of the spirit world reserved for hypocritical priests who had forsaken their vows.

Thunderbird: Like many fabulous birds, the Thunderbird of North America was considered to be the source of high winds or storms. A sacred bird to Native American Indians, the Thunderbird represents a force against evil, a creature with highly acute senses that can never be surprised by evil. The Thunderbird can never be summoned or invoked in a battle against evil; it comes of its own will or not at all. Its attack is always signaled by the thunder of its great wings.

As a spiritual force, the Thunderbird is often referred to as a singular creature, but in legend and story, it is sometimes spoken of as more than one creature, suggesting it is a species of bird. Descriptions of the Thunderbird vary as well. Pacific Indians describe a bird so immense that it has a lake on its back, which is the source of rain. Mountain Indians conceive of the Thunderbird as a small red bird that shoots lighting from its wing tips and makes thunder with the beating of its wings.

Trickster: The **trickster** figure appears in many mythologies around the world: in Greece as Hermes; as Coyote in the American Southwest; as Eshu-Elegba and Ananse in Africa; as Susa-no-o in Japan; and as Loki in Norse mythology. In many cultures, he is the culture hero, responsible for bringing the arts to his people. Stories about Trickster, particularly in Native American Indian and African lore, depict a character getting by on his wits against more powerful enemies.

Typhon and Echidna: **Typhon** was the last child of Gaea, Mother Earth. She bore him to fight against Zeus and the Olympian gods. He was gigantic with over a hundred flaming heads. Some accounts say these heads were serpents' heads that appeared beneath his waist. Other accounts say that he was human to the thighs. In any case, he was incredibly strong but ultimately defeated by Zeus and trapped under Mount Aetna. His mate was **Echidna** (a.k.a. *Echidne*). Echidna was a beautiful woman from the waist up. Below the waist she was dragon or serpent. She was also the mother of monsters, including the Hydra, Ccrebrus, Chimera and others.

Another half human, half dragon appears in Greek mythology as well but was not considered a monster. His name was **Cecrops** and was considered a king and hero and possibly the founder of the royal house of Athens.

Unicorns: The unicorn originally had many different descriptions, but the most common image is that of the white horse with flowing mane and tale and the single spiral horn sprouting from its forehead. Unicorns can be both fierce and gentle. Its horn can pierce anything, though it has to be careful of ramming it into a tree and getting stuck. The unicorn's horn has magical properties, chief of which was the ability to either detect or nullify poisons. For this reason, the horn was much sought after. Unicorns can easily be trapped by using a virgin as bait. The pure maiden sits in the woods and the unicorn will approach and place his head in her lap. It is then easy prey for hunters. Besides humans, the other natural enemy of the unicorn is the lion.

Wendigo: A North American Indian spirit, the wendigo inhabits the woods of Canada. It is a man-eating ghost that usually preys on hunters. Its tactics include whispering noises and making sounds that drive the hunter or woodsman into reckless terror. The victim then runs into the wendigo's ambush. It seems to also have had the power to possess people. Wendigo possession could be stopped in its early stages by a shaman.

Werewolves: Stories of men turning into beasts are common in most cultures. In Roman myth, Jupiter turns **Lycaon** into a wolf as punishment for the man's savagery. In most cases, the werewolf or were creature gives up his/her human form completely to take on the shape of the animal. These transformations normally occur at night and the person returns to human form with daylight. One way to tell such a shape-changer is to see if wounds inflicted on the animal form appeared on the human the next day. The **wolfman** image, along with the legends of silver bullets and wolfsbane, are creations of Hollywood and have little to do with actual folklore.

While European tradition has the werewolf, other cultures have their versions. South America has the **were-jaguar** while African folktales mention **hyena men**.

Vampire: Stories of spirits or demons or undead creatures that require the blood of the living for sustenance are part of the mythology of many parts of the world. In *The Odyssey*, for example, Odysseus descends into the underworld but is unable to speak with the shades of the dead until he feeds them the blood of a sacrificed sheep.

Other stories of vampirism involve corpses, not just spirits or ghosts, that rise out of the grave and seek the blood of the living. A twelfth-century English chronicle by William of Newburgh tells of an evil man who died without confessing, but was given a Christian burial nevertheless. He would rise out the grave every night and walk the town's streets, his flesh rotting and infecting the air with a plague that killed many. Finally he was exhumed so that the corpse could be burned, but it was found to be bloated and when struck with a spade, the man's body gushed with the warm blood of the people he had killed with the disease he had spread. The corpse was burned and the plague ended.

In Europe, stories of blood-sucking spirits and animated corpses merged, and "true" printed accounts of vampires began to appear in the sixteenth century. An account from Belgrade in 1732 describes a vampire being dispatched by driving a stake through its heart and burning the body.

In 1610, **Elizabeth Bathory**, the so-called vampire countess of Hungary, was suspected and convicted of using the blood of murdered peasants in her potions. She was actually convicted of sorcery, but was not described as a vampire until many years later.

Literary vampires became popular in English fiction in the nineteenth century, but Bram Stoker's *Dracula* in 1897 set the standard for all that followed. Our contemporary conception of the vampire as elegantly dressed, erotically attractive and intriguingly foreign can be traced to Stoker's *Dracula* and its film adaptations.

A number of standard "rules" govern vampires and vampirism. For one, a vampire must spend the night searching for its victims, but at dawn must return to its grave. Anyone bitten by a vampire becomes a vampire upon death. One can tell a vampire by examing the corpse; if the corpse is not decayed or has some color, then it is likely a vampire. Holy water will burn the flesh of a vampire, causing it to shriek in pain.

The legends built up around vampires give them a variety of powers including the ability to merge with shadows; shapechange, particularly into bats or wolves, though sometimes ticks and spiders; and the ability to mesmerize with their eyes. Vampires also have a variety of weaknesses. In some stories, vampires cannot enter a home without being invited in. They shun religious symbols. Garlic, mustard seed and other herbs can keep them away. They can be killed with a stake through the heart, though this may not be a permanent solution. Permanently destroying a vampire requires not only the stake, but beheading the vampire, stuffing the mouth with garlic and burning the body.

Yeti: The word "yeti" is Tibetan, which originally referred to a mountain spirit or demon, but has come to describe a creature known also as the **Abominable Snowman**, which is something of a misnomer since it seems to be neither abominable nor live only in the snow. Conflicting accounts of sightings of the elusive creature and contradictory and questionable physical evidence make the yeti out to be either a bit smaller than an average-sized man or nearly ten feet tall. What is consistent is that the yeti lives in the Himalayan mountains, is human-shaped and covered with fur, and seems to be an herbivore. In Russia, it is known as the **alma**, and is more ape-like in appearance with long arms and short legs. In China, legend tells of the **wildman**, who is covered with grayish-red fur and looks like plaster models of Peking man.

CHAPTER EIGHT

DRESS AND COSTUME

Sherrilyn Kenyon

C ostuming takes on a very important role in fantasy writing. It sets the tone for a story and can also tell the reader much about the character. Hooded robes or other voluminous garments appear any time the writer wants to add mystery to a character or conceal the character's identity. Clean, well-made silk dresses and capes imply wealth, while dirty, threadbare rags show poverty. An eye-patch gives a character an evil air, but replace that patch with a belled cap and he becomes a jester. Just as in the theater, a costume can tell your audience volumes about a character in very few words.

Unlike historical writers, fantasy writers aren't bound by any set of rules. They are free to pick and choose whatever fashions and forms work best for their story. But in order to help keep the medieval pageantry so often associated with this genre, the following list should prove invaluable whether you are dressing kings or peasants.

MATERIALS

Black-work: A gorgeous Renaissance invention, black-work was simply embroidery done with black silk.

Brocade: A tightly woven fabric with a raised pattern. Originally, the pattern was done with either gold or silver threads, but over time other threads were used. This was a material strictly reserved for only those who could afford it.

Canvas: A coarse cloth made of flax or hemp. It was worn by all.

Calico: A white cotton imported from India. Reserved for the rich.

Cambric: A fine white linen.

Damask: A silk fabric that was woven with various, often elaborate, patterns and designs. This was an expensive cloth reserved for royalty and nobility.

Embroidery: Though not a fabric, embroidery was highly prized and often decorated even the poorest of fabrics. Peasant designs were simple, often nothing more than just geometric. Noble clothing was much more elaborate and the stitches were often done with gold and silver thread.

Flannel: A lightweight woolen fabric, flannel was often used as undergarments, bandages and wash rags. It was available to all.

Freize: A thick woolen cloth that was often used for outer garments. Worn by all classes.

Fustian: A type of scarlet cloth, it was a lightweight silky material that also bore a resemblance to velvet. It was an expensive fabric worn by those who could afford it.

Gold and Silver Tissue: A lightweight fabric that had gold or silver threads woven into it. For the most part, it was reserved for royalty. However, richer nobility and even a few enterprising wealthy merchants might also acquire a bolt every now and again.

Holland: A very finely woven lawn material that was often used for shirts and undergarments. Usually reserved for the rich.

Kersey: A woolen cloth, often ribbed, worn by the wealthy.

Lawn: A finely woven linen reserved for the wealthy.

Linen: Cloth made from flax and used by all.

Musterdevilliers: A gray woolen cloth reserved for the middle and upper classes.

Russet (more commonly known as homespun): A coarse woolen cloth that was most often reddish-brown or gray colored. Russet was a favored material of the lower classes, but could also be found among the poorer nobility.

Samite: A silken cloth that was often woven with gold. Reserved for the wealthy.

Satin: Fabric made of silk that was shiny on one side. Reserved for the wealthy.

Scarlet: Not to be confused with the color, scarlet cloth was most often red, but could also be a number of other colors. It was a softer cloth that draped in folds. Usually reserved for nobility, it could also be found in the possession of outlaws.

Serge: A woolen fabric used for clothing and all types of other supplies: bed-covers, hangings, funeral drapes, shrouds and so on. It was used by all.

Silk: An expensive cloth woven from silk threads in the Orient. Originally reserved only for royalty, it gradually became used by the rich who could afford it.

Taffeta: A plain-woven glossy silk reserved for the rich.

Tartan: A twilled woolen fabric named for its tartan coloring and design.

COLORS

Black: First associated with the Vikings, black was worn by all and eventually became the color worn by mourners, the elderly and scholars.

Blue: Light blue was worn by all, but dark blue was worn by higher-ranking nobles and royalty until it became associated with scholars and apprentices.

Crimson: A bright red worn by the wealthy.

Flame: A bright red-orange reserved for the wealthy.

Gold Cloth: Reserved for royalty.

Green: All shades. Worn by all.

Murrey: Deep purple red. Worn by the rich.

Parti-colored: Clothes that were often made up of several different colors like a Harlequin doll.

Purple: Reserved for royalty and very high-ranking nobility.

Red: Worn by all.

Red-browns: Extremely popular and worn by all.

Scarlet: A vibrant shade first reserved for royalty and then worn only by the nobility.

Silver Cloth: Reserved for royalty.

Siskin: Light greenish-yellow worn by the wealthy.

Slate: A gray blue. Worn by all.

Tan: A light brown worn by the nobility.

Tartan: A plaid pattern of Scottish origin, the unique colors and pattern of which denote the wearer's clan or family.

Tawny: A brownish-yellow color that was popular. Worn by all.

Watchet: A light greenish-blue worn by all.

White: Worn by all, but preferred by the nobility and royalty.

Yellow: Worn by all.

WOMEN'S CLOTHING

Aprons: Used by middle- and lower-class women, they could be a variety of colors.

Barbe: A pleated piece of linen similar to the barbette and widows, it was worn underneath the chin of widows and over the chin to denote a noblewoman.

Barbette: A linen band that wrapped around the head, under the chin. It was usually pinned.

Butterfly Headdress: Worn at the back of the head, it was made of wire covered with fabric, and was draped with a fine gauzy veil that draped over the wearer's forehead and down her back. The almost right angle differentiated it from the hennin.

Caps: Made of linen, these were often worn over frets or with barbettes or wimples.

Caul (a.k.a. Fret or Crispinette): A coarse hair net made out of silk, gold or silver. It was worn only by royalty and nobles.

Chaplet: A padded roll that was worn on the head much like a hat. It was often bejewelled and embroidered. Variations of this could be horn-shaped or heart-shaped to where it dipped low around the forehead of the wearer. Some were extremely wide and high. It was most fashionably worn with the houppelande.

Cloak: An outer garment worn to keep the wearer warm in cool weather. Ofter semicircular or square, its shape was dictated by whatever was currently fashionable. Most fastened with a chord or brooch. However, there were a few styles in the early Middle Ages that fit over the head. Wealthy and nobles often lined their cloaks with fur.

Cote-hardie: A gown that was cut tight to the hips and then fell in folds to the ground. A button of rows down the front were used to fasten it.

Crispinette: see Caul.

Dagged or Dagging: Scallops cut into the fabric for decorative purposes.

Diadem: In the Middle Ages, it was a crown or golden chaplet that denoted royalty. In fantasy, they can either be the former, or are more akin to chain mail in that they are made of finely riveted silver or gold. Oftentimes jewels are interwoven with the metal. These elaborate pieces drape over the forehead and down the back. They are worn by priestesses, enchantresses, demons, ladies and thieves.

Fillet: A stiffened piece of linen, it was molded into a wide headband that was worn like a hat. Often it was placed over the barbette or a veil.

Fitchets: A hole cut into the cote-hardie that allowed the wearer access to their purse, which was hung on the girdle.

Fret: see Caul.

Girdle: A leather or metal belt worn about the hip. The style and length varied depending on the fashion of the day. Sometimes a purse was tied to it.

Gloves: Made out of leather or fabric, they were worn during winter for travel. The wealthy and nobles had gloves lined with fur and some of these were scented with flower oils.

Headdress: This name referred to the combination of a wimple and veil, or the fillet and barbette, or barbette and veil, or a cap and veil or barbette.

Hennin: The high pointed headdress that most people associate with the Middle Ages. It often had a piece of sheer veil worn over it, or it could have a lirapipe attached to the point. It was constructed on a wire frame either left bare or covered with fabric.

Hose: Either thick like a sock or thin like the modern-day counterpart, they were fastened about the knee with a garter.

Houppelande: A long gown that fell loose from the shoulders. It was belted at the waist and the collar was often high and tight.

Kirtle: Generic name for a dress. It could take a number of shapes and did so throughout the period. It was most often used to refer to the tight-fitting undergown or smock.

Lirapipe: A long streamer that was attached to a chaplet, hennin or heart-shaped headdress.

Mantle: A cloak worn indoors for state functions. It was attached to the dress with brooches or was tied with chords.

Pelisse: A jacket-type covering that was often worn over a dress and sometimes for outdoors.

Purse: A sack made of leather or cloth, it was drawn closed with cord or leather straps that were usually long. The chords were then fastened to the girdle and the purse hung down to about midthigh.

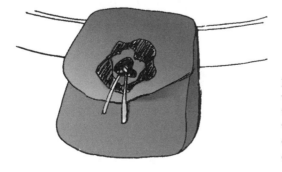

PURSE: Unlike the women's handbags of today, medieval purses were worn on the belts of both men and women.
©1998, Chivalry Sports, Inc.

Sideless Surcoat: This was an outer dress worn over a smock or kirtle. The sides were left open and cut to the hip. The neck could be square or round depending on the fashion. It was worn by the rich and often as court dress, or for state functions.

Sleeves: Due to the rapidly changing fashions, these were often made to come off so that the owner could update the sleeves without throwing out the costly yardage of the dress. Women were also known to give a sleeve as a token to a knight or lover.

Smock (a.k.a. Undertunic): The chemise or gown worn beneath a dress. In some styles, it was fully concealed and in others either the sleeves or skirt (or both) were visible.

Supertunic: A strip of material with a hole cut out for the head. It could have the sides sewn shut, or were sometimes left unsewn. In the Middle Ages, it appeared around 1200 and was worn only by the lower classes. The sides were sewn up and the ends of it were tucked into the sides while they worked. Though similar, it should not be confused with the sideless surcoat worn by the rich and nobility.

Tippet: A white piece of linen that was attached to the upper arm and worn to trail down to the floor. It was a purely decorative piece.

Undertunic: Another name for the chemise or smock. It was worn beneath a gown and, depending on the cut of the gown, was hidden completely or seen.

Veil: These could be long or short depending on fashion. Some were worn down the back while others were wrapped about the shoulders. Often a circlet or band was worn to help hold it in place. If not, then it was pinned to the hair.

TUNIC (left) and **SUPERTUNIC**
©1998, Chivalry Sports, Inc.

Widows: A wimple worn over the chin with a series of pleats down
   the front.

Wimple: This covered the throat and was often tucked into the
   neckline of the dress. Most often it was worn with a veil over it.

MEN'S CLOTHING

Braies or Breeches: Pants. The lower classes tended to wear looser
   pants and the nobles or wealthy wore more form-fitting ones.
   Many of these either had feet made into them (some of which
   had leather sewn onto the botton so they could be worn without
   shoes) or with loops to secure them on the foot when they were
   worn with boots. They were usually secured at the waist with a
   drawstring.

Cap: Any of a variety of small, usually brimless hats.

Chaperon: Similar to the woman's chaplet, it was made of material
   rolled up around the head. Extra material was placed up top and
   allowed to drape to one side. It was often worn with a coif.

Chaplet: Same as that worn by the women.

Cloak: Like the women, these took on a variety of shapes and styles
   and were worn to keep the wearer warm in the winter.

Codpiece: When the hose were so long that they met and were tied
   together at the waist, a small triangular piece covered the joining.
   This codpiece could be made of a similar or contrasting color
   and was obviously seen with the shorter gypons and
   houppelandes.

Coif: Similar to the barbette, they were made of white linen and
   covered the head and ears. Black coifs denoted scholars and
   elders.

LONG BREECHES (left)
and **SHORT BREECHES**

©1998, Chivalry Sports, Inc.

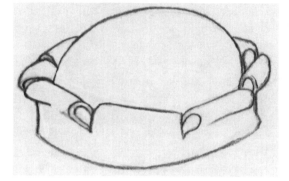

CAPS: Italian Rennaissance cap (left) Medieval muffin cap (right) and a simple rolled cap (bottom) with a cut brim.

©1998, Chivalry Sports, Inc.

Cote-hardie: Worn over the gypon, it originally went to the knee, then was shortened to where it barely reached the hips. The front was fastened with buttons. Poorer men wore a cote-hardie of medium length.

Cowl (a.k.a. *Hood):* These covered the head of the wearer during inclement weather and often came to a point that draped down the wearer's back.

Dagging: Scallops cut into the material to decorate the gorget, hem of the tunic or sleeves.

Doublet: A tailored tunic worn over the undertunic. The front of it was often stuffed to make the wearer appear more broad-shouldered. The length of it depended on fashion.

Folly-bells: Worn by noblemen and jester alike, these small bells were hung on little chains from the girdle.

Garnache: A supertunic that was allowed to drape over the shoulder to below the elbow. Like the supertunic, it was either left open at the sides or sewn together.

Gorget: The cape part of a hood or cowl that covered the shoulders.

CLOAK: This man wears a cloak over his supertunic and boots to protect himself from the weather.

©1998, Chivalry Sports, Inc.

COWL: This hood and gorget fit over the head and shoulders.

©1998, Chivalry Sports, Inc.

Gloves: Usually made of leather for the rich and linen for the poor, they were worn out-of-doors. Nobles and high officials would often wear them indoors as well.

Girdle: A belt that wrapped around the waist, the style and length of which varied according to fashion.

Gypon: Another name for a doublet.

Hose: Made of linen or wool, these were pulled over the braies up to the knee and were gartered or cross-gartered to the shin.

GORGET: This plain gorget covered the shoulders. Other styles might have a pattern along the bottom edge.

©1998, Chivalry Sports, Inc.

GIRDLE: standard girdle worn by men or women (left) and soldier's girlde.

©1998, Chivalry Sports, Inc.

Wealthier men and noblemen often wore loose hose that reached all the way up their inseams.

Houppelande: A loose gown that hung from the shoulders and was belted to the waist. The collar was high and tight. Richer men wore it long or short, and merchants and the poor wore it calf-length. A slit was made at either side or down the center to allow for greater mobility.

Jerkin: Identical to the houppelande except that the collar was cut low into a circle or square.

Kilt: A knee-length pleated skirt worn by Scottish men. Kilts were usually made of tartan to display the wearer's clan or family.

Lirapipe: This was the name given for the hood when the point of it was extended and left to dangle down the back to the wearer's feet. Sometimes it was coiled around the head or neck.

Pallium: A togalike garment, it was draped over the shoulders and hip.

KILT: The tartan of this Scot's kilt, cloak, cap and leggings indicates his clan.

©1998, Chivalry Sports, Inc.

Phyrgian cap: A cone-shaped cap made of wool or linen, the brim of which was folded up.

Purse: Men wore purses similar to the women's.

Supertunic: A strip of material with a hole cut out for the head. Some of these also had a slit cut up the center to allow the wearer to ride a horse. The sides were often left open, but could be sewn shut. Supertunics generally hung down to midcalf.

Swords and Daggers: Neither of these were worn with civilian dress. However, both men and women often kept a small knife with them that they used for eating.

Tippet: A long streamer that hung from the elbow, down the wearer's leg.

Tunic: A typical shirt, the style and cut of which varied according to fashion.

Undertunic: An undershirt. More pious laity would sometimes have this made out of horsehair or another coarse material (hence the term "hair shirt").

SHOES

Poorer people wore sandles or ankle-length shoes that were little more than leather tied onto their feet. Boots were mostly worn by

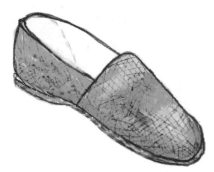

SHOE: Even this simple shoe was more advanced than most medieval peasants could afford.

©1998, Chivalry Sports, Inc.

men and they took on a variety of styles from shin-length to thigh-length. Wealthy men often had them lined with fur and would turn down the tops to show off the lining. Women wore shoes made of leather and wealthy women would sometimes have them made of fabric.

CHILDREN'S CLOTHING

Both boys and girls were dressed identically to their parents. Babies were swaddled in blankets or lightweight linen and their limbs tied,

CHILDREN: Note the similarities between these children's garb and the adult garments shown earlier.

©1998, Chivalry Sports, Inc.

CLERGY: A variety of clergymen—and their garb—is shown here.

much as you see the character Flora Danan swaddled in the film *Willow*. The thought behind this was that infants, whose movements can be somewhat spastic, would hurt themselves with their flailings about.

CLERGY

Nuns wore simple dresses, the style and color of which were determined by their order. Most wore veils and once the wimple came into fashion, they wore the two together. Crucifixes were often tied to their girdles and some wore wedding rings to symbolize their marriage to God and the Church. Although not sanctioned as part of their uniform, many sisters wore silk chemises beneath their coarse dresses. Some of these chemises were even dyed red! And on the opposite end of the spectrum, the extremely pious would sometimes wear horsehair shirts beneath their robes to chafe their skin and remind them of the suffering of Christ.

Monks and priests wore homespun robes, the color and style again dictated by their order. Most wore a wooden cross around their neck, and leather sandals or shoes on their feet. Bishops, archbishops and popes wore silks, the style and color of which is virtually unchanged to today.

Priestesses and sorceresses are seen in a variety of outfits. In Kinley MacGregor's story "Born of Fire," her priestesses wear golden robes similar to monk's robes. In Pamela McCutchinson's *Golden Prophecies*, we see priestesses dressed as Romans. And in *Wizard of Seattle*, by Kathy Hooper, sorcerers and sorceresses are dressed in everyday clothing.

Since wizards and sorcerers are often associated with religious figures (most likely due to the mystic legends of the Druids), they are often depicted in the same type of homespun robes, the colors of which tend to be black, white, brown or navy. The somewhat cliché image of the wizard's robes are dark garments embroidered with stars or moons; leave this kind of garb for the Disney movies, not your novel. A much more realistic representation is that of Merlin in the film *Excalibur*. There, Merlin wears monk-like robes and a metal skull cap.

CHASTITY BELTS

Although chastity belts have been used in a number of fantasy novels over the years, they were not a part of the European Middle Ages, although there is evidence to show that they were used in the Far East during that period. Chastity belts have a variety of forms, the most common of which is the belt made of a magical, nonrusting metal that either the heroine or her lover must quest to find a way to open it. We see just such an example in David Vierling's *Armor Amore*.

Another type of chastity belt is that made of cloth and bound with a magical spell to keep all men at bay, or one that has a magical knot that only a designated lover can undo. This latter is the type Marie de France uses in her novel, *Guigemar*. In this epic, the lady begs for the hero's shirt and he wraps it around her in such a manner that no man can remove it without cutting it. The heroine swears only to love the man who can undo the knot without violence and, of course, that is only the hero.

CHAPTER NINE

ARMS, ARMOR AND ARMIES

Michael J. Varhola

F ew fantasy stories would be complete without powerful warriors, skilled soldiers and the armies they head (or fight against), not to mention the tools of their trade—weapons and armor.

This chapter is designed to provide writers with an overview of ancient and medieval arms, armor and armies so that they can effectively include these things in their stories. Other aims are to give writers authentic terminology they can use in their stories, point them in the right directions for doing more research, and help them think about how and why arms and armor were used and developed.

ARMS

When arming characters, there are several things that writers should take into account. Among these are what the people in question use their weapons for, what their level of technology is and what their material resources are.

The sorts of weapons a culture uses says much about that culture and are determined by their chosen forms of combat. For example, long, slashing swords and javelins might be favored by warriors who fight from chariots or horseback. Missile weapons like bows and slings are likely to be preferred by warriors who make their living hunting when not waging war. Maces, picks and other heavy, crushing weapons are the sort that will be used by soldiers who need to penetrate the defenses of heavily armored opponents. Long, sharpened paddles used for rowing canoes might be the primary weapons of a riverine jungle people. Steel-bladed swords, spears and arrows might be issued to the professional soldiers of a wealthy city state.

The technology level of the people in question and their available material resources will dictate the material form of the weapons to a very great extent. For example, are they operating at the level of a Stone Age, Copper Age, Bronze Age, Iron Age or even some age unknown in our world? Warriors of a primitive people unable to work metal and living in an area devoid of appropriate rocks might utilize "Bone Age" technology, arming the edges of heavy wooden clubs with bone shards and making spear- and arrowheads from sharpened pieces of bone.

Writers should also consider the attitudes that people of their cultures have toward their weapons, for example, the warriors of the various Germanic peoples (Goths, Saxons, Vikings) had a spiritual reverence for fine weapons. The antithesis of this attitude was found in the Roman republic, where soldiers regarded weapons as necessary tools to be brought forth when needed and then put away until needed again.

Weapons Terms

Most weapons can be divided into several broad types, which are explained below. For some, subgroups or various regional or variant names are also provided in parentheses. Not all are exactly synonymous, but are at the least in the same family of weapons. For example, a gaesum and a pilum are both types of javelins, but are not identical in form or function.

Weapons inflict three broad types of damage: crushing (clubs, maces), cutting (axes, broadswords) and piercing (arrows, spears, lances, longswords).

axe: Many shapes, sizes and varieties of this weapon have been used throughout the world for about fifty thousand years. Stone Age peoples used flint-headed axes with wooden hafts; medieval men-at-arms used heavy, steel-headed two-handed axes like the **bardiche** to hack through plate armor; and warriors in India used axes with hafts and heads forged entirely of steel, the weapons ornately decorated with koftgari etch work. Axes were used extensively by primitive or barbarian warriors because they could serve as both tools and weapons.

bow: Bows have been used by hunters, warriors and soldiers the world over since prehistory. **Self-bows** consist of a single piece of flexible wood. **Composite bows** are made of one or more

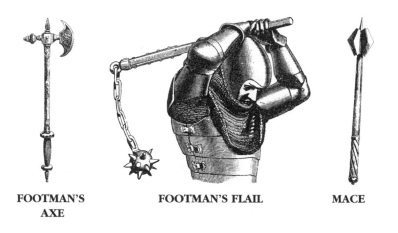

FOOTMAN'S   FOOTMAN'S FLAIL   MACE
AXE

pieces of wood reinforced with layers of horn and sinew. In all cases, the string is markedly shorter than the bow itself in order to provide tension.

Short self-bows can have pulls ranging from 40 or 50 pounds for the primitive hunting bows of forest peoples, who operate at short ranges, to 70 or 80 pounds for an English longbow with typical ranges of 230-250 yards, to about 110 pounds for some types of East African bows. Composite bows allow for much stronger pulls, the Turkish variety of this weapon having a pull of 150 or 160 pounds with typical ranges of 360-400 yards.

club: Basically an extension of the fist, simple wooden clubs were the first hand weapons and were used universally. Their descendants, **composite clubs**, were similarly widespread, and consist of wooden clubs with stone or metal heads, sometimes simply round but more often armed with metal flanges or spikes. Examples of these include **maces**, **morning stars** and **flails**.

crossbow: Crossbows have advantages over bows in that they allow mechanical power to be substituted for muscle and can be kept readied to fire longer than can bows. Disadvantages include having a rate of fire much less than that of bows.

Crossbows probably appeared in Europe in the eleventh century and were developed into progressively more powerful weapons over the course of the next few centuries. The lightest had wooden bows and could be cocked by hand. The most powerful, called **arbalests**, had steel bows and could only be armed by use of a windlass, goat's foot lever or similar device. Such weapons could pierce armor and constituted such a threat to armored knights that for a time the Church banned their usage against Christians (a ban about as effective as those being called for against handguns today).

Crossbows fire bolts, or quarrels, broad-fletched projectiles less than half the length of arrows.

dagger: Usually double-edged and used for both slashing and thrusting, the dagger is a universal weapon. Daggers were often used as secondary weapons to be resorted to after being deprived of a primary weapon (their concealability enhanced this usage), or used as an offhand weapon.

Daggers were also made for special purposes. For example, the Indian **peshkabz** had an acute point and a reinforced spine, so that it could be rammed through mail armor; and the French **misericorde** was long and narrow, so that it could be thrust through openings in the armor of knights who had been knocked to the ground.

Amongst people with limited metalworking abilities, long copper, bronze or iron daggers sometimes served as primary weapons.

javelin: Such light spears are designed for hurling, rather than melee, and generally have about twice the range of thrown close-combat spears. Some, notably the **pilum**, were forged with a soft metal neck that bent upon impact. This made it impossible to hurl back, hard to withdraw from a wound; and, if stuck in a shield, weighed it down and made it difficult or impossible to use. (Gallic **gaesum**; Roman **pilum**)

lance: In its simplest form, a spear used by a mounted warrior whose horse is equipped with spurs. Used by such a soldier, a lance could be couched under his arm when charging in order to put

DAGGER: Judging by this dagger's handle and blade, it most likely came from India or Persia.

HALBERD: The metal head of this type of polearm was mounted on the end of a 6 to 8 foot long wooden pole.

the weight of the horse behind the impact of the weapon. During the Middle Ages, the lance developed several features, including hand grips and guards, and specialized heads. The term "lance" is often erroneously used to refer simply to a spear. No other melee weapon can inflict as much shock and damage as a lance wielded by a mounted warrior with stirrups, as the weight of the horse is behind the attack.

polearm: Any weapon consisting of a head mounted on a haft, the former usually of metal and the latter usually of wood. The spear, a dagger blade mounted on a pole, is the simplest form of polearm. Throughout the world, innumerable types have been used, ranging from the modified peasant tools to highly specialized arms designed to penetrate heavy armor. Examples include the **bill**, **guisarme** and **fauchard**, weapons used by European peasants in time of war; the **bec de corbin**, **Lucerne hammer** and **halberd**, all designed to help infantrymen stand up to or even overcome heavy cavalry; and the Japanese **naginata** and Indian **hoolurge**, both polearms with broad cleaving heads.

sword: No class of weapon has been so revered or romanticized as the sword. Swords represent a relatively high level of technology and economic development, in that they were made almost entirely of metal and were thus expensive and labor-intensive. Swords were produced in a great variety shapes and sizes, and several general types are described below, loosely in the order of their technological development.

bastard sword: Also called a hand-and-a-half sword, this is a weapon that can be wielded with either one hand or two. Examples include the **khandar** of India and what was called a **sword of war** during the European Middle Ages.

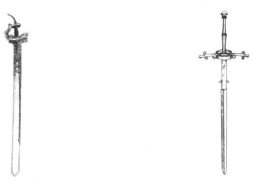

KHANDAR: The "bastard," or hand-and-a-half, sword of India.

"**ZWEIHAENDER:** The two-handed sword of the German landsknecht."

broadsword: A sword three or more feet in length with a rounded or spatulate tip used for chopping or slashing. Examples include the iron swords of Dark Age barbarians and of Middle Eastern chariot peoples.

khopesh: A bronze sword of ancient Egypt about two feet long with a heavy, cleaverlike, D-shaped blade. What is most interesting about the khopesh is that its form was adopted throughout the ancient world and it became the grandfather of an extended family of cleaverlike shortswords that includes the **falcata** of Spain, the **kopis** of Greece, the **sax** of the Danes and the **kukri** of Nepal.

longsword: A double-edged, long-bladed sword with an acute point that could be used for slashing or thrusting. Most of the swords carried by the knights and men-at-arms of the Middle Ages were of this sort, although these can be divided into more than a dozen broad types. Representing a higher technology level than most broad- or shortswords, such weapons were deadlier and almost always made of steel. **Rapiers** are an example of an especially thin, long version of such a weapon.

protosword: A wooden club shaped like a sword and fashioned with acute, swordlike edges, or armed with chunks of stone, glass or other sharp objects. Such weapons were made by peoples who recognized the superior form of the sword, but were unable to produce true metal swords. Examples include the **macahuitl** of the Aztecs, and the shark-toothed **tebutje** of the Gilbert Islanders of Micronesia.

scimitar: A curved, single-edged slashing sword, typical of Middle Eastern and especially Arabic peoples. The **saber** is a type of scimitar designed for equestrian troops.

shortsword: Broad-bladed, usually double-edged swords about two feet in length were popular amongst many peoples. Roman soldiers carried the steel **gladius**; Celts wielded leaf-shaped bronze shortswords; West Africans used broad-bladed iron shortswords. Shortswords were often made by people who had not achieved a high level of metalworking ability and used a relatively soft metal, such as copper or low-carbon iron. Broad, thick blades helped to make such weapons strong enough for use in battle.

two-handed sword: Heavy, two-handed weapons of this sort tended to be five or six feet in length, twenty-five or more pounds in weight, and used for hacking. The best examples of such weapons came into use from the fifteenth century onward. Specific examples include the **zweihaender** of the German landsknecht mercenaries and the **no-dachi** of Japan.

stirrups: Although not a weapon as such, stirrups caused one of the great revolutions in the history of warfare. They allowed mounted warriors to use high-impact weapons like lances and to more effectively fire bows from the saddle. Since the earliest days of European warfare, disciplined formations of heavily armored infantrymen, exemplified by Roman legionnaires, had dominated the battlefield and could withstand attacks from cavalry, which were largely relegated to the role of skirmishers. Stirrups were invented around 200 B.C. in China, during the early Imperial period. They were introduced in Europe one thousand years later by Muslim invaders. The first European warriors to adopt them were probably the mounted troops of Charlemagne, who heralded in a millennium of battlefield dominance by cavalry.

ARMOR

Throughout history, various sorts of armor have been developed to protect combatants, and weapons have been improved upon and specialized for the purposes of penetrating that armor.

In fantasy art, movies and literature, warriors are often depicted wearing little if any body armor. In reality, however, most historical warriors endeavored to equip themselves with as much protection as possible, and unarmored or lightly armored soldiers were generally hacked to bits by those who were better equipped. Armor stands between a soldier and the weapons that others are trying to kill him with, and its value cannot be underestimated. Armor can deflect or absorb weapon blows that would otherwise maim or kill their wearer.

The following section is an overview of the use of armor and provides authentic terminology. After all, anybody can write, "Duke William donned his helmet," and that might be good enough. If you have to, however, it is nice to be able to write, "Duke William donned his spangenhelm, then pulled his ventail up to cover his throat and jaw, tying off the corners of the mail flap to the sides of his coif."

Armor can be broadly divided into helmets, shields and body armor.

Helmets are one of the most crucial and universally worn pieces of armor, even among nonwealthy troops. Head wounds are the most bloody, disabling and lethal, and nothing is more important than preventing them. Broadly speaking, a helmet can include anything from a bronze skull cap, a thick cotton turban, an iron great helm, a conical steel helm with a noseguard or a hood of mail.

Shields are devices held in the user's nonweapon hand and actively used to block weapon blows or enemy missiles. Shields can be of any shape, size or material. Shields must strike a balance between sturdiness and maneuverability; a shield made of plate steel may stop any weapon, but would be impossible to lift; one made of paper might be easy to carry and move about, but obviously wouldn't stop weapon blows very well. Most have a wood core or frame, a covering of leather and metal fittings if available. Other materials have included wickerwork, turtle shell and even reinforced cloth and silk.

Body armor in some form has been worn for thousands of years in every place that human beings have made war upon each other. The materials such armor was constructed of depended on what was available, the technology level of the society constructing it and the needs of those wearing it. For example, the peoples of Mesoamerica made armor of quilted cotton because cotton was readily available, they did not have metalworking technology, and they really did not need anything considerably better against the Stone Age weapons they faced.

Throughout the ancient world, many sorts of body armor were used, including coats of mail, scales, rings and plates. Armor ranged in complexity from leather cloaks studded with metal worn by Assyrian soldiers to the extremely complex panoply of the Samurai, which consisted of dozens of specialized pieces of finely crafted metal and silk armor. Padded clothing was always worn under armor to reduce chafing and help absorb blows.

For many centuries after the fall of Rome in the fifth century A.D., most European warriors wore leather armor, sometimes augmented by metal studs or rings; waist-length, short-sleeved coats of mail and remnants of Roman armor.

By the eleventh century, the best-equipped warriors wore a **hauberk**, a knee-length coat of mail; and a **spangenhelm**, a conical helmet made of four sections of wood and leather set in a metal frame and with a nasal, a metal bar protecting the nose and upper face. Shields during this period tended to either be a few feet wide and round, or about four-feet high and kite-shaped, the latter type favored by cavalrymen. Vikings, Normans and many early crusaders were equipped in this way.

Mail was gradually augmented with additional pieces. By the thirteenth century, it was being reinforced with **coats of plates**, typically cloth or leather vests with rows of metal plates sewn into them—pieces of plate metal to protect the elbows, knees and shins. Cylinder-shaped **great helms** were adopted by many warriors, and the kite shield was abbreviated into the **heater** shield.

Armor of the fourteenth and early fifteenth centuries included many plate metal components, including breast- and backplates. Armor of this period is now referred to as **transitional armor**, as it represented a shift from all-mail to all-plate armor. **Close helmets**, which fit tightly around the head and enclosed it entirely, replaced the bulky great helms.

European body armor reached its developmental peak in the fifteenth century. Armor was almost entirely made of plate metal components and was characterized as **full-plate**. Shields were either smaller or abandoned altogether because of the greater protective value of armor.

The progressive competition between weapon smiths and armorers was abruptly settled in the sixteenth century with the spread of firearms. Armorers tried to counter this by creating increasingly heavy breastplates, but eventually had to concede the contest.

Complex, expensive, highly protective suits of armor were still made for a few centuries, but used only for tournaments and pageants. Battlefield armor was abandoned piece by piece until by the eighteenth century, even helmets were abandoned—for a time.

Since then, firearms have continued to evolve and become more and more deadly, while no effective defenses have been developed to counteract their effects. Even modern bulletproof vests are not completely protective against firearms. Such armor is really only effective against handgun ammunition or explosive fragments, and generally cannot withstand rifle fire; protects only the torso and its vital organs, not the limbs or head; and is not provided to regular soldiers in any case. Bulletproof helmets do exist and are issued to U.S. military personnel, and some form of helmet is worn by the soldiers of most armies. If anything, this is a reminder of the importance of head protection, one of the first and most universal forms of personal defense.

Armor Terms

Several specific sorts of helmets, shields and armor, along with various armor terms, are described below. Pieces described as being plate armor are usually worn in conjunction with other pieces to form transitional-plate or full-plate armor.

aventail: A flap of mail that hangs down from the back of a helmet to protect the wearer's neck.

bard: Armor for a horse, which could be constructed of much the same materials as armor for humans. Individual pieces included the **chanfron** or **champfrein**, a piece designed to protect the horse's head.

bevor (a.k.a. beaver): A piece of mail or plate armor that protected the chin and lower face, often attached to the bottom of a helmet with hinges if made of plate, or part of a coif if made of mail or padded cloth.

breastplate: A metal plate designed to protect the torso. In their simplest form, breastplates may be square or round pieces, a few hands across in width and worn strapped onto the chest. Those worn by ancient Greek and Italian warriors were of bronze and cast to look musculatured. Steel breastplates came into use in the Europe during the 1200s to augment chain mail and by the 1500s, were one of many plate steel components of full-plate armor.

BARDING

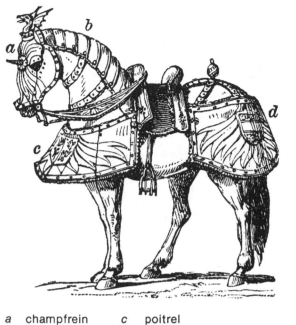

a	champfrein	*c*	poitrel
b	criniere	*d*	croupiere or buttock-piece

Backplates were a typical counterpart to the breastplate, but were notably absent among some armies. For example, many Greek soldiers had only breastplates, causing rout in battle to be thought of as tantamount to suicide as it left an unprotected back exposed.

breaths: Narrow slits or holes in the close helms and great helms of the Middle Ages used to breath through.

coif: A hood of mail, often attached to a coat of mail. In India, mail with an attached coif was often referred to as **ghughuwa**.

couter: A piece of plate armor that protects the elbow, attached to the upper and lower arm guards by hinges.

cuisse: A broad piece of formed plate armor that protected the thighs. Such armor typically wrapped around the front and sides of the thighs but left their backs unprotected.

fauld: A mail skirt worn under plate armor to protect the groin.

flutes: Corrugations in some plate armor of the late Middle Ages that gave it additional strength but did not add to its weight. A characteristic of what is known as Maximilian Armor.

CHAINMAIL COIF: Coifs were also made of cloth and worn by commoners for protection against the elements.

gauntlet: A heavy leather or metal glove. Those of the Middle Ages designed for use with plate armor often had articulated steel fingers.

gorget: A heavy piece of plate armor designed to protect the neck.

greave: A piece of armor, usually of metal but possibly of hardened leather, used to protect the shins. Greaves were used from the earliest times, from Bronze Age Greek warriors to sixteenth-century European knights.

haute-piece: A ridge of metal on plate shoulder armor designed to prevent horizontal cuts to the neck.

helm, helmet: A piece of armor designed to protect the head. There are innumerable names and variations, but a few notable ones follow.

   arming cap: A padded, lightweight cloth helm worn underneath a heavier metal helmet, or by itself by troops of modest means.

   barbute: A Renaissance helm with an opening for the face shaped like a rounded "T," the barbute is based on an ancient Greek helmet and was revived because of the Renaissance veneration for the classical world.

   close helmet: A plate-armor helmet of the late Middle Ages that fitted very closely around the head and was looked through by means of narrow sights or eye slits. Such helmets often consisted of two or more pieces that were bolted together around the head of the soldier. Examples include the **armet**.

   great helm: A heavy, round helm of the early Middle Ages that looked a bit like a bucket or can with eye slits. The great helms of knights often had their heraldic devices mounted on top of them.

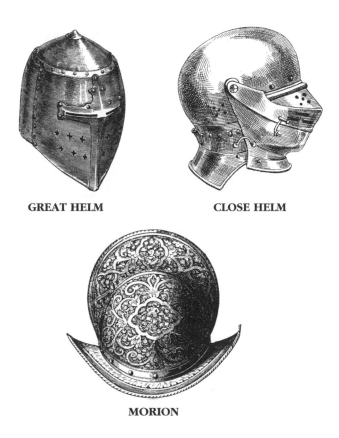

GREAT HELM   **CLOSE HELM**

MORION

khula-kud: A Persian or Indian helmet, traditionally consisting of a round steel cap, a noseguard extending down from the brim, an aventail and a pair of hollow metal pipes attached to either side of the front, used to hold plumes.

morion: A broad-brimmed, high-crested helmet of the Renaissance, usually associated with the Spanish Conquistadors.

lance rest: A metal hook attached to the breastplate of plate armor and used to help keep a lance level during a charge.

lorica segmentata: This characteristic armor of the Roman legions consisted of horizontal bands of iron protecting the abdomen and torso, with smaller vertical pieces to protect the shoulders. A knee-length skirt of metal-studded leather strips protected the lower part of the body.

mail: A type of armor made up of interconnected links of metal. In most examples, each ring of metal is attached to four others, creating a tough, flexible mesh, which is called the "four-in-one pattern.'' Such armor was worn throughout Europe, Asia and North Africa.

Mail is often referred to (somewhat redundantly) as **chain mail**.

pauldron: Pieces of plate armor designed to protect the shoulders.

poleyn: A piece of plate armor that protects the knee, which is attached to the thigh and shin armor by means of pins or hinges.

sabaton (a.k.a. *soleret):* A piece of plate armor used to protect the top of the feet.

scale armor: Armor consisting of scales of metal, horn or leather on a coat of cloth or leather. Such armor was used by the Byzantine and later Roman armies, and was characteristic of the cataphractoi and clibinarus heavy cavalrymen.

shield: Shields are probably the earliest type of armor designed specifically for defense, and many sorts have been carried by troops through the ages. A few notable varieties are described below.

> *buckler:* A very small shield, usually a few hands wide and made entirely of metal. Such shields required great skill to use effectively.

> *heater:* A three-sided shield with a straight upper edge and two curving sides meeting at the bottom in a point, widely used during the Middle Ages.

> *hoplon:* The large, round shield of the ancient Greek heavy infantrymen.

> *scutum:* The large, semicylindrical rectangular body shield carried by Roman legionaries.

side wing: A piece of plate armor attached to knee guards to help defend against blows to the side of the leg.

surcoat: A loose tunic worn over armor during the Middle Ages that was usually emblazoned with a soldier's colors or heraldic markings.

tasset: A broad piece of plate armor used to protect the thigh.

vambrace: A piece of forearm armor.

ventail: A square of mail attached to the upper chest by two corners, the other two hanging loose across the chest when not in use. In battle, the wearer pulls the ventail up to protect his throat and jaw, tying off the loose corners to the sides of his coif.

The Parts of Armor: Front View

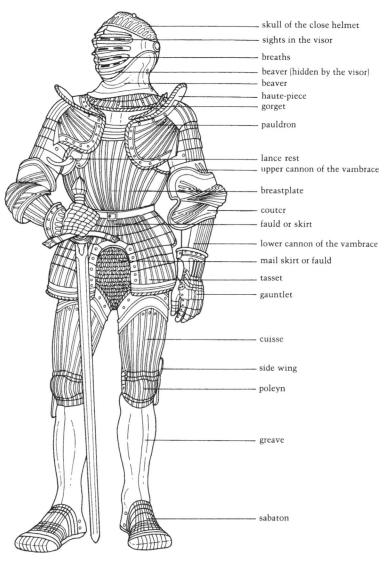

- skull of the close helmet
- sights in the visor
- breaths
- beaver (hidden by the visor)
- beaver
- haute-piece
- gorget
- pauldron
- lance rest
- upper cannon of the vambrace
- breastplate
- couter
- fauld or skirt
- lower cannon of the vambrace
- mail skirt or fauld
- tasset
- gauntlet
- cuisse
- side wing
- poleyn
- greave
- sabaton

MAXIMILIAN ARMOR, GERMANY, 1520: The flutes or corrugations gave the armor added strength without additional weight. "Maximilian" armor is often considered to be the height of achievement of the armorer's craft.

The Parts of Armor: Rear View

- plume tube
- comb
- plume tube also placed here
- rear neck guard
- gorget
- pauldron
- backplate
- culet
- mail skirt or fauld
- spur slit

visor: A piece of a helmet covering the face, usually capable of being lifted on hinges or removed.

ARMIES

Writers creating armies should understand the difference between warriors and soldiers. Warriors are the combatants of primitive or nonurbanized cultures and are judged largely on the basis of individual skill and ability. They tend to go into battle in loose mobs or grouped into warbands, and are led by warriors who lead by virtue of strong personality or hereditary status.

Soldiers are the combatants of organized or urbanized societies and are trained to fight in units rather than as individuals. Soldiery draws its strength from numbers and cooperation at every level. Soldiers are organized into units, go into battle in formations and are led by officers that have been appointed over them by the state or promoted based on merit and experience.

Troops can be formed on the battlefield in many ways, and different eras, places and conditions have dictated various ways of doing so. In the classical world, units of troops tended to be drawn up in a straight line, with the strongest unit on the right flank. Infantry typically formed the core of such armies. Units of cavalry were deployed on the flanks to prevent an enemy from surrounding one end of the army. Units of cavalry might be deployed to the rear of the army and deployed as needed once a battle began.

In battle, commanders tried to force the enemy to retreat, rout or surrender; completely annihilating an enemy was not always a desirable, necessary or possible goal. Soldiers were deployed in order to maneuver around an enemy and attack its flanks or rear, or break through its lines to do the same. Once this occurred, all or much of the breached army might break and run. At that point, cavalry was typically deployed to harry or eliminate the fleeing enemy.

Writers interested in describing battles should read about historic examples. Almost any detailed information about a battle will be useful, regardless of the period. The actions of the Second Punic War (218–202 B.C.), fought between Hannibal's Carthaginians and Rome's legions, are ideal reading for such purposes. Reading about the first defeat of Rome at the Battle of Lake Trasimene—Hannibal's quintessential victory with his double envelopment of the Roman army at Cannae, and his ultimate defeat before the gates of Carthage at the Battle of Zama—will make writers infinitely more qualified to discuss the actions on a field of battle.

Writers should also be aware that the vast majority of combatants have no idea what is going on around them in a battle, and even commanders might have skewed ideas of what is happening. Tolstoy captures much of this battlefield confusion in episodes throughout *War and Peace*, his classic novel of the Napoleonic wars.

Quality of Troops

Writers can mentally classify the soldiers of their armies according to their level of skill, training and experience. These terms might be used to describe troops of certain types. For example, an experienced soldier might very well refer disdainfully to "green" soldiers, and a commander would certainly be cognizant of which of his troops were his veterans.

Various units might have identifying names rather than generic descriptions: one company of green levies might be identified by their village of origin and called "The Mill Village Militia"; a regiment of veteran mounted lancers might be named for their commander and called "Arikon's Winged Lightning"; and a king's elite palace bodyguard might be named for his mystical guardian and called "Blue Dragons."

Regular troops will make up the bulk of most professional armies. They are soldiers with training in arms and maneuver, many of whom will have seen some limited action, such as border skirmishes or putting down urban riots. Such troops will stand their ground in the face of all normal battlefield threats and with proficient leadership, can be very reliable.

Green troops may have little or no training, or be relatively well trained but have no experience. Thus, they may be as good with their weapons as regulars on the training field, or may even be able to march better. However, such troops have not been exposed to real action, and without strong leadership and steady units on their flanks, they are liable to break under any sort of duress; for example, during the War of 1812, Maryland militia troops at the Battle of Bladensburg broke and ran when rockets were fired over their heads.

Veteran troops have had extensive training and considerable experience. Units of such soldiers will invariably have a history and will practice rituals or pageants that recall their glories. Such troops might also be entitled to special honors, such as wearing a special device on their uniforms, carrying silver-plated weapons or being awarded extra pay. Most legionaries of the Roman Empire were veteran troops, and legions displayed their histories with standards that they carried into battle. The officers in charge of a unit of regulars will usually be a group of veterans.

Elite troops are the best soldiers, which will be formed into units. Some armies may have no elite troops at all, such as those with little experience at warfare, and they will be a prized component of those that do. Elite units in history include the **Sacred Band of Thebes**, a two hundred-man unit that helped make the Greek city-state of Thebes formidable. They died to a man defending their city against the armies of Alexander the Great, who afterward wept for their valor. Elite soldiers are usually the leaders of veteran soldiers.

Heroes are unique soldiers with extensive training, experience and special abilities, like magic weapons, great strength or supernatural companions. They will lead units of veteran or elite soldiers or entire armies, or even operate independently. Beyond them are superheroes, demigods, demons, deities. . . . The possibilities in a fantasy milieu are unlimited.

The above notes are useful guidelines but can be bent as needed. Historically, even elite units have broken inexplicably, and green troops have stood their ground under harrowing circumstances. Some very dramatic scenes can be created by considering these facts.

Types of Troops

Troops can be divided into several types based on their role in battle. Many of these troop types had specific names as well, usually based on the sort of equipment they used. For example, many classical world infantrymen were named for the type of shield they carried (Greek **hoplites** were named for their hoplon, a large, round shield).

Infantry. The most versatile arm of a military force are **foot soldiers**. They can operate under the greatest variety of conditions and with the least expense and equipment. Such troops also tend to be the least glamorous or rewarded of any sorts of soldiers.

Heavy infantry are as heavily armored as possible (which may not be very heavy in some cultures) with close-combat weapons and perhaps secondary hurled weapons, and trained to fight toe-to-toe with the enemy in close formations. Examples include the Roman **legionary**, armed with javelins, shortswords and daggers; the Greek **hoplite**, armed with twelve to eighteen-foot-long pikes; and medieval **men-at-arms**, armed with armor-crushing weapons like battle axes, maces and flails.

Light infantry wore light or no armor, or perhaps only shields and helmets. Typically, they served as skirmishers, launching missiles at the front ranks of an enemy force before close combat, dispatching wounded soldiers on the battlefield or chasing down retreating foes. Examples include the **velites** of Rome, armed with javelins; the **peltasts** of Greece, also armed with javelins; and the **pindaris** of India, armed with pikes and miscellaneous weapons.

Missile troops typically wore no armor and could not engage the enemy in close combat. Such troops were often among the most highly trained of an army. Examples include the Balearic **slingers** of the ancient world and the English **longbowmen** of the Middle Ages.

Cavalry. The first sort of effective cavalry was **chariotry**. Forces of chariot troops conquered much of Asia and India in the second millennium B.C. Chariots are even more limited than horses in the kinds of terrain they can operate on, however, and once horses were bred strong enough to carry an armored man, more maneuverable individual cavalrymen eclipsed the chariotry, beginning around 500 B.C.

Heavy cavalry used hand weapons like swords, spears and axes; wore heavy armor; and fought in close formation, often stirrup to stirrup. The horses of such units were often as heavily armored as the men, equipped with bard of quilted cloth, scales, mail or plate. Examples include the Byzantine **cataphractoi**; the armored **knights** of the Middle Ages; and the **Mamluk slave soldiers** of medieval Egypt.

Light cavalry wore little armor and were used to skirmish against, harry or pursue the enemy, usually using missile weapons, such as javelins or bows. Prior to the introduction of stirrups, most cavalry were of this sort. The best example of such troops were the **Mongol mounted archers**, who could fire accurately from the saddle while moving at a full gallop.

Soldier Terms

Many of the following terms are selected to help writers think about how to organize their armies, for example, the names of various types or units or ranks. In addition to general troop types, there are also listings for various ranks, types of units and specific troop types to help writers think about the special kinds of soldiers they can include in their armies.

Many of the following terms apply to the Roman and Macedonian armies, both excellent models for the armies of a fantasy world.

acies: A single Roman battle line. **Triplex acies** designates a three-line battle formation.

agema: A Greek term for an army in the field, and in the Macedonian army, an elite unit.

alae: The "wings" of a Roman battle line, usually formed by cavalry.

Amazon: A female warrior, this term originally referred to a tribe of woman warriors believed by the Greeks to live along the shores of the Black Sea. The term has subsequently been used to refer to any groups of female combatants.

antesignani: Roman soldiers who fought in front of the battlefield standards (i.e., usually first-rate troops) as opposed to the **post-signani**, troops who fought behind the standards.

aquila: The eagle battlefield standard of the Roman legions.

arquebusier: A soldier of the late Middle Ages or Renaissance who was armed with an arquebus, or handgun, a type of matchlock firearm.

artillerymen: In ancient and medieval times, the soldiers who crewed ballistae, catapults and bombards, who were often considered mere laborers rather than true soldiers.

auxilia: Auxiliary foreign troops attached to Roman armies. Most of Rome's cavalry, archers and slingers were auxiliaries, such troops typically being drawn from Gaul, Syria and Spain, respectively.

battalion: A unit of about one thousand men, or ten companies. From the Swiss *battaile*, units of axemen and halberdiers raised during the Burgundian-Swiss War (1474–1477) against the French.

berserkers: Warriors able to work themselves up into a frenzy before going into battle so as to fight more effectively in hand-to-hand combat. Such warriors might imbibe hallucinogenic or other drugs, such as the **Hashashim of Syria**, who ambushed and assassinated European knights on Crusade.

blunderbuss woman: A member of an elite female corps under the command of the king of Dahomey, Africa. Blunderbuss women

and their counterparts, the **razor women**, were equal in status
to men and were actually considered to be better troops. At their
peak, they numbered some 2,400 and were used not just as body-
guards, but on the battlefield.

captain: In the ancient world and Middle Ages, a general term for
the commander of a force of one hundred or more men; a company commander.

cataphractoi: Heavily armored cavalrymen, cataphractoi were armored from head to foot in mail reinforced with plate; even their
horses were completely covered in scale armor. A sixth-century
Persian document lists the arms and armor required of each individual cataphractus: lance, sword, mace, battle-ax, two bows and
a bowcase, a quiver with thirty arrows, two extra bowstrings,
mail, breastplate, helmet, greaves, arm guards, buckler and bard.

Similar troops included the **clibinari** of the late Roman Empire. Because the extensive arms and equipment required by such
troops was so expensive, each clibinarus tended to be of aristocratic background.

centurion: In the Roman army, a high-ranking, noncommissioned
officer in charge of a century. Such veteran soldiers were the
backbone of the Roman army.

century: A unit of the ancient Roman army numbering eighty to one
hundred men at full strength.

cohort: A unit of the Roman army, numbering 480 to 800 men at
full strength and composed of six to eight centuries.

company: A basic unit of troops, usually consisting of about of one
hundred or more troops and led by a midrank officer or senior
noncommissioned officer. Specific examples include the Roman
century (c. 80-100 men), the Macedonian **syntagma** (c. 256
men) and the Greek **pentekostos** (c. 128 men).

conquistador: Spanish adventurer-soldiers who conquered much of
the New World in the sixteenth century. Firearms, horses, modern tactics, ruthlessness and treachery allowed them to overcome
Aztec, Mixtec and Mayan forces that were vastly superior in
numbers.

cuahchic: Shock troops of the Aztecs. Such troops were all elite
veterans who opted to serve in the elite assault units rather than
assume command as captains. Cuahchics were distinguished by
mohawk-style haircuts, and typically armed with obsidian-edged
clubs (**macahuitls**), padded body suits, and shields.

colonel: Literally, the leader of a column. In western armies, a typical command for a colonel is a brigade, or about two thousand men.

*crossbowman (*a.k.a. *arbalestier):* A soldier armed with a crossbow. Such fighters began to come into use near the end of the twelfth century.

Crusader: European knights and soldiers who participated in the various religious Crusades that began in 1096, usually with the Holy Land as a goal.

engineer: Soldiers assigned the duties of constructing fortifications, field works and obstacles, or the removal of the same. Prior to the rise of modern armies, the engineer was considered a civilian rather than a soldier. The word is derived from Latin and means ingenious, and points to the high regard in which expert engineers were held.

escrimador: Filipino warriors trained in the use of a straight fighting stick who are reputed to have defeated Magellan's swordsmen in combat.

federati: Gothic warriors and aristocracy who were given military training by the Roman army in the third century A.D. This double-edged program meant trained Goths formed a buffer between the Romans and more fearsome enemies, but also that the Goths acquired skills (both military and administrative) that would later be used against Rome.

general: The leader of a body of at least several thousand men, a group usually characterized as an army. In armies with complex structures, a great variety of officers might serve under a general, including colonels, majors, captains and lieutenants. In simpler armies, all the main officers under the general might simply be referred to as his captains.

handgunner: A soldier armed with a handgun or hand cannon, early forms of firearm.

hastati: The heavy spearmen of the Roman army who occupied the first line in a three-line battle formation (*see* Acies). Literally, someone who used a hasta, or spear.

hoplite: Heavy infantry of classical Greece, named for the large body shields they carried called hoplon.

horns of the bull: An enveloping tactic used by Zulu armies. The army would attack in a half-moon formation, fixing the enemy with the central section of the army, allowing the flanking units to encircle the enemy and closing inward like a huge pair of horns.

Huscarl: Danish mercenaries in the pay of the Saxon kings of England. The main weapon of these staunch warriors was the two-handed Danish axe, which they swung in a huge arc. Huscarls wore the Saxon **byrnie** for protection, and used the Norman-style kite shield, as well as an older round shield. Despite their skill and fortitude, they were defeated at the battle of Hastings in 1066 by Norman cavalrymen.

ile: A cavalry unit in Greek and Macedonian armies.

Immortal: A class of ancient Persian infantryman.

Jannisary: Christian child raised to be a soldier by the Ottoman empire. Jannisaries were fierce, dedicated soldiers and often used as shock troops.

knight: This was the name applied to mounted warriors of aristocracy in western Europe from the ninth century onward. The **paladins of Charlemagne** were among the first knights of the European ages.

legion, Roman: The basic strategic division of the Roman army differed in size and composition over the centuries, but at full strength tended to range from 4,200 to 5,200 men. In the first century B.C. when Julius Caesar was battling the Gauls, a 4,800-man legion consisted of ten **cohorts**, each composed of three **maniples**, one each of **principes**, **hastati** and **triarii**. Each maniple was composed of two centuries of eighty men, so sixty centuries made up a legion.

A legion might also have attached to it cohorts of auxiliary cavalry and infantry, many of them specialists, such as Gallic cavalrymen, Syrian archers or Spanish slingers. Some 1,200 auxiliaries per legion was typical.

A Roman field army typically consisted of four or more legions.

levy: A commoner, usually a peasant, called up for military service.

line units: The regular units that made up the line of battle as opposed to guard or elite units.

men-at-arms: Typically, well-equipped and armed warriors of the Middle Ages of non-noble birth. Such men-at-arms were trump cards in close combat. So heavily armored and equipped were they, however, that they often could not fight very long, and the victor was often the man who could outlast his opponent.

marines: Troops trained to fight on shipboard or to attack from a ship. They were distinct from sailors in that marines were stationed on vessels but did not actually operate them. Indeed, in some military systems, marines are employed on shipboard to prevent sailor mutinies or to protect the ship's officers.

militia: Municipal citizen armies began to rapidly form in Europe around the eleventh and twelfth centuries. These armies not only defended their cities, but often furthered the ends of the city abroad. Some of them were quite puissant. The **militia of Ghent**, Belgium, for example, were not only an exceptional field force armed with bows, pikes and swords, they were also widely considered specialists in siege.

mounted infantryman (a.k.a. *dragoon, hobilar):* A soldier who moved about on horseback or other means other than his own feet, but fought on foot as an infantryman rather than mounted as a cavalryman.

musician: Military musicians conveyed signals or made field calls, such as a signal to attack or retreat. In armies where soldiers were trained to march, musicians used percussion instruments to beat a cadence by which a pace was set.

oarsman: Rowers aboard oar-driven ships were most common in the Mediterranean Sea during the classical age of Greece and the dominion of Rome. Contrary to common belief, oarsmen were more often freemen than slaves and received decent pay for their services. Outside of the Mediterranean, oarsmen were usually also warriors, for example, the Viking raiders of the ninth century onward.

orbis: A ring-shaped tactical formation used by Roman troops, especially during an emergency, such as surprise attack by a numerically superior foe.

peltast: In ancient Greece, a light infantryman, named for his lightweight shield, or pelte, and armed with javelins.

petardier: A soldier who hurled pots of pitch or other combustibles onto the enemy from the walls of a castle. During the English Civil War, such troops were referred to as **grenadiers**. Eventually, this latter term took on a different meaning for an elite sort of soldier.

phalanx: Classic ancient Greek and Macedonian formation in which highly trained heavy pikemen, formed in blocks of eight- to sixteen-men deep, locked their shields into a wall and pointed their pikes straight forward. The first four or five pikes extended beyond the front of the formation, presenting a steel hedgehog to an enemy. When phalangists charged, the phalanx hit an enemy formation like a freight train.

The phalanx could be deployed in a variety of shapes, including a straight line, diagonal line, square, crescent or wedge. Disadvantages were that it could only move in a forward direction, could not be used on the same breadth of rough terrain as other infantry formations and was especially vulnerable on its flanks and rear. More fluid Roman formations were used to overcome and defeat the formidable phalanx.

priest: Holy men have fought alongside their flocks throughout the world. Mesoamerican priests served as elite troops or commanders; Hindu **brahmins** who were unable to find posts as priests took up arms as mercenary soldiers; and Buddhist **warrior monks** fought alongside the samurai of Japan.

Priests also fought with other soldiers during the Middle Ages. For example, during the A.D. 1066 Norman Conquest of England, a **warrior bishop** accompanied the invasion force, wearing a chain mail hauberk and armed with a heavy spiked club. Christian holy men were forbidden by their religion to shed blood, so the club and mace were popular weapons with them.

principe: The soldiers in the middle rank of a Roman three-line military formation.

rank and file: Companies of soldiers parade, or maneuver, in ranks and files. Ranks go from left to right, and files go from front to rear. In European armies, junior soldiers were called **rankers** as opposed to their officers, who took up their posts outside of the mass of soldiers lined up in ranks and files.

razor women: An elite force of female soldiers employed by the king of Dahomey, Africa, most notably in the nineteenth century. At times this force may have been utilized as a special bodyguard, but at one point it was 2,400 strong and apparently battle-ready. Their main weapons were long, two-handed razors, called **nyek-ple-nen-toh**, which could fold into their hafts like giant straight razors. *See* blunderbuss woman.

regiment: A grouping of several companies under a staff of additional officers (typically a major, lieutenant colonel and colonel). In the sixteenth century when companies or bands of soldiers were so grouped and placed under a staff, they were said to be regimented.

scout: Soldiers deployed ahead of or to the sides of an army to detect the presence of the enemy. Examples include the Greek **prodromoi** and the Roman **exploratores**.

sergeant: An enlisted soldier who has achieved leadership through experience and time in service, rather than holding rank by virtue of a commission from the government. Often called noncommissioned officers (NCOs). In the Middle Ages, sergeant was the term given to the leaders of bodies of men-at-arms. (Roman **optio**, assistant to a centurion, and **centurion**, a company sergeant; Indian **nayak**, a corporal, and **subadar** and **havildar**, grades of sergeant)

shield wall: A tactic in which combatants armed with large shields stood side to side, creating an unbroken defensive wall. The Vikings were famous for this maneuver, and are even said to have charged, swords pointed straight forward, while employing it.

shock troops: Soldiers used to force a breach in an enemy line by means of rapid, concentrated assault. Such troops usually had at least veteran status, and were as well or better armed and equipped than regular soldiers. Examples include the cuahchics of the Aztecs and the **janissaries** of the Ottoman Empire of Turkey.

slinger: A soldier armed with a sling. Men used these most primitive of missile weapons en masse through the thirteenth century. A trained slinger could accurately fire a projectile more than 225 yards.

squad: A small unit, usually the smallest battlefield division, comprised of around ten men. Examples include the Roman **contubernium** of eight infantrymen and **decuria** of ten cavalrymen, and the Macedonian **lochoi**, a file of sixteen men.

syntagma: A 256-man square of sixteen men in sixteen files, or lochoi, constituting the basic unit of the Macedonian phalanx.

testudo: A formation used in the Roman army in which shields guarded each side of a unit, including the top. Such a "tortoise" formation was used, among other things, to withstand massed sling or arrow fire.

Trabanter Guard: A ceremonial guard of troops composed of the henchmen and lackeys that surrounded a great man. A member of such a guard was called a trabant. From the German for "satellite."

triarii: Roman soldiers used as the final rank in the legion's three-line battle formation. By the time of the battle of Cannae in 216 B.C., the triarii were so rarely used in battle that it was customary to detail them to guard the Roman camp or to fall upon the enemy camp.

turmae: A unit of sixty-four Roman cavalrymen. During the second century, four turmae were attached to each legion of Roman soldiers, for a total of 128 troopers. In the third century, however, increased cavalry needs led to an increase to twenty turmae per legion, for a total of 640 troopers, or five times as many.

Vandal: One of a tribe of Germanic peoples probably originating in Denmark who conquered Roman-held Spain and North Africa in the fifth century A.D.

velites: Lightly armed Roman legionaries deployed at the front of a battle formation to skirmish with the enemy. When the enemy came within closing range of the velites, they retreated through gaps in the hastati, the next troops in the Roman line.

Viking: Viking warriors were among the most feared people of the Dark Ages, raiding coasts from Ireland to North Africa mainly in the ninth to eleventh centuries. Known for their skill and fierceness, Viking warriors went into battle wielding swords, battle axes and spears. (They also used bows, but these were held in the lowest regard.) Common warriors wore little or no armor, while leaders often wore chain mail, sometimes reinforced with additional pieces of metal. Round shields and conical helmets were also commonly used.

BEASTS OF WAR

From the earliest times, people have fought against animals, first as both hunted and hunter, and later upon the field of battle. Horses usually come to mind when people think of animals on the battlefield, but many other sorts of animals have fought alongside men as well. This variety in the real world hints at the possibilities for a fantasy world, where war beasts might be magically controlled or augmented, possess supernatural qualities or be of a mythological or otherworldly nature.

Horses allow for speed and mobility in battle unparalleled by foot soldiers. Nonetheless, they have their limitations and require proper care and lots of water and grain. Grass is not sufficient for horses expected to cover great distances, carry heavy burdens and fight. Horses also cannot operate on the same breadth of terrain as infantry, and fare badly in rough terrain, marshlands and mountains.

Before about 500 B.C., horses did not have the strength to support the weight of an armored man and were thus yoked to chariots. Chariot-mounted forces represented a revolution in warfare and swept over less well-equipped forces, reshaping the political face of the ancient world. The Aryan hordes that swept into India in the sixteenth century B.C. and crushed the Harrappan culture were charioteers, as were the Hyksos armies that overran and dominated Egypt for one hundred years.

Eventually, horses were bred to the point were they could support the weight of a combatant. Nonetheless, for many centuries the value of cavalry was limited and could not stand up to heavy infantry. The invention of stirrups allowed cavalry to truly come into its own, as they allowed warriors to use couched lances and effectively fire weapons from the saddle.

Stirrups came into wide usage in Europe around 500 A.D., and issued in an age of equestrian dominance that lasted for one thousand years.

Dogs, man's oldest friend, were used in combat from the earliest times, guarding the hearths of primitive men and accompanying them on the hunt. As armies developed throughout the ages, dogs were a part of them, from the first-known usage of large mastiffs in combat in Tibet during the Stone Age.

Assyrians, Babylonians, Greeks and Persians all subsequently used war dogs in great numbers, typically as sentries or as forward elements on the battlefield, where they could harry enemy scouts and help alert an army to the presence of the enemy. The Corinthians even treated great war dogs as heros and honored them with monuments. The classical historians Pliny the Elder and Plutarch discussed the role of dogs in warfare several times and described how they were equipped with armor and spiked collars, and used as shock troops to break up formations of enemy soldiers. The Huns, too, employed war dogs; mounted warriors carried their dogs perched on their saddles until they were sent into the fray. North American Indians also used dogs, both as sentries and in combat.

Elephants are the biggest and most intrinsically deadly of all creatures marched onto the battlefield. Alexander the Great witnessed such creatures in battle while campaigning in India and was so impressed with them that he added them to his own armies around 325 B.C.

Elephants were an important component of ancient armies for many centuries and were so widely used that one species, the African Forest elephant, became completely extinct. Such elephants were smaller than their Asian and African cousins, measuring less than eight feet at the shoulder (The Asian elephant is about ten feet at the shoulder and the African elephant is some eleven to twelve feet at the shoulder.)

Elephants were used in much the same way that armored vehicles are used today. Elephants could be equipped with **howdahs** to transport infantry or used as mobile firing platforms for archers or javelin men; they could have catapults or other weapons mounted on them (such as rockets in India) and be used to mount assaults on enemy positions; and they could be armed with iron headplates and used to batter down fortified gates or sections of wall. Elephants were particularly effective against cavalry, causing horses to panic. Some elephants are even purported to have been trained to wield huge swords with their trunks.

Other sorts of animals were also used for every sort of purpose. **Birds** carried messages from one part of an army to another, or from the defenders of besieged castles. **Monitor lizards** were used in ancient and medieval India to carry scaling ropes into besieged places. And **lions** and other great cats were used by Egyptians as combatants on the battlefield.

A clever fantasy writer could incorporate many such beasts into his stories. Possibilities include, but are obviously not limited to, fierce predators like wolves, tigers or bears cut from their leads to tear into the fray; huge creatures like elephants or dinosaurs equipped with fighting platforms for whole crews of soldiers; or squadrons of warriors mounted on winged horses, giant bats or huge pterodactyls.

CHAPTER TEN

ANATOMY OF A CASTLE

Michael J. Varhola

C astle is a word that brings to mind images of stout battlements, drawbridges over slime-filled moats and dank dungeons. But for one thousand years of European history, castles were more than a source of colorful imagery; they were a critical bastion of security for the inhabitants of a chaotic, dangerous world.

Castles are some of the most interesting, evocative settings for fantasy stories and can be used in innumerable ways. Indeed, unique, well-described castles are virtually characters themselves. Thus, it is important for fantasy writers to understand what constitutes a castle, why castles have the parts they do and how these elements function as part of the whole. In short, to write about such structures intelligently, writers need to have a working knowledge of the anatomy of a castle. Writers should also understand the differences between castles and other sorts of defense works, such as fortresses or walled cities.

Castles will not be part of all fantasy milieux, but some sort of fortifications will be a part of most of them. For example, in an empire with strong borders and safe and secure internal areas, there will be no need for functional castles but there may be border fortifications, possibly including large barracks to house soldiery, watchtowers or long curtain walls (like **Hadrian's Wall** in Scotland or the **Great Wall** in China).

Except as noted, the emphasis of the following information is upon the castles of Europe and the Middle East during the period A.D. 500 to 1500. However, much of it can be applied to fortifications in general, and notable facts about other sorts of fortifications are also mentioned. Information in this chapter is divided into three sections: the defensive components of a castle, castle life and sieges.

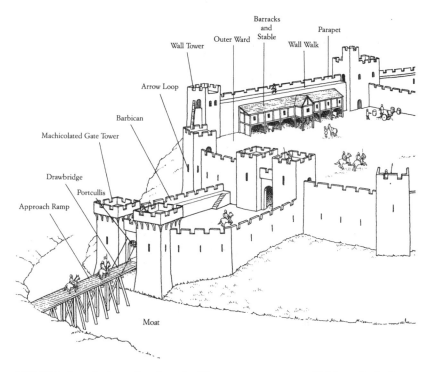

CASTLE: A typical medieval castle. The square towers and high walls indicate that this castle predates the invention of gunpowder.

Attached to each section is a detailed listing of important terms, some of which are technical or even a bit esoteric. These glossaries are intended not just to define useful terms, but also to provide writers with terms they can use to convincingly include castles, their inhabitants and sieges in their stories.

Historical notes appear throughout the sections and may not apply to fantasy writers who are not concerned with the precise time lines along which castles developed. Still, it is important to realize that military architecture evolved over many centuries and represented a long tradition of experience.

CASTLES AND OTHER FORTIFICATIONS

Castles were fortified dwellings deliberately built for the security of a local lord and his or her followers in areas subject to little or no central political control. The primary purpose of true castles is defense, and any other uses are incidental or auxiliary.

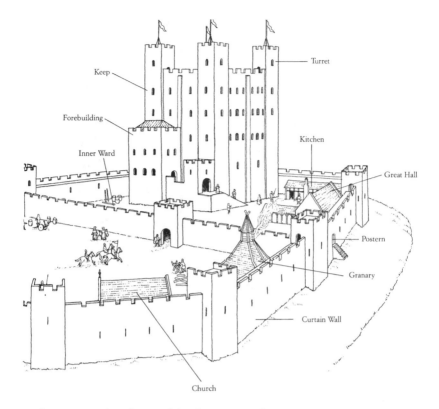

Keep

Forebuilding

Inner Ward

Turret

Kitchen

Great Hall

Postern

Granary

Curtain Wall

Church

Symptomatic of anarchic, fragmented societies, castles were not built casually or for their aesthetic value and were rarely constructed inside strong national states. Rather, they were built for protection against raiders, foreign invaders or aggressive neighbors. From modest fortifications that sheltered a dozen warriors and their dependents, castles evolved through the Middle Ages into complex, durable citadels that housed hundreds. Some of the most well-situated, well-constructed and well-stocked castles never succumbed to their enemies, whether by assault or siege.

From at least 2000 B.C., and perhaps much earlier, until the first century A.D., fortified cities were the major sort of defense in use. In the ancient world, city-states like those of Greece and republics like Rome fortified their urban areas, guarding their walls with citizen armies. Such states also built fortresses—fortified military bases—to guard mountain passes, rivers and other strategic sites, and manned them with professional soldiers, usually far from home. Examples include the **Great Wall** of China and the **Limes** in Germany.

CHINA'S GREAT WALL: The world's largest curtain wall.

During the Dark Ages and early Middle Ages, urban centers persisted as little more than fortified communities. Such towns, along with fortified dwellings, cannibalized Roman forts and other structures, were not true castles. Many fortified cities from the Middle Ages exist to this day, and some have even had their defenses reconstructed. These include Nuremburg and Rothenburg in Germany, Avignon and Carcassonne in France and York in England.

True castles were built in Europe starting in the ninth century. Castle evolution coincided with the rise of feudalism, a hierarchical social system described in chapter one. Castles were usually built or controlled by the ruler of an area and used to defend its frontiers from invasion. Such castles would be given to leaders who had sworn fealty to the noble.

The lord of a castle usually had military control over the area immediately around the castle and maybe within a few hour's travel from it. He lived in the castle with his family, his soldiers and their families, and a variety of craftsmen, servants and serfs. Frequently, the latter did not actually live in the castle but on its lands and near enough that they could quickly repair it in times of crisis.

Castles were the rocks upon which the tiny states of feudal lords existed, and a suitably built, stocked and manned castle could allow a lord to wield great power within his realm and possible political importance outside of it. Historically, lords were able to tax people passing through their realms; imprison their enemies or shelter other people's; practice heretical, anachronistic or illegal religions; and engage in mass murder or torture of undesirable inhabitants (as did Vlad Tepes, the inspiration for Dracula, and a disturbing number of other nobles in the Carpathian Mountains and surrounding region). These activities, whether sanctioned by a greater outside power or not, were possible in large part because of the security afforded by a strong castle.

In their simplest forms, castles were little more than fortified towers, or **keeps**. The Norman **motte-and-bailey** castles of the eleventh century, built by the vassals of William the Conqueror in England after he defeated the Saxons at Hastings in 1066, are among the simplest of all and constructed of an earthen hillock (motte) surmounted by a stone or wooden tower at one end of a palisaded yard (bailey). The knight commanding the castle lived in the tower, and his household and serfs dwelt in buildings in the bailey.

Some of the largest and most complex castles have at their heart massive keeps, often centuries older than the rest of the castle. Such a keep might have originally been the entire fortification, and then been augmented throughout the ages as conditions required and resources allowed. One or several concentric curtain walls might surround the keep, surmounted by **battlements** and reinforced with large towers at their corners and smaller ones in between.

Effective castles made the most of local geography, such as rivers, coasts and heights, using man-made defenses to augment natural barriers. Indeed, building upon high ground is one of the most fundamental canons of castle architecture, making a staunch ally of gravity. Being situated upon a hill allowed a castle's approaches to be protected by several or even a dozen successive gates, or interlocked smaller forts, called **wards**. Defenses on heights also forced enemy soldiers to charge uphill laden with weapons and armor, to fire their missile weapons further upward, and to have critical walls and structures situated out of reach of their siege engines. Likewise, high above their opponents, defenders could see attackers from afar and dump rocks, hot oil and other weapons onto their assailants. Good castles also needed a reliable source of potable water, as thirsty defenders could quickly be brought to heel. Thus, the presence of deep wells or unhampered access to rivers or, in their absence, constructions like cisterns were common.

Castles were often built by invaders to dominate and control a conquered country. (Nicollo Machiavelli discusses these uses of castles in *Art of War* and *The Prince*. Both of these books are must reading for anyone interested in warfare and politics during the Renaissance.) One of the best examples of this are the hundreds of castles built by William the Conqueror to control England after his victory at Hastings. Most of these were hastily built, economical motte-and-bailey castles, but they also built huge, square-towered affairs that came to represent a school of castle architecture. Indeed, the lack of Saxon defensive castles is one of the reasons William so quickly conquered England. It is completely inaccurate in *Robin Hood* and similar movies when the Saxons gaze upon Norman castles and claim that these massive stone structures were seized from their grandfathers. Most of their grandfathers would have actually lived in wattle-and-daub lodges.

Castles could not be safely ignored by an invading army. If ignored and left in the rear of even a strong army, mounted raiding parties could harass the invading force, cutting its supply lines or burning its camps. If the castles were attacked, months might be lost trying to take them, adding time and expense to a campaign and even stalling it altogether. And if an army was not strong enough, it might not even have been able to successfully capture or besiege a castle, especially if a relief force arrived from an allied castle. Thus, castles had both deterrent and defensive functions.

Fortification construction was a critical art and science, and often represented a major portion of a state's budget. Construction of simple fortifications, like motte-and-bailey castles, could be accomplished in a matter of weeks. More complex structures, like the walls of towns and cities, took years or even decades to complete, and might be refined and improved upon over the centuries. Ken Follet's *Pillars of the Earth* is a historical novel that traces the building of a medieval English cathedral over a period of decades, a story concept that could readily be applied to the construction of a major castle.

In fact, many castles evolved over a period of centuries. A good example of this is one of the most impressive castles ever built, the **Krak des Chevaliers** in Syria, which began in the eleventh century as a small Arab fortress. Acquired by the Crusader knights of St. John in 1142, it was enlarged into a rectangular castle. In the thirteenth century, a curtain wall was added, turning it into the massive concentric fortress that remains today.

Castle architecture evolved over the centuries, and the needs of the various ages can often be seen today in castles that were built over hundreds of years. For every sort of defensive construction, some siege weapon or technique was devised to overcome it. And for every siege technique, some countermeasure was developed to neutralize or lessen its effect. For example, some castles built in the twelfth and later centuries made use of shorter, thicker walls, sometimes reinforced with stone plinths at the bases of their towers, in order to better resist the latest form of siege weapon, the **trebuchet**.

The thirteenth century—a period of warfare, especially in the Middle East and southern and eastern Europe—represented a period of advancement in castle architecture. Developments included cross-shaped arrow slits; wooden shutters to provide greater protection for soldiers standing between merlons; and increased construction of round, rather than square, towers. On the other hand, while castle architecture did not develop much militarily in the fourteenth century, effort was put into making living areas more comfortable for the nobility. During this period, the nobility often lived in manors or buildings that looked like castles but were not militarily functional.

In areas where stability increased and national boundaries began to develop, castles became less important. In less secure areas, however, especially border regions, castles remained crucial. In Scotland, for example, where highland brigands posed a threat, fortified tower houses, with their characteristic L- or Z-shaped floor plans, were typical of the sixteenth century.

Castle Construction

While most surviving castles are of stone, castles were, however, built with whatever was expedient. Some materials do not lend themselves to lasting hundreds of years, which is why castles made from them no longer exist. Examples of these range from simple motte-and-bailey castles to massive, complex timber fortresses built by the Russians and Vikings. In the former case, however, earthworks still exist and can be explored. This is also the case with the much earlier Bronze and Iron Age earthworks.

Castles might have been made of timber where no other materials were available in sufficient quantity. Timber was also cheaper and easier to work with, allowing for much quicker construction (perhaps half as long, all other factors being the same). The main disadvantages, however, included wood's vulnerability to fire and the fact that it would eventually rot. In other areas, stone was simply not available and other materials had to be used. For example, in the Low Countries (Belgium, Holland and Luxembourg), brick was often used as a medium of construction.

Similarly, high ground was not always available and other measures had to be resorted to. When it was not possible to build on hills and ridges, other sorts of terrain could be exploited. In the Low Countries, castles often had large, wet moats, or were built in the midst of coastal marshes, their brick foundations rising directly from the muddy waters. Such fortifications were called **wasserburgs**.

Windows were never built at ground level, as this would have provided vulnerable entry points. Windows above ground level were often barred or shuttered, and shutters were sometimes provided with arrow slits or loopholes.

Square towers were the easiest to build and, with many notable exceptions, predominated until about the fourteenth century. However, the introduction of gunpowder artillery had the most profound effect on the development of fortifications, and quickly rendered useless many that had been powerful redoubts for centuries. Round towers, as a function of their shape, were able to absorb more damage from artillery fire, and also deflected projectiles more effectively than a flat surface. As gunpowder artillery came into use and spread (from their first likely use in Europe in 1326), so did the need for thicker, stronger and more curved defenses. Eventually, gunpowder siege weapons became too powerful for traditional defenses to withstand, and castle architecture became decorative rather than functional. After this, defenses were designed to absorb damage rather than deflect it, with a return to earthworks (or walls with an earthen core sheathed in stone) and walls that became lower and thicker. This sort of architecture was exemplified by the work of the seventeenth-century French military architect Marquis de Vauban, whose legacy can be seen in polygonal, star-shaped forts built through the ninteenth century.

Castle architecture evolved throughout the world in response to the changing modes of warfare. Europe is by no means the only home to great castles, it is just one of the most familiar to us. In India, military engineers built castles that used a system of concentric walls with the outermost wall the lowest and each successive inner one taller—exactly the opposite of the trend of European fortifications.

Japanese castle architecture is noteworthy and interesting, and was the product of a science all its own. The most incredible examples represent a synthesis of artistic sensibility and functionalism that is not seen anywhere else in the world; castles are usually utilitarian or beautiful, but those of Japan tend to be both, making use of complex systems of curtain walls and moats. A good example is the **Himeji Castle** near Kobe. Because effective gunpowder weapons were introduced later in Japan than in Europe, castles were effective well into the seventeenth century.

In a fantasy milieu like that of medieval Europe, most castles will be of small or medium size and controlled by minor nobility, like barons. However, in this setting, and certainly in a less traditional fantasy setting, castles might be the strongholds of many other sorts of inhabitants. These could include martial orders of priests in a fortified temple; a company of skeletal mercenaries led by an undead lord in a ruinous castle deep in a tangled wood; or a castle guarding a trading center that is maintained and manned at the expense of a major mercantile guild. Each castle that a writer describes or his characters visit can be made into a unique, memorable, significant subject.

Writers should consider factors like technology or magic when determining the properties of castles and other fortifications in their worlds. If cannons or other very powerful weapons are available, then high, square-towered castles will be an anachronism, and lower, earthen fortifications may be the norm. Similarly, if wizards or other spell-casters who can easily reduce or bypass the sturdiest walls are common, then traditional castles will be rather moot. There is no sense spending time and resources to build something that is really of no use. Other aspects of castle architecture might be affected by the presence of magic, even subtly. For example, illusory magics might be used to cloak the presence of sally ports, or elemental magics might be used to call up rainstorms, to provide water for the besieged and mudslides for attackers camped in areas denuded of trees used for building siege engines.

Well-conceived, strategically placed castles can serve as ideal centers of action in a great many fantasy stories, and can be used to say

HIMEJI CASTLE

much about those who dwell in them. Writers can include frontier forts of wooden towers and timber palisades manned by fur-clad hillmen; massive curtain walls of cut-and-fitted stone surrounding mercantile cities, their walls lined with the volunteer men and women of a republican state; or ancient citadels perched on mountainous peaks, the redoubts of xenophobic warlords and their minions.

To the peoples of medieval Europe, castles were homes, fortifications and bastions of security in a chaotic world. They remained so for a full millennium until, beginning around the fifteenth century, gunpowder artillery made castles inviable and the rise of national states and their armies made castles unnecessary.

Castle Terms

Where multiple terms exist for a given structure, the term closest to English is given with other terms provided parenthetically.

arrow slit: A narrow opening in a wall or **merlon** through which bows or crossbows could be fired. The inside surfaces were often angled, both to reduce the size of the hole from the point of view of an attacker and to allow a defending soldier to direct his fire in an arc (of up to about 60 degrees). Arrow slits were often crossletted (in the form of a cross) to more easily accommodate crossbows.

barbican: A stone building buttressed with towers almost always used as a gatehouse but sometimes as simply an **outwork**, and equipped with a drawbridge if situated on a moat.

bartizan: A small, round tower mounted on a wall or larger tower, and typically pierced with arrow slits or murder holes, or could even be a garderobe (latrine).

bastion: A structure bulging out from a curtain wall, looking a bit like a tower the same height as the rest of the wall. Its primary function was to allow flanking fire along the face of a wall.

battlement: The fighting area at the top of a wall, generally consisting of an area for soldiers to stand (either upon the top of a thick wall or on a catwalk), a parapet to protect soldiers up to torso level, and alternating embrasures and merlons.

buttress: A pillar of stone mounted against a wall of tower to reinforce it. Flying buttresses, characteristic of cathedral architecture, are attached to the building with a stone bridge rather than being up against it.

catwalk: A wooden platform that was mounted on a walk otherwise too narrow to fight upon, and used as a fighting surface, often in conjunction with permanent stone battlements, or as part of hoardings.

crenellations: Rows of alternating merlons and embrasures upon a battlement.

curtain wall: A straight section of defensive wall, generally at least twenty feet tall and five feet thick. Walls were usually somewhat thicker at their bases than their tops. For simplicity, writers can assume that a wall's base will be about 10 percent thicker than its top for every ten feet of height. Thus, a wall thirty feet tall and ten feet thick near the top will be 30 percent thicker, or thirteen feet wide, at its base. Tall walls were also reinforced with plinths and buttresses.

drawbridge: A gate that could be lowered or raised (rather than opened or closed like a door) using chains in conjunction with winches and counterweights. Contrary to popular conceptions about castles, only those with moats were likely to be equipped with a drawbridge. Timber planks at least a half-foot thick were needed for a drawbridge, which must be strong enough to support armored horsemen.

earthworks: A basic form of fortification, consisting of a ditch with compacted sides surmounted on one side by a rampart, built from the excavated earth. If means allowed, the ramparts were often equipped with a timber palisade. Simple castles might consist of nothing more than earthworks (e.g., a motte and bailey was made up of earthworks, augmented by a hillock and wooden or stone tower); during the Dark Ages, most fortifications would have been of this sort.

embrasure: The open space in a battlement between a pair of merlons. From about the thirteenth century, these were often reinforced with a set of shutters, often a single piece that could be angled to protect a man from frontal attack but allow him to fire downward.

gatehouse: The gate is perhaps the most vulnerable spot on a castle, and a strong structure was needed to keep it from becoming an Achilles' heel. A typical gatehouse consisted of a large square tower some two or three levels tall, often flanked with a pair of taller towers. Anyone entering the castle this way had to enter the gatehouse via the outer gate, pass through it and then enter the castle through an inner gate. During an attack, anyone within the gate would likely have been subject to attack through murder holes in the ceiling.

Gatehouse roofs could be equipped with battlements and armed with catapults, ballistae, cauldrons and braziers, or they could be manned by archers or arbalestiers. Typically, the outer gateway would be set with an iron-reinforced single or double door and/or a drawbridge, the inner gate with a reinforced door, and either with a portcullis.

boardings: A superstructure mounted on and projecting in front of a curtain wall, consisting of a sturdy wooden catwalk, a wooden wall set with embrasures or arrow slits, a peaked roof connected

to the battlements, and murder holes in the floor to allow attacks
against opponents at the base of the wall.

keep: A tall, heavily fortified structure that is the defensive heart of
a castle. The keep typically served as the residence of the castle's
lord, and the site of an assaulted castle's final defense. Early castles
might have consisted entirely of a keep. Many of those of the late
Middle Ages did away with the keep altogether, and concentrated
on the strength of other defensive structures, such as curtain
walls, towers and gatehouses. (French *donjon*; German
bergfried)

loophole: A hole in a wall designed for shooting a firearm through.

machiolations: A construction that projected the floor of the battlements over the front of a wall, and was often set with murder
holes to allow attacks against enemies against the wall below;
essentially like permanent stone hoardings.

merlon: The raised section of a battlement, set on a parapet and
flanking embrasures, usually three or four feet wide and four feet
tall; thus, a four-foot-tall merlon set upon a three-foot-high parapet
would create a seven-foot-high obstacle upon the rampart. Merlons may have arrow slits.

moat: A ditch surrounding a fortified area, which could have been
either dry or wet (full of water). Wet moats could have been
stone-lined channels full of rainwater, or connected with a stream
or river; indeed, such a body of water could even border one or
more sides of a castle.

motte and bailey: A style of castle typical of eleventh-century
Europe. Most of these were simple fortifications consisting of a
tower built on top of a motte (hillock), which dominated a palisaded bailey (yard) containing the domestic buildings of the lord's
household. Such castles were typically built entirely of earth and
timber.

murder hole: A hole, trapdoor or slit in a floor that allowed attacks
against a passageway or area below, often located in the gatehouse of a castle. (French *meurtrieres*)

outwork: A fortified structure that projected from or was completely outside of the walls of a castle, for example, a gatehouse
on the far side of a moat that served as a first line of defense.

palisade: A wall made of wooden stakes or timber beams, and often
used in conjunction with some other sort of defense, such as
earthworks. Palisades could comprise the primary curtain walls

of simple castles, be used for temporary field fortifications, or be raised to block breaches in stone walls.

parapet: A low wall, usually about three feet tall, built upon a rampart to provide cover for soldiers. Cover provided by parapets was augmented by merlons.

pilaster: A pillarlike construction used to reinforce walls.

plinth: Also called **batters** or **splays**, these were sloping supports that strengthened the bases of walls or towers and hindered attacks against them.

portcullis: A grill of metal or reinforced timber that could be lowered into a gateway and lifted by means of a winch and counterweights.

sally port: A small, heavily defended gate that could be used to launch surprise attacks against a besieging enemy. Such gates could also be used, if necessary or possible, as routes of escape or passages for secret messengers or emissaries.

CASTLE LIFE

Even as the physical parts of a castle had certain characteristics, so did the homes and work areas of the people who lived within it and in its environs. The common people—peasants—lived predominantly in agricultural villages. Most of the peasants were serfs, the lowest level in the feudal system. They were tied to the land where they were born and which they worked, their rights and responsibilities determined by custom and the lord of the region. Most peasants lived in modest dwellings: wood-framed, thatch-roofed and walled with wattle and daub (lattice walls covered with a muddy mortar) with one or two common rooms, which were also shared with livestock. For security reasons, their hamlets were almost always within a short distance of the castle or fortified town, so that they would have a place to take refuge in time of danger.

The lord of the castle had broad powers over the area he controlled. These included taxing the local populace a portion of the food they produced; calling upon them to provide labor or other services; rights to all wood and timber on the surrounding lands; and hunting rights to all game. (Robin Hood is traditionally considered to have been outlawed because he poached a local lord's deer.)

Lords did not always treat their serfs well, but they needed them since they were the economic base upon which the castle existed. Thus, the lord offered them protection and allocated various resources to them such as wood for construction and fuel. Hunting, on the other hand, was a jealously guarded privilege that was rarely relinquished by the nobility.

Within the castle, space tended to be limited and was utilized to its fullest extent, integrating defense and daily life. Attics of towers were used as rookeries for pigeons, which were raised for food. The lower levels of towers, when they were not solid bulwarks of stone, were used for storage areas, wellhouses and dungeons. Small courtyards were used for herb and vegetable gardens, while larger courtyards were used for stables, the huts of castle staff and workshops of craftsmen like blacksmiths.

In small, early castles, the great hall was used not just for communal meals, but as a common area where most of the inhabitants of the castle slept at night and where much of the work and social activity took place during the day. (This descends from the Germanic/Viking tradition of using great timber lodges in the same way.) In larger castles, living and work areas became as specialized as space allowed and the needs of the inhabitants required. The lord and his family had their own apartments. Soldiery were housed either in barracks or in small groups within furnished tower rooms. Servitors like cooks, gardeners and craftsmen lived in huts along the inside walls of the castle.

Often, men and women were virtually segregated from each other, with each sex having their own activities and responsibilities. Commoners pursued their assigned tasks; knights, men-at-arms and the lord and his sons trained for warfare or performed daily administrative duties; and women performed various vital crafts, such as tapestry weaving, and answered to the lady of the castle, who often oversaw the day-to-day functions of the castle.

The role of women in the life of a castle should not be dismissed. Historically, when a lord and his men were away at war or on hunting expeditions, or if they were killed, a lady was often responsible for ensuring that business continued as usual. Many ladies were necessarily excellent administrators and could run a castle as well as their husbands could, even to the extent of defending it in time of siege. And sometimes, when the regional social order allowed it or was not strong enough to oppose it, women might rule in their own right following the death of a husband or father (and in fantasy milieux, of course, this can become even more likely).

Castle walls were thick, but, being built for defense rather than comfort, they were of uninsulated stone. Thus, castles tended to be chilly, damp, drafty and musty. Their subterranean areas would be even danker, the walls encrusted with feathery white niter. Because of these conditions, tapestries were hung on walls, cutting down on drafts and providing a form of insulation.

Furniture tended to be sturdy and made of wood. Benches were used at all levels of society throughout the Middle Ages, as were stools. Actual chairs were much less common and were used by lords, judges or merchants, but not necessarily by anyone else around them. Castles did not have closets, so various sorts of chests and wardrobes were used to store clothing and other possessions. Beds tended to be short, not because people were that much smaller, but because many well-born people slept sitting upright. This was the result of a diet consisting almost exclusively of meat which led to all sorts of digestive problems that caused less discomfort when sitting up than when lying prone.

Castles built in settings unlike the European Middle Ages may have characteristics different than those described above, and when writers are designing and describing their castles, they must take into consideration the individual cultures of the inhabitants of each castle. In a fantasy world, such considerations might extend to other races or species as well. For example, Muslim emirs would have areas dedicated to their **seraglio**, or harem; most medieval Indian rajas would have some sort of torture chamber; Christian lords would certainly have a chapel or maybe even a cloister for monks (indeed, a templar castle is essentially a combination cloister/barracks for religious soldiers); and stables would be of great importance in many traditions, for the horses of mounted European warriors or the elephants of Indian ones. The needs of nonhuman peoples might be even more specialized or elaborate.

Castle Life Terms

The following list describes some of the people that lived in the castles and the various rooms, sections or areas within a castle that might be relevant to a story. Writers should be able to envision how such areas might be modified for use in a fantasy environment. For example, in some worlds, an aviary might take up all of the largest tower in a castle and be home to the giant raptors ridden by the castles' knights.

armory: A room where arms and armor were stored, usually guarded by a stout, iron-bound door to which the castellan and perhaps one or two other people would have access.

aviary: A chamber, often in a tower, where the birds of prey used for hunting were kept, usually under the supervision of a falconer, a commoner trained in handling such creatures.

barracks: Areas full of bunks or pallets that served as living quarters for the men-at-arms dwelling there. Higher-ranking soldiers like sergeants might have shared a tower room together, and single knights might have had their own rooms.

castellan: An officer in charge of all the affairs of a castle who answered directly to the lord. Duties of a castellan included keeping the castle in good repair and ensuring it was well stocked for any eventuality. In some cases, able castellans served as guardians for lords who had been orphaned but had not yet reached their majority. (French *chatellan*)

chapel: An area within the castle dedicated to worship. The word ''shrine'' might more properly apply to the small temples of non-Christian religions.

cisterns: Large containers used for holding water, especially in areas where a well could not provide enough water for all of the needs of a castle or where a water supply could be denied in time of siege. Such containers could be several stories deep and were typically cut out of solid rock; similarly, small, natural caverns could also form the basis for cisterns. Historically, many besieged areas were able to hold out against attackers because of water stored in this fashion. Likewise, defenders of otherwise virtually impregnable fortifications sometimes had to surrender when overcome by thirst.

crypt: A room that was often built beneath the chapel, the crypt could contain the remains of the former lords of the castle and their families. An excellent place for morbid trysts, secret meetings or forbidden rituals.

dungeon: An area used for imprisonment and torture. Such areas were common in the castles of most cultures. (French *oubliette*)

garderobe: Situated on an outside wall or in a small overhanging tower, this area was a latrine with a hole that overlooked an area outside the castle onto which defecation could drop.

great hall: The central social area of a castle, a great hall usually had one or more long banquet tables, and walls lined with weapons, banners and other trophies won in tournaments and battles. It was in this area that communal meals were eaten, guests entertained and strategy discussed with a lord's vassals. The great hall could have been the central area of the keep, or a less military building in the main courtyard of the castle. It was frequently the sleeping area for many of the castle's inhabitants.

harem: An area set aside by non-Christian, particularly Muslim lords, to house their wives or concubines. Such areas were often guarded by eunuchs (castrated men) or female warriors.

kennel: An area used for housing the dogs of a castle. In some castles, dogs were simply allowed to roam freely and allowed to feed on the refuse in eating areas. Dogs often had important roles in castles, with hounds being used in hunting, and mastiffs used as guards or in war.

kitchen: In small or simple castles, food for the lord and his retainers could be cooked in the hearth of the great hall itself. Larger castles, particularly those set up to cater to nobility, would have separate, more elaborate areas.

library: In regions where literacy was not the norm, castle libraries were not common or extensive, or could have represented the legacy of former inhabitants. In the castle of a cultured lord or an order of monks, however, not to mention a wizard, sage or alchemist in a fantasy milieu, a library would be of prime importance.

smithy: Blacksmiths, or farriers, worked iron into implements like horseshoes, nails and tools, but did not fashion weapons or armor. A smithy would likely face onto the courtyard of a castle.

stable: An area for housing horses and storing the equipment used with them. The stables of large castles in cultures where horses or other mounts were important often had special officers in charge of them. Ideally, stables were not underneath or too near to living areas.

storage: Cool, dry areas were needed to store all the supplies necessary for running a castle and sustaining it through long winters and sieges. Basements beneath the keep and the lower level of towers were the primary storage areas.

well: Wells were often dug deep into the basement of a castle's keep or within another large tower.

workshops: Areas used to produce goods necessary for a castle that might not otherwise be available. Castles and their attached villages were often isolated from other communities and had to be self-sufficient. Thus, coarse cloth, furniture, barrels and other goods would manufactured in the castle or adjacent village, often in the homes of skilled peasants.

SIEGE

Sieges can make for exciting reading, even though historically they tended to be dreary, protracted affairs, punctuated by episodes of violence, and culminating in either withdrawal or a bloody assault.

Literally, the word "siege" comes from French and means "to wait," and most sieges were lengthy, tedious battles of attrition, often as ruinous to the besiegers as to the besieged. This section describes both the process of siege and other methods used to capture castles and fortified areas.

Castles were generally taken either by assault or by siege. A quick assault and overrun of a castle was most desirable, especially if this could be achieved by surprise. A successful siege, on the other hand, could take weeks, months, even years, and stood to decimate even the besiegers through disease, attrition, attack from relieving forces, or surprise attacks from the castle called **sallies**, which were made through small gates called sally ports.

The actual means of capturing fortified positions changed little from the earliest sieges right up through the fifteenth century, with the exception that siege weapons gradually became more powerful and destructive. This power culminated in the development of gunpowder weapons, which led to the decline of traditional fortifications.

Sieges were actually conducted very early in human history. Jericho, founded some eight thousand years ago and perhaps the oldest city in the world, fell to siege many times in its history, several times even before Joshua marched around its walls and brought them crashing down. The first protracted, complex sieges date from at least 1500 B.C., when the Assyrians were attacking neighboring Mesopotamian city-states, and when Aryan steppe dwellers were sweeping into northern India and overrunning the mud-brick citadels of the Harrappans.

Some peoples had a knack for **poliorcetics**, as the science of siege was known, and others did not. For example, the Romans excelled at siege and were able to take positions considered impregnable, like Herod's palace-fortress at Masada in what is now Israel, overlooking the Dead Sea (at considerable cost and time, nonetheless). Even peoples who were proficient at siege often had to pay a heavy price for their success.

Traditionally, defenders of a besieged castle were allowed to surrender unconditionally. If they did not surrender and their stronghold was subsequently taken, they were usually subjected unhesitatingly to slaughter, rape and enslavement.

The familiar assault upon the walls resulting in the taking of the castle was usually the culmination of months or even years of preparation and activity. Such assaults were costly in terms of men and equipment, and less glamorous but more effective techniques of conquest were tried first.

The first step in a siege was to surround and completely cut off the castle, preventing the besieged from escaping or from being relieved by outside forces. Thus, the besiegers themselves were often in a precarious position with opponents to their fronts and backs. There is no more famous example of this phenomenon than Julius Caesar's first century B.C. siege of the Gallic fortified town of Alesia in France. Just as Caesar was compelled to do, besiegers often built earthworks to protect themselves from missile fire or attacks from the castle or their flanks.

Attackers usually had considerably more men at their disposal than the besieged. Otherwise, the besieged would not likely subject themselves to the perils of being holed up in their strongholds. Writers can assume at least twice as many men in the besieging army outside as there are within the besieged castle.

Wooden fortifications were more vulnerable to attack than stone structures. Fire could be used to burn down the walls, axemen could hack them down and weapons like catapults and rams were considerably more effective against such structures than against stone. Many other specialized methods were also developed for reducing a castle's defenses. **Sapping** could be very effectively employed against stone castles. **Sappers** would burrow into a wall, supporting the excavated area with timbers. When sufficient material had been removed from the wall or tower, the sappers packed the area with combustibles (from the fifteenth century onward, gunpowder was also used) and set fire to them. When the timbers burned away, the wall section collapsed, leaving a breach that could then be assaulted by troops.

Sappers and axemen were vulnerable to attack from boulders, boiling oil and missiles dropped on them from above. Therefore, whenever possible, they approached the castle walls and labored under wheeled galleries, or moved up through covered trenches that were gradually being dug toward the fortification. Troops also worked at the base of a castle with no cover if the means of providing it for them were not available, but horrible casualties often resulted from this.

Hoardings, **bastions** and **machiolations**, defensive structures that projected out over a wall, were developed largely to help defenders prevent mischief by attackers like sappers. Through holes in floors of such projections, defenders could monitor the base of their walls, areas that would otherwise be blind spots to someone positioned on top of a straight wall.

Mining was another way to undermine castle walls. Out of sight of the castle, usually behind **mantlets** or even from within a nearby building, a shaft was dug downward and then gradually up toward the castle walls (shafts were angled in this way to help prevent defenders from flooding them).

Deep or steep-walled moats made close approach to a castle difficult, especially if they were filled with water. Even a dry moat that had to be crossed was an area devoid of cover that could easily become a deadly killing ground for attacking troops. Before troops could assault walls or employ engines like siege towers, rams or sows, moats had to be negotiated. A common way to make moats passable to engines was to fill them with rocks or bundles of sticks (**fascines**); the filled area would then be covered with planks to ensure smoother crossing for the wheeled engines. Portable boats and pontoon or folding bridges could be deployed to allow passage by troops.

Escalade, or attack by use of ladders, was an often final and very hazardous method for capturing a castle. While archers, arbalestiers and artillery engines attacked the defenders manning the walls, foot soldiers ran forward with tall ladders and clambered up toward the battlements, fighting desperately to get onto them. Defenders would launch missile fire, drop large rocks and pour boiling oil or molten lead upon the climbers. They would also use polearms to push away the ladders before assaulting soldiers could make it to the top.

Siege towers, if available, could also be used to attack battlements. They were maneuvered up to the walls, and upon reaching

ESCALADE: Often a hazardous final method for capturing a castle.

them, the attackers dropped their attack ramps onto the battlements, allowing troops to pour out onto the defenders.

Most castles were not constantly subjected to attack and gradually fell into disrepair. Wooden structures like hoardings or catwalks rotted away over the years, and often were not maintained until a time of crisis, when they could be replaced relatively quickly. Whereas a large stone castle might take several years to build, the wooden superstructures could be added or replaced in a matter of weeks.

In addition to the replacement of wooden structures, castles often had to be prepared for siege in other ways. These included clearing the moat of debris; diverting a waterway so as to fill it, if appropriate; and repairing any crumbling masonry. Clearing all trees and vegetation within the largest possible radius of the site was also done to deny the enemy cover from missile fire, deny them wood for campfires or field quarters, and to prevent construction of siege engines.

Siege engines were large, cumbersome, often expensive pieces of equipment and were rarely transported by an attacking army, especially as it was not always known at what point in a campaign a siege might occur (after all, any given lord might capitulate, become an ally, conclude a treaty, etc.). Rather, the tools and knowledge needed to build siege engines were brought and the weapons were constructed at the site of the siege.

Ironically, many of the biggest, most impressive and most expensive weapons did not turn out to be the war-winners that they were expected to be, often exhibiting lackluster performance. A good example is the **Helepolis**, the "City-Taker," a siege tower built for the 304 B.C. siege of Rhodes. It was 140 feet tall with a dozen levels for troops and equipment, covered with iron plates, armed with thirty catapults and ballistae of varying sizes, and propelled forward by a crew of two hundred men operating a massive capstan mounted in its lower level. Several hundred more men pushed and pulled the machine as well. Despite its imposing appearance and size, the Rhodians managed to damage the Helepolis and the besiegers withdrew it from the fray, fearing for the fate of their expensive weapon.

Writers should be certain to take the special nature of a magical world into consideration when describing scenes of siege warfare. For example, a priest dedicated to elemental gods might cast his blessings upon a catapult boulder prior to its being fired; peoples native to subterranean regions might sap or mine more quickly or efficiently than normal humans; and large, winged creatures might be used to transport attackers over walls.

Siege Terms

Many terms are marked with a (d), indicating an item that it was used primarily by the defenders of a fortified area, or an (o), indicating an item used primarily by attackers. This represents the way various devices were typically used, however, and should not act as a restriction upon writers.

ballista: An engine like a large crossbow used to fire heavy javelins, employing twisted skeins of sinew for power. Ballistae were so powerful that a single bolt fired from one could skewer several men and penetrate almost any armor. Such weapons tended to be used as defensive weapons rather than by besiegers because they were not very effective against stone and required less space to operate than catapults. Along with catapults, ballistae were used in virtually every major siege for at least three thousand years. (Greek *oxybeles*; Latin *ballista, scorpio, cheiroballistra*)

battering ram (o): A heavy beam used to batter down doors or, more slowly, walls. In its simplest form, it was a big log carried by a dozen soldiers and used to stave in the door of a small castle. In its more complex form, a ram was shod with a wedge-shaped metal head, mounted on a carriage so that it could be swung rhythmically, and either protected by a wheeled shed or mounted within a siege tower. Rams are among the oldest, and the most rudimentary, of siege engines. (Latin *testudo*)

cat: A wheeled shed used to protect troops while they moved toward a fortified position. Cats were often used to house battering rams or **screws**, and were sometimes attached to the rear of a siege tower, allowing additional troops to follow behind it.

catapult: A siege engine using an arm powered by great twisted skeins of cords to hurl rocks. Missiles of this sort had to be fired in great concentration and over a long period of time if they were to break through strong curtain walls or demolish towers, but could more easily clear walls of defenders, damage battlements or crush wooden structures like hoardings. Like ballistae, catapults were used in almost every siege from around 1500 B.C. until about A.D. 1500. (Greek *lithobolos*; Latin *onager*)

cauldron (d): A large, cast-iron pot mounted over a brazier, which was used to boil oil or melt lead that could then be poured over walls or through murder holes onto attackers (causing horrible, lethal wounds against which armor was of little defense).

crow (d): A device consisting of a long, counterweighted pole and line that could be lowered over a wall by defenders and used to hook onto a besieging soldier, jerk him off the ground and swing him into the castle.

fascines: Large bundles of sticks (usually five to six feet high and three to four feet across) with a variety of uses including reinforcing field fortifications and filling moats.

gallery (o): A covered wooden passageway constructed for the protection of besiegers, often made resistant to fire by being covered with green hides. Galleries were used to allow attackers to approach walls, dig siege ditches and so on, and were often constructed in stages, gradually getting longer and closer to the castle.

gastrophetes: Meaning "belly bow," this was an early form of crossbow developed around 400 B.C. and apparently used as a siege weapon in classical Greece. Also called **Heron's gastraphete**.

hoist (o): A heavy frame mounted with a large counterweight and a lever, one end of which was equipped with a basket large enough to hold several attackers who could then be lifted up to the top of a wall.

ladder, siege (o): A tall ladder that was flung against the wall of a castle and used to scale it by besiegers. Such ladders frequently consisted of a single long timber set with crosspieces. (Greek *sambuca*; Mughal *narduban, zeenah pae* [a broad ladder])

mantlet (o): A large, wooden shield, propped up by supports or on wheels, which was used to shelter at least two besieging troops, typically those needing cover while loading slow weapons like crossbows. Mantlets could gradually be moved forward toward the walls of a castle. (Mughal *turah*)

petard (o): A crude explosive device employed by means of a hoist and used to blow breaches in walls.

ram catcher (d): A device consisting of a hook or fork on a long beam, which was lowered by defenders to catch a battering ram or screw being used against a wall, and then was rapidly lifted, breaking or dislodging the attacking engine. Grappling hooks on ropes might be used in the same manner.

redoubt: A small field fortification, often built on a natural or built-up piece of high ground, and typically consisting of earthworks reinforced with a palisade or fascines. Besiegers often built such structures. (French *bastille*)

screw (o): Sometimes called a **pick** or **sow**, this device was placed against a wall and used to bore a hole into it. Attackers using such a device typically needed the protection of a gallery. (Latin *musculus*)

siege engine: Any machine specially designed to assist in sieges.
Many types exist, but they can be broadly classified into missile
weapons and nonmissile weapons. Engineers specially skilled in
the construction of such weapons were very important members
of ancient and medieval armies. On the other hand, the troops
that operated such engines were generally the most lowly regarded, and were often considered little better than laborers.
Such engines used enormous amounts of timber and were so
massive in size and weight that they were usually built on-site
(or, less frequently, prefabricated and transported to the site of
a siege).

Missile weapons can be divided into four main categories: **ballistae**, **catapults**, **springnals** and **trebuchets** (all discussed separately). A wide variety of terms were used for such weapons
throughout the Middle Ages, although these can often be applied
to more than one of the four classes of weapons and are not
technical nomenclatures. These names can be put to good use
by writers, and include **beugle**, **blida**, **scorpion**, **onager**, **bri-
cole**, **calabra**, **fronda**, **engin**, **espringale**, **fundibulu**, **manga-**

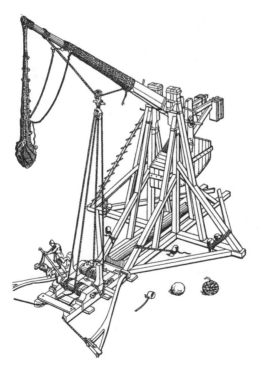

TREBUCHET: Typically,
these massive siege engines
were over 60 feet tall and
could hurl a 300-pound rock
nearly 300 yards.

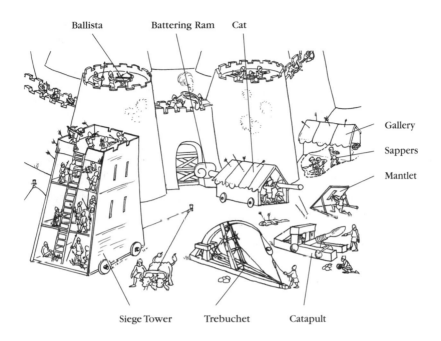

Ballista   Battering Ram   Cat

Gallery

Sappers

Mantlet

Siege Tower   Trebuchet   Catapult

Art by Sharon Daugherty. © Writer's Digest Books.

num, martinet, matafunda, mategrifon, petrary, robinet, springald, tormentum and **tripantum**.

Proper names were often applied to large or powerful weapons (for example, "Wolf of War," "God's Hammer"), and such names might be emblazoned on the engine itself.

Nonmissile siege engines included **towers**, **rams**, **screws** and **mantlets** (also discussed separately).

springnal: A siege engine using the tension of a flexible arm to fire rocks or javelins. The arm would typically be made from laminated layers of planks and bent into firing position with a windlass. Of the four main classes of siege weapons, the springnal is the simplest and quite possibly the oldest. Those designed to fire rocks would have tended to be less powerful than catapults (not to mention trebuchets) and those configured for javelins would have been less accurate than ballistae. Nonetheless, it was doubtless a formidable weapon. Also referred to as a "spring engine."

tower, siege (o): Towers had to be taller than the walls they were being used to attack or dominate. Thus, they might be as small as thirty feet tall, but much larger ones are known to have been used. For example, at the siege of Lisbon in 1147, two towers eighty-three and ninty-five feet tall were used.

Because they were used to help clear walls of defenders, towers were sometimes called **bad neighbors**; they were also known as **belfries**.

Ropes and pulleys, powered by teams of oxen, were used to drag towers toward enemy walls. They were set up so that the oxen moved away from the walls, dragging the tower forward via the pulleys mounted in front of the tower. Another slower method was to have men inside the tower ratchet the wheels forward using crowbars. (French *beffroi, malvoisin*; Mughal *seeba*)

trebuchet: A huge, powerful siege engine that used a massive counterweight to hurl large rocks, or even dead cattle and horses; a typical trebuchet could hurl a three hundred-pound rock about three hundred yards. The trebuchet came into use in the twelfth century and was the only major siege engine of the Middle Ages that did not have its origins in antiquity. Of all non-gunpowder missile engines, these were the biggest, slowest, most destructive and most expensive. Writers should not underestimate the size of these monsters: They could be well over sixty feet tall, have an arm sixty feet long, be equipped with a counterweight that weighed twenty or even thirty thousand pounds, and required crews of dozens or even hundreds of men.

INDEX